THE COMING KING AND THE REJECTED SHEPHERD

New Testament Monographs, 4

Series Editor
Stanley E. Porter

THE COMING KING AND THE REJECTED SHEPHERD

Matthew's Reading of Zechariah's Messianic Hope

Clay Alan Ham

SHEFFIELD PHOENIX PRESS

2005

Copyright © 2005, 2006 Sheffield Phoenix Press

First published in hardback, 2005
First published in paperback, 2006

Published by Sheffield Phoenix Press
Department of Biblical Studies, University of Sheffield
Sheffield S10 2TN

www.sheffieldphoenix.com

A CIP catalogue record for this book
is available from the British Library

Typeset by Forthcoming Publications
Printed by Lightning Source

ISBN 1-905048-01-7 (hardback)
ISBN 1-905048-70-X (paperback)
ISSN 1747-9606

To Diane

CONTENTS

Chapter 2

Chapter 3

ABBREVIATIONS

1 Apol.	Justin Martyr, *First Apology*
1 Clem.	*1 Clement*
1 En.	*1 Enoch*
1QM	*War Scroll*
1QpHab	*Pesher Habakkuk*
1QS	*Rule of the Community*
2 Bar.	*2 Baruch*
4QXII	*The Greek Minor Prophets Scrolls* (= 4Q82)
4QCommGen	*Commentary on Genesis* (= 4Q252)
4QpIs	*Pesher Isaiah* (= 4Q163)
8Hev	*The Greek Minor Prophets Scrolls from Nahal Hever*
11QMelch	*Melchizedek* (= 11Q13)
AB	Anchor Bible
'Abot R. Nat.	*'Abot deRabbi Nathan*
ABRL	Anchor Bible Reference Library
ACCS	Ancient Christian Commentary on Scripture
AnBib	Analecta biblica
ANET	James B. Pritchard (ed.), *Ancient Near Eastern Texts Relating to the Old Testament* (Princeton, NJ: Princeton University Press, 3rd edn, 1969)
ANF	*Anti-Nicene Fathers*
ANRW	Hildegard Temporini and Wolfgang Haase (eds.), *Aufstieg und Niedergang der römischen Welt: Geschichte und Kultur Roms im Spiegel der neueren Forschung* (Berlin: W. de Gruyter, 1972–)
Ant.	Josephus *Jewish Antiquities*
ANTC	Abingdon New Testament Commentaries
Apoc. El.	*Apocalypse of Elijah*
Apoc. Sedr.	*Apocalypse of Sedrach*
APOT	R.H. Charles (ed.), *Apocrypha and Pseudepigrapha of the Old Testament in English* (2 vols.; Oxford: Clarendon Press, 1913)
ArBib	The Aramaic Bible
Artap.	Artapanus
ASNU	Acta seminarii neotestamentici upsaliensis
ATDan	Acta theologica Danica
AThRSup	Anglican Theological Review Supplement Series
b.	Babylonian Talmud
Barn.	*Barnabas*
BASORSup	*Bulletin of the American Schools of Oriental Research*, Supplements

BBR	*Bulletin for Biblical Research*
BDAG	Walter Bauer, Frederick W. Danker, William F. Arndt and F. Wilbur Gingrich, *A Greek–English Lexicon of the New Testament and Other Early Christian Literature* (Chicago: University of Chicago Press, 3rd edn, 1999)
BDB	Francis Brown, S.R. Driver and Charles A. Briggs, *A Hebrew and English Lexicon of the Old Testament* (Oxford: Clarendon Press, 1907)
BDF	Friedrich Blass and Albert Debrunner, *A Greek Grammar of the New Testament and Other Early Christian Literature* (trans. and rev. Robert W. Funk; Chicago: University of Chicago Press, 1961)
Ber.	*Berakot*
BerOl	Berit Olam: Studies in Hebrew Narrative and Poetry
BETL	Bibliotheca ephemeridum theologicarum lovaniensium
BHS	*Biblia hebraica stuttgartensia*
Bib	*Biblica*
BIS	Biblical Interpretation Series
BJRL	*Bulletin of the John Rylands University Library of Manchester*
BJS	Brown Judaic Studies
BR	*Bible Research*
BWANT	Beiträge zur Wissenschaft vom Alten und Neuen Testament
BZ	*Biblische Zeitschrift*
BZAW	Beihefte zur *ZAW*
Cal.	Suetonius, *Gaius Caligula*
CBET	Contributions to Biblical Exegesis and Theology
CBQ	*Catholic Biblical Quarterly*
CCSL	Corpus Christianorum: Series latina
CD	Cairo *Damascus Document*
cod.	codex
Comm. Matt.	Jerome, *Commentary on Matthew*
ConBOT	Coniectanea biblica, Old Testament
CRINT	Compendia rerum iudaicarum ad Novum Testamentum
CV	*Communio Viatorum*
Decal.	Philo, *On the Decalogue*
Deut. Rab.	*Deuteronomy Rabbah*
Dial.	Justin Martyr, *Dialogue with Trypho*
Did.	*Didache*
DJD	Discoveries in the Judaean Desert
DJG	Joel B. Green and Scot McKnight (eds.), *Dictionary of Jesus and the Gospels* (Downers Grove, IL: Intervarsity Press, 1992)
DJS	Documents of Jewish Sectaries
DLNT	Ralph P. Martin and Peter H. Davids (eds.), *Dictionary of the Later New Testament and Its Developments* (Downers Grove, IL: Intervarsity Press, 1997)
Dom.	Suetonius, *Domitian*
DPL	Gerald F. Hawthorne, Ralph P. Martin and Daniel G. Reid (eds.), *Dictionary of Paul and His Letters* (Downers Grove, IL: Intervarsity Press, 1993)

Eccl. Rab.	*Ecclesiastes (Qohelet) Rabbah*
EDNT	Horst Balz and Gerhard Schneider (eds.), *Exegetical Dictionary of the New Testament* (3 vols.; Grand Rapids: Eerdmans, 1990–93)
EKKNT	Evangelisch-katholischer Kommentar zum Neuen Testament
Epid.	Irenaeus, *Demonstration of the Apostolic Preaching*
EstBib	*Estudios bíblicos*
ETL	*Ephemerides theologicae lovanienses*
EurUS	European University Studies
EvQ	*Evangelical Quarterly*
Evt	*Evangelische Theologie*
Exod. Rab.	*Exodus Rabbah*
FRLANT	Forschungen zur Religion und Literatur des Alten und Neuen Testaments
Fug.	Tertullian, *On Running away from Persecution*
GCT	Gender, Culture, Theory
Gen. Rab.	*Genesis Rabbah*
GKC	*Gesenius' Hebrew Grammar* (ed. E. Kautzsch, revised and trans. A.E. Cowley; Oxford: Clarendon Press, 1910)
Gosp. Thom.	*Gospel of Thomas*
GTJ	*Grace Theological Journal*
Haer.	Irenaeus, *Against Heresies*
HALOT	Ludwig Koehler and Walter Baumgartner, *The Hebrew and Aramaic Lexicon of the Old Testament* (rev. Walter Baumgartner and Johann Jacob Stamm; trans. M.E.J. Richardson; 5 vols.; Leiden: E.J. Brill, 1994–2000)
Hist.	Tacitus, *Histories*
Hist. Eccl.	Eusebius, *Ecclesiastical History*
HKNT	Handkommentar zum Neuen Testament
HTKNT	Herders theologischer Kommentar zum Neuen Testament
HTR	*Harvard Theological Review*
HUCA	*Hebrew Union College Annual*
Hul.	*Hullin*
IBHS	Bruce K. Waltke and M. O'Connor, *An Introduction to Biblical Hebrew Syntax* (Winona Lake, IN: Eisenbrauns, 1990)
ICC	International Critical Commentary
impv.	imperative
Int	*Interpretation*
ITC	International Theological Commentary
JAAR	*Journal of the American Academy of Religion*
JANESCU	*Journal of the Ancient Near Eastern Society of Columbia University*
JAOS	*Journal of the American Oriental Society*
JB	*Jerusalem Bible*
JBL	*Journal of Biblical Literature*
JES	*Journal of Ecumenical Studies*
JETS	*Journal of the Evangelical Theological Society*
JJS	*Journal of Jewish Studies*
Jos. Asen.	*Joseph and Aseneth*

JSJSup	Supplements to the Journal for the Study of Judaism
JSNTSup	*Journal for the Study of the New Testament*, Supplement Series
JSOTSup	*Journal for the Study of the Old Testament*, Supplement Series
JTS	*Journal of Theological Studies*
Jub.	*Jubilees*
J.W.	Josephus, *Jewish War*
K&D	C.F. Keil and R. Delitzsch, *Biblical Commentary on the Old Testament*. X. *Minor Prophets*, by C.F. Keil (trans. James Martin; repr., Grand Rapids: Eerdmans, 1988)
KJV	King James Version
KNT	Kommentar zum New Testament
L&N	J.P. Louw and E.A. Nida (eds.), *Greek–English Lexicon of the New Testament: Based on Semantic Domains* (2 vols.; New York: United Bible Societies, 2nd edn, 1989)
LEC	Library of Early Christianity
Let. Arist.	*Letter of Aristeas*
Lev. Rab.	*Leviticus Rabbah*
LXX	Septuagint
m.	Mishnah
Marc.	Tertullian, *Against Marcion*
MBCNTS	The Mellen Biblical Commentary New Testament Series
Midr. Ps.	*Midrash Psalms*
MS(S)	manuscript(s)
MT	Masoretic Text
NA27	Barbara Aland, Kurt Aland, Johannes Karavidopoulos, Carlo M. Martini and Bruce M. Metzger (eds.), *Novum Testamentum Graece* (Stuttgart: Deutsche Bibelgesellschaft, 27th edn, 1993)
NAB	*New American Bible*
NAC	New American Commentary
NASB	*New American Standard Bible*
NCB	New Century Bible
NEB	*New English Bible*
NET	New English Translation
NGS	New Gospel Studies
NKJV	New King James Version
NICNT	New International Commentary on the New Testament
NIDOTTE	Willem A. VanGemeren (ed.), *New International Dictionary of Old Testament Theology and Exegesis* (5 vols.; Grand Rapids: Zondervan, 1997)
NIDNTT	Colin Brown (ed.), *The New International Dictionary of New Testament Theology* (3 vols.; Exeter: Paternoster Press, 1975)
NIV	New International Version
NJB	*New Jerusalem Bible*
NJPS	*Tanakh: The New JPS Translation*
NLT	New Living Translation
NovT	*Novum Testamentum*
NovTSup	*Novum Testamentum*, Supplements
NRSV	New Revised Standard Version

NTS	*New Testament Studies*
NTTS	New Testament Tools and Studies
OBO	Orbis biblicus et orientalis
OECT	Oxford Early Christian Texts
OTL	Old Testament Library
OTP	James Charlesworth (ed.), *The Old Testament Pseudepigrapha* (2 vols.; Garden City, NY: Doubleday, 1983–85)
Paed.	Clement of Alexandra, *Christ the Educator*
Pers.	Persian
Pesiq. R.	*Pesiqta Rabbati*
pf.	perfect
Pirqe R. El.	*Pirqe deRabbi Eliezer*
PRSt	*Perspectives in Religious Studies*
Pss. Sol.	*Psalms of Solomon*
ptc.	participle
PTS	Patristische Texte und Studien
PTSDSSP	The Princeton Theological Seminary Dead Sea Scrolls Project
PVTG	Pseudepigrapha Veteris Testamenti Graece
Q	Quelle ('source')
RB	*Revue biblique*
REB	Revised English Bible
RestQ	*Restoration Quarterly*
RevScRel	*Revue des sciences religieuses*
RSV	Revised Standard Version
Ruth Rab.	*Ruth Rabbah*
Sanh.	*Sanhedrin*
SBLDS	SBL Dissertation Series
SBLRBS	SBL Resources for Biblical Study
SBLSCS	SBL Septuagint and Cognate Studies
SBLSP	SBL Seminar Papers
SBT	Studies in Biblical Theology
ScEs	*Science et esprit*
SCJ	*Stone-Campbell Journal*
Sib. Or.	*Sibylline Oracles*
SJT	*Scottish Journal of Theology*
SNTG	Studies in New Testament Greek
SNTSMS	Society for New Testament Studies Monograph Series
SP	Sacra Pagina
Song Rab.	*Song of Songs Rabbah*
Spec. Laws	Philo, *On the Special Laws*
SSEJC	Studies in Scripture in Early Judaism and Christianity
SSN	Studia semitica neerlandica
ST	*Studia theologica*
STDJ	Studies on the Texts of the Desert of Judah
StPB	Studia postbiblica
Str–B	Hermann L. Strack and Paul Billerbeck, *Kommentar zum Neuen Testament aus Talmud und Midrasch* (7 vols.; Munich: Beck, 1922–61)

SVTP	Studia in Veteris Testamenti pseudepigrapha
Syr.	Syriac
T. Ab.	*Testament of Abraham*
T. Benj.	*Testament of Benjamin*
T. Dan	*Testament of Dan*
T. Gad	*Testament of Gad*
T. Job	*Testament of Job*
T. Jos.	*Testament of Joseph*
T. Jud.	*Testament of Judah*
T. Levi	*Testament of Levi*
T. Sim.	*Testament of Simeon*
T. Zeb.	*Testament of Zebulun*
TDNT	Gerhard Kittel and Gerhard Friedrich (eds.), *Theological Dictionary of the New Testament* (trans. Geoffrey W. Bromiley; 10 vols.; Grand Rapids: Eerdmans, 1964–76)
THS	Tyndale House Studies
Tg.	Targum
THKNT	Theologischer Handkommentar zum Neuen Testament
TJ	*Trinity Journal*
TLNT	Ceslas Spicq, *Theological Lexicon of the New Testament* (trans. and ed. James D. Ernest; 3 vols.; Peabody, MA: Hendrickson, 1994)
TLOT	Ernst Jenni and Claus Westermann (eds.), *Theological Lexicon of the Old Testament* (trans. Mark E. Brodie; 3 vols.; Peabody, MA: Hendrickson, 1997)
TNTC	Tyndale New Testament Commentary
TOTC	Tyndale Old Testament Commentaries
TSAJ	Texte und Studien zum Antiken Judentum
TUGAL	Texte und Untersuchungen zur Geschichte der altchristlichen Literatur
TynBul	*Tyndale Bulletin*
UCOP	University of Cambridge Oriental Publications
USB4	Barbara Aland *et al.* (eds.), *The Greek New Testament* (Stuttgart: Deutsche Bibelstiftung, 4th rev. edn, 1993)
Vesp.	Suetonius, *Vespasian*
Virt.	Philo, *On the Virtues*
VT	*Vetus Testamentum*
VTSup	*Vetus Testamentum*, Supplements
Vulg.	Vulgate
WBC	Word Biblical Commentary
WMANT	Wissenschaftliche Monographien zum Alten und Neuen Testament
WUNT	Wissenschaftliche Untersuchungen zum Neuen Testament
x	Number of times a form occurs
ZAW	*Zeitschrift für die alttestamentliche Wissenschaft*
Zebah	*Zebahim*
ZNW	*Zeitschrift für die neutestamentliche Wissenschaft*
ZTK	*Zeitschrift für Theologie und Kirche*

PREFACE

In the fall of 1997, the late Dr William Farmer graciously invited me to observe his Seminar on the Gospel of Matthew at the University of Dallas (UD). That semester I wrote for Dr Farmer a paper, entitled 'The Last Supper in Matthew', which examined the Old Testament antecedents to the cup-saying recorded in Mt. 26.28. At his encouragement, I sent the completed paper to Dr E. Earle Ellis, whose seminar on New Testament Theology I had completed while a PhD student at Southwestern Seminary. To my delight, Dr Ellis recommended my paper for publication in the *Bulletin for Biblical Research*. In the course of researching this paper, I had noticed for the first time what others had seen before, that one of the texts standing behind Mt. 26.28 is Zech. 9.11. This discovery was for me the genesis of the research for this manuscript, the topic and method of which were patterned after the work of these two professors, who largely influenced my own study of the use of the Old Testament in the New Testament. While I had the privilege to participate with the UD seminar for two more years, I regret that this work was not completed before Dr Farmer's death in the winter of 2001.

Many people deserve my thanks for their guidance and encouragement. To name any is to leave some out, but I must recognize several people in particular. I am indebted to those from whom I have learned: my professors, including Dr Thomas Tanner, Dr Robert Lowery, and Dr Gary Hall of Lincoln Christian College and Seminary; Dr Lorin Cranford, Dr Bruce Corley, and Dr Siegfried Schatzmann of Southwestern Seminary; and the members of the Seminar on the Gospel of Matthew at UD, particularly Dr Jeffrey Bingham. I do want to express my appreciation for the students and faculty of Dallas Christian College. I am especially grateful for my teaching colleagues: Dr Mark Hahlen, who provided insight into the enigmatic book of Zechariah; Dr Tony Springer, who increased my understanding of the early Church Fathers; and Dr Cara Snyder, who read the entire manuscript for clarity and style. For their support and prayers, I want to express my gratitude to Dr Rodney Combs, Mark Yarbrough, and my friends from the North Point Christian Church. And I am most grateful for my family: my wife, Diane, for her love and encouragement and for her interest in my research; our children, Elizabeth, Emily, and Allan, for their patience; my parents, Roger and Beverly Ham, for their example of Christian faith and the study of scripture; my grandfather, Wilbur Chapman, for his encouragement to pursue my educational dreams; and my grandmother, Jessie Ham, for her daily prayers for the completion of this project.

Clay Alan Ham
23 August 2004

INTRODUCTION

The Gospel of Matthew uses the Old Testament extensively. The frequent appearance of references to the Old Testament clearly demonstrates this. At least 41 times[1] Matthew employs an Old Testament passage either as an explicit or implicit citation.[2] Depending on how one identifies such citations, their number in Matthew may actually be as high as 64.[3] Matthew also alludes

1. W.D. Davies and Dale C. Allison, Jr, *The Gospel according to Saint Matthew* (ICC; 3 vols.; Edinburgh: T. & T. Clark, 1988–97), I, pp. 34-56, list 41 quotations in Matthew: 1.23a; 2.6, 15, 18, 23; 3.3; 4.4, 6, 7, 10, 15-16; 5.21, 27, 31, 33, 38, 43; 8.17; 9.13; 11.10; 12.7, 18-21; 13.14-15, 35; 15.4a, 4b, 8-9; 19.4, 5, 18-19, 19; 21.5, 13, 16, 42; 22.32, 37, 39, 44; 26.31; 27.9-10.

2. Stanley E. Porter, 'The Use of the Old Testament in the New Testament: A Brief Comment on Method and Terminology', in Craig A. Evans and James A. Sanders (eds.), *Early Christian Interpretation of the Scriptures of Israel: Investigations and Proposals* (JSNTSup, 148; SSEJC, 5; Sheffield: Sheffield Academic Press, 1997), pp. 79-88, has delineated well the difficulty in defining various terms used to describe the use of the Old Testament in the New Testament. The present work adopts the descriptions suggested by Douglas J. Moo, *The Old Testament in the Gospel Passion Narratives* (Sheffield: Almond Press, 1983), pp. 18-21: 'explicit quotations' clearly mark the Old Testament reference with an 'introductory formula', and 'implicit quotations' are 'relatively lengthy, word-for-word parallels' without an introductory formula. In the present work, the words 'quotation' and 'citation' are used interchangeably.

3. Wilhelm Dittmar, *Vetus Testamentum in Novo: Die alttestamentlichen Parallelen des Neuen Testament im Wortlaut der Urtexte und der Septuaginta* (Göttingen: Vandenhoeck & Ruprecht, 1903), pp. 1-72, lists 49 citations; while he accepts all but 5.31, 33 from the list in n. 1, he adds 1.23b; 7.23; 18.16; 21.9; 23.39; 24.15; 24.30; 26.64a; 27.43a, 46. Eugen Hühn, *Die alttestamentlichen Citate und Reminiscenzen im Neuen Testament* (Tübingen: J.C.B. Mohr [Paul Siebeck], 1900), pp. 1-49, lists 50 citations. Having used Dittmar's work, Hühn presents a similar listing; Hühn excludes 18.16; 24.30; 26.64a; 27.43a from Dittmar's list but adds 3.17; 5.31, 33; 11.29; 22.24. Barbara Aland, Kurt Aland, Johannes Karavidopoulos, Carlo M. Martini and Bruce M. Metzger (eds.), *The Greek New Testament* (Stuttgart: Deutsche Bibelgesellschaft, 4th edn, 1994), pp. 887-90, lists 52 quotations; these include all but 2.23 from the 41 in n. 1, while adding 1.23b; 10.35-36; 12.40; 18.16; 19.7; 21.9; 22.24; 23.39; 24.30; 26.64a, 64b; 27.46. Barbara Aland, Kurt Aland, Johannes Karavidopoulos, Carlo M. Martini, and Bruce M. Metzger (eds.), *Novum Testamentum Graece* (Stuttgart: Deutsche Bibelgesellschaft, 27th edn, 1993), pp. 770-806, offers the longest listing with 61 quotations; these include all those listed in

frequently to the Old Testament, perhaps as many as three hundred times.[4] Taken together these citations and allusions show how prominent is the use of the Old Testament in Matthew's Gospel.

the UBS4 except 5.31, 33; 19.7; 26.64a, but the NA27 adds 7.23; 9.36; 11.5, 29; 13.32, 42, 50; 16.27; 17.10; 24.15, 29; 26.38; 27.35. The NA27 list of 61 plus 2.23; 3.17; 27.43a (mentioned in Davies and Allison, Dittmar, and Hühn) equals 64 potential citations from the Old Testament in Matthew's Gospel. In any case, according to UBS4, pp. 888-89, Matthew cites from the Old Testament approximately twice as often as Mark or Luke does and more than three times as often as John does.

Comparing these lists of quotations, and thereby arriving at a definitive number of citations, is difficult for several reasons. One, the distinction between 'implicit quotation' and 'allusion' remains elusive. For example, while the NA27 lists Mt. 13.32 as a quotation of Ps. 104.12, the UBS4 lists it as an allusion. Using the criteria suggested by Moo, the reference in Mt. 13.32 is more likely an allusion. Two, the nature and listing of combined citations makes the counting of quotations quite complicated. Mt. 19.18-19, for instance, clearly cites both Exod. 20.12-16 and Lev. 19.18; thus, it appears in these listings as two quotations. Whereas Mt. 24.29 incorporates wording from Isa. 13.10 and 34.4, it may not meet the criteria for an implicit citation and likely should not appear in a list of quotations even one time. Three, in some instances, the identification of the citation's source differs from one list to another. Here Mt. 22.24 provides a good example. While the NA27 identifies both Gen. 38.8 and Deut. 25.5 as sources for the citation, the UBS4 lists only Deut. 25.5. Mt. 22.24 clearly cites Deut. 25.5, but it probably does not cite Gen. 38.8, although Gen. 38.8 illustrates the practice of Deut. 25.5. Therefore, Mt. 22.24 possibly cites one passage and alludes to another. Four, some citations do not clearly refer to a specific Old Testament passage: for example, 2.23; 26.56 and perhaps 5.31; 19.7.

4.   The UBS4, pp. 891-901, lists over two hundred allusions and verbal parallels, while the NA27, pp. 770-806, lists approximately three hundred. Porter, 'Use of the Old Testament in the New Testament', pp. 81-88, has convincingly demonstrated that the term 'allusion' is difficult, at best, and thus warrants clear definition. Laurence Perrine and Thomas R. Arp, *Literature: Structure, Sound, and Sense* (San Diego: Harcourt Brace Jovanovich, 5th edn, 1988), p. 623, define an allusion as 'a reference to something in history or previous literature'. That 'something' may be a person, place, concept, tradition, event, or text. An allusion assumes that the author(s) and reader(s) share a common knowledge of that 'something' and thus relies on such a knowledge for its impact. (On the process of a reader's actualization of an allusion, see Ziva Ben-Porat, 'The Poetics of Literary Allusion', *PTL: A Journal for Descriptive Poetics and Theory of Literature* 1 [1976], pp. 105-28.)

More specifically, a literary allusion presupposes a tradition that existed in textual form and thus exhibits a linguistic similarity to the evoked text. While citations from the Old Testament in the New Testament are generally word-for-word renderings of some length and are often, though not always, introduced with a formula, Moo, *Old Testament in the Passion Narratives*, p. 20, distinguishes an allusion from a citation or quotation in that an allusion uses 'Scriptural words and phrases without introduction and without disrupting the flow of the narrative'. The presence of an allusion to an Old Testament text by a New Testament author depends on, in the words of Kevin Vanhoozer, *Is There a Meaning in This Text? The Bible, the Reader, and the Morality of Literary Knowledge* (Grand Rapids: Zondervan, 1998), p. 257, 'what the author *could have done* in tending to his words'.

Research Problem

With such recurrent use of the Old Testament in Matthew, opportunities abound for studying the origin, purpose, and meaning of Matthew's appeals to the Old Testament. However, in spite of these opportunities a small set of ten quotations has almost entirely dominated the study of Matthew's use of the Old Testament.[5]

Formula Quotations in Matthew's Gospel

These ten so-called formula quotations (1.22-23; 2.15, 17-18, 23; 4.14-16; 8.17; 12.17-21; 13.35; 21.5; 27.9-10) share three characteristics. One, they are introduced by a similar redactional formula, hence the name 'formula quotations'. This introductory formula usually includes the words: ἵνα πληρωθῇ τὸ ῥηθὲν διὰ τοῦ προφήτου λέγοντος.[6] Two, the formula quotations

Thus, a biblical allusion presupposes that a New Testament author is interpreting an Old Testament text (often with reference to the original Old Testament context behind the allusion, according to C.H. Dodd, *According to the Scriptures: The Sub-Structure of New Testament Theology* [London: Nisbet, 1952], pp. 126-33) or, more precisely, that the New Testament author is using the Old Testament phraseology to explain the meaning of a New Testament event, generally one in the life and ministry of Jesus, as one which fulfills the Old Testament.

5. So Donald Senior, 'The Lure of the Formula Quotations: Re-assessing Matthew's Use of the Old Testament with the Passion Narrative as Test Case', in Christopher M. Tuckett (ed.), *The Scriptures in the Gospels* (BETL, 131; Leuven: Leuven University Press, 1997), pp. 89-115 (89), asserts: 'While there have been innumerable studies attempting to understand the purpose and meaning of Matthew's appeal to the Old Testament, the most characteristic note in recent scholarship has been an emphasis on the so-called "formula quotations". In fact, with few exceptions, virtually all studies of Matthew's use of the Old Testament concentrate on the formula quotations as the most characteristic and revealing feature of the gospel's perspective in this matter'.

6. Variations in the introductory formula include an additional designation of the prophetic or divine source of the citation (ὑπὸ κυρίου in 1.23; 2.15, Ἰερεμίου in 2.18; 27.9-10, and Ἡσαΐου in 4.15; 8.17; 12.17; 13.35) and an alternative subordinate conj. beginning the phrase (ὅπως in 2.23; 8.17; 13.35, τότε in 27.9). Mt. 2.23 also contains the pl. description τῶν προφητῶν rather than the sg. τοῦ προφήτου. Mt. 3.3 contains an introductory phrase with remarkable similarities to the one used with the formula quotations (οὗτος γάρ ἐστιν ὁ ῥηθεὶς διὰ Ἡσαΐου τοῦ προφήτου λέγοντος); however, it does not contain the pass. verb πληρωθη. Other texts (2.5; 11.10; 13.14-15) employ formulas with less similarity, and Mt. 26.56 uses a formula with πληρόω (ἵνα πληρωθῶσιν αἱ γραφαὶ τῶν προφητῶν) but without any Old Testament quotation.

On the origin of introductory formula itself, Ulrich Luz, *Matthew 1–7: A Commentary* (trans. Wilhelm C. Linss; Minneapolis: Augsburg Press, 1989), p. 158, finds 'no direct models in the Old Testament and in Jewish texts'. On the lack of parallels in the Mishnah and the Dead Sea Scrolls, see respectively Bruce M. Metzger, 'The Formulas Introducing Quotations of Scripture in the New Testament and the Mishnah', *JBL* 70 (1951), pp. 297-307, and Joseph A. Fitzmyer, 'The Use of Explicit Old Testament Quotations in

function as editorial commentary from the evangelist; they are not spoken by Jesus or other characters in the gospel narrative.[7] To emphasize this personal reflection by the evangelist, German scholarship has used the term *Reflexionszitate*[8] to distinguish these ten texts from other explicit citations or *Kontextzitate*, which are more closely linked to their context. Another designation, *Erfüllungszitate* or 'fulfillment quotation', has been suggested by Wilhelm Rothfuchs to underscore the theological purpose of the quotations.[9] Three, these quotations exhibit a mixed text form less close to the LXX than other references to the Old Testament in Matthew.[10] Often the wording of these

Qumran Literature and in the New Testament', in *idem, Essays on the Semitic Background of the New Testament* (London: Geoffrey Chapman, 1971), pp. 5-58. Since πληρόω is found infrequently in the LXX for the fulfillment of prophecy, only a few texts supply a possible, albeit doubtful, model for the Matthean formula: for example, 1 Kgs 2.27; 8.15, 24; 2 Chron. 6.4, 15; 36.22; Ezra 1.1 and most notably 2 Chron. 36.21 (τοῦ πληρωθῆναι λόγον κυρίου διὰ στόματος 'Ιερεμίου). The closest synoptic par. is Mk 14.49: ἵνα πληρωθῶσιν αἱ γραφαί. Even if one accepts that the Matthean introductory formula may have originated from this expression in Mk 14.49, the redactional characteristics of the introductory formula (notably Matthean language and adaptation to the context and/or to the quotation) suggest that the introductory formula has been created by the Matthean evangelist. So argue Senior, 'Lure of the Formula Quotations', p. 102; Luz, *Matthew 1–7*, p. 159; Graham Stanton, 'Matthew', in D.A. Carson and H.G.M. Williamson (eds.), *It is Written: Scripture Citing Scripture: Essays in Honour of Barnabas Lindars* (Cambridge: Cambridge University Press, 1988), pp. 205-19 (215). According to Dennis Gordon Tevis, 'An Analysis of Words and Phrases Characteristic of the Gospel of Matthew' (PhD dissertation, Southern Methodist University, 1983), pp. 39-40, the phrase's distribution throughout the gospel in contexts with a redactional function strongly suggests that it comes from the final redactor of Matthew.

For the most detailed studies of the introductory formula, see Wilhelm Rothfuchs, *Die Erfüllungszitate des Matthäus-Evangeliums: Eine biblisch-theologische Untersuchung* (BWANT, 8; Stuttgart: Kohlhammer, 1969), pp. 27-44; George M. Soares Prabhu, *The Formula Quotations in the Infancy Narratives of Matthew: An Enquiry into the Tradition History of Mt. 1–2* (AnBib, 63; Rome: Pontifical Biblical Institute, 1976), pp. 45-62.

7.   With the exception of Mt. 3.3, all other explicit citations in Matthew are spoken by Jesus (4.4, 7, 10; 5.21, 27, 31, 33, 38, 43; 9.13; 11.10; 12.7; 13.14-15; 15.4, 8-9; 19.4, 5, 18, 19; 21.13, 16, 42; 22.32, 37, 39, 44; 26.31) or other characters within the narrative (chief priests in 2.6 and Satan in 4.6).

8.   The term *Reflexionszitate* appears as early as H.J. Holtzmann, *Die Synoptiker—Die Apostelgeschichte* (HCNT, 1; Freiburg: J.C.B. Mohr [Paul Siebeck], 1889), p. 41.

9.   Rothfuchs, *Erfüllungszitate*, pp. 20-26. Raymond E. Brown, *The Birth of the Messiah: A Commentary on the Infancy Narratives in Matthew and Luke* (ABRL; New York: Doubleday, 1993), p. 97, calls the term employed by Rothfuchs more 'descriptive than analytical'; in any case the preferred expression in English has been 'formula quotation', since Sherman E. Johnson, 'The Biblical Quotations in Matthew', *HTR* 36 (1943), pp. 135-53 (135).

10.   Presumably Eugene Massebieau, *Examen des citations de l'ancien testament dans l'évangile selon Saint Matthieu* (Paris: Librarie Fischbacher, 1885), pp. 93-94, was first to

citations does not correspond to the LXX but shows striking similarities to the MT or, in some instances, even variant Hebrew wordings, Aramaic Targumim, and other Greek translations.[11] These three characteristics make the formula quotations 'almost a Matthean peculiarity'[12] and have provided the impetus for the course of Matthean scholarship over the past fifty years, a course which has been primarily concerned with the origin, text form, and purpose of the formula quotations.

In 1954,[13] Krister Stendahl published his *The School of St Matthew*; it was the first detailed study of the use of the Old Testament in Matthew[14] and one

connect the two observations that this group of citations in Matthew which are introduced with a formula also shows an awareness of the Hebrew text; Massebieau calls them 'citations apologétiques'. B.F. Westcott, *An Introduction to the Study of the Gospels* (London: Macmillan, 7th edn, 1888), p. 229, clearly identifies a group of 'original renderings of the Hebrew text' which are cited by the evangelist himself.

11. Krister Stendahl, *The School of St Matthew, and Its Use of the Old Testament* (ASNU, 20; Lund: G.W.K. Gleerup, 1954; repr., Philadelphia: Fortress Press, 1968), pp. iv, 97-127 (page citations are to the reprint edition). So also Robert H. Gundry, *The Use of the Old Testament in St Matthew's Gospel with Special Reference to the Messianic Hope* (NovTSup, 18; Leiden: E.J. Brill, 1967), pp. 89-127.

12. Brown, *Birth of the Messiah*, p. 97. Among the other Synoptic Gospels only Lk. 22.37 has a clearly uncontested formula citation, but it uses a form of τελέω rather than πληρόω. The Gospel of John contains ten fulfillment formulas. Eight use the pass. form πληρωθῇ following ἵνα (Jn 12.38; 13.18; 15.25; 17.12; 18.9, 32; 19.24, 36), while two use a form of λέγω (12.39; 19.37). In contrast to Matthew, the formula in John exhibits greater verbal and conceptual variation. Only in 12.38-39 does John name a particular prophet; generally the text makes a less specific reference to 'the Scripture' (13.18; 17.12; 19.37) or refers to the words of Jesus rather than the Old Testament (18.9, 32). Also, the citations in John refer to passages from all three divisions of the HB: Torah, Nebiim, and Ketubim. On the Johannine quotations, see Rothfuchs, *Erfüllungszitate*, pp. 151-77; Edwin D. Freed, *Old Testament Quotations in the Gospel of John* (NovTSup, 11; Leiden: E.J. Brill, 1965); and Craig A. Evans, 'On the Quotation Formulas in the Fourth Gospel', *BZ* 26 (1982), pp. 79-83.

13. The work was reprinted in 1968 with a preface, in which Stendahl qualified somewhat his thesis that the mixed text form of the formula quotations was created by a Matthean 'school'.

14. Stendahl's work follows from earlier works, in particular George D. Kilpatrick, *The Origins of the Gospel According to St Matthew* (Oxford: Clarendon Press, 1946), pp. 56-57, who had already noted that the formula quotations do not show a dependence on the LXX, whereas other citations in Matthew follow the LXX rather closely. Kilpatrick, *The Origins of the Gospel*, p. 95, suggests different backgrounds for the two types of quotations: 'It may be that quotations which derive from lectionary associations keep closer to the LXX, while those which exhibit some freedom would come from the stock quotations of the sermon'. Stendahl, *School of St Matthew*, p. 205, would later say that these 'stock quotations' are the *pesher* interpretation of the 'school' of Matthew. For a brief survey of research before Stendahl, see S.E. Johnson, 'Biblical Quotations in Matthew', pp. 135-53, and Norman Hillyer, 'Matthew's Use of the Old Testament', *EvQ* 36 (1964), pp. 12-26.

of the first works by a New Testament scholar to make extensive use of the Dead Sea Scrolls. Stendahl conceives of Matthew's Gospel as a handbook produced by a school for teachers and church leaders,[15] a school whose closest parallel is the Dead Sea Scrolls sect. He attempts 'to trace the influences of a school on the composition and the actual material of the gospel',[16] in particular through a detailed study of Old Testament quotations in Matthew. According to Stendahl, the text form of the quotations Matthew has in common with Mark and Luke is the LXX; however, the formula quotations often show a striking closeness to the MT or 'show deviations from all Greek, Hebrew and Aramaic types of text known to us, while at the same time they intermingle influences from these'.[17] For this reason, Stendahl sees the formula quotations as a distinct group of citations with a distinct text form, which he attributes to the creative work of the 'school' of Matthew.[18] He claims then that the school treated the Old Testament texts in a manner similar to the *pesher* interpretation found in the Habakkuk scroll (1QpHab).[19]

Stendahl's conclusion has not generally been accepted, due in part to the perceptive critique by Bertil Gärtner's 'The Habakkuk Commentary (DSH) and the Gospel of Matthew'.[20] Questioning the presumption that 1QpHab makes use of various versions, Gärtner sees in the word play found in 1QpHab and CD that the Dead Sea Scrolls sect may have had its own textual tradition of the Minor Prophets.[21] More importantly, Gärtner challenges Stendahl's understanding of the term *pesher*. While *pesher* relates to an interpretation of consecutive Old Testament texts, Matthew relates the Old Testament to a consecutive story to show messianic fulfillment.[22] The use of *pesher* for the formula quotations in Matthew then is misleading. So too is Stendahl's notion that these quotations arose within a school, rather than in the early missionary preaching to the Jews.[23]

---

15. According to Stendahl, *School of St Matthew*, pp. 20-35, the ordered structure, extensive discourse material, and concern for church leadership in Matthew's Gospel give the work a character of a handbook produced by a school for teachers and church leaders.

16. Stendahl, *School of St Matthew*, p. 12.

17. Stendahl, *School of St Matthew*, p. 97.

18. Stendahl, *School of St Matthew*, p. 127.

19. In the words of Stendahl, *School of St Matthew*, p. 31, 'The main object of our study on the school of Matthew will be to prove the close affinity between the type of O.T. interpretation to be found in a certain group of Matthew's quotations and the way in which the Sect of Qumran treats the book of Habakkuk'.

20. Bertil Gärtner, 'The Habakkuk Commentary (DSH) and the Gospel of Matthew', *ST* 8 (1955), pp. 1-24.

21. Gärtner, 'The Habakkuk Commentary', pp. 4-6.

22. Gärtner, 'The Habakkuk Commentary', pp. 12-14.

23. Gärtner, 'The Habakkuk Commentary', pp. 22-24.

Georg Strecker's *Der Weg der Gerechtigkeit* devotes an introductory section to the formula quotations.[24] In it he puts forward some ideas which differ from Stendahl. Strecker doubts that the wording of the quotations themselves is the work of the evangelist, since he has concluded that the quotations do not contain words characteristic of Matthew nor does their wording appear to be influenced by the context. That Matthew has assimilated both quotations common with Mark and Q and his own quotations, apart from the formula quotations, to the wording of LXX suggests to Strecker the improbability of the same redactor adapting some quotations to the LXX and others to the MT.[25] According to Strecker, therefore, the evangelist has most likely taken the formula quotations from a *Zitatensammlung*, that is, a written collection of prophetic passages, sometimes called a testimony book.[26] Strecker also claims that, by quoting the Old Testament in the formula quotations, Matthew has 'historicized' the life of Jesus, showing that the life of Jesus belongs to a past sacred epoch.[27] By doing so, Matthew has used these Old Testament citations to create stories within his narrative about the life of Jesus.[28]

In 1967, Robert Gundry presented an extremely detailed study of the quotations and allusions in Matthew, entitled *The Use of the Old Testament in St Matthew's Gospel*.[29] Gundry attempts to refute the idea of a distinct text for

24. Georg Strecker, *Der Weg der Gerechtigkeit: Untersuchungen zur Theologie des Matthäus* (FRLANT, 82; Göttingen: Vandenhoeck & Ruprecht, 3rd edn, 1971), pp. 49-85. The work was first published in 1962; all references are to the 3rd edition.

25. Strecker, *Der Weg der Gerechtigkeit*, pp. 21-29.

26. Strecker, *Der Weg der Gerechtigkeit*, p. 50. The testimony hypothesis is most often associated with J. Rendel Harris, *Testimonies* (2 vols.; Cambridge: Cambridge University Press, 1916–20). For Harris's discussion of the possible use of testimonies in the Synoptic Gospels, see esp. II, pp. 58-70. Even if one does not accept the school hypothesis, Stendahl's analysis of the multiple textual traditions in the formula quotations seems to have shown convincingly that the formula quotations are *ad hoc* compositions and not taken from a previous source.

27. Strecker, *Der Weg der Gerechtigkeit*, p. 82.

28. While Strecker's conclusion about the 'historicizing' use of the formula quotations influenced the scholarship which followed him, it has since been challenged. See especially Gundry, *Use of the Old Testament*, pp. 189-204, and Brown, *Birth of the Messiah*, p. 100.

29. Gundry, *Use of the Old Testament*, pp. 9-150. Stanton, 'Matthew', p. 210, holds that 'Gundry's careful presentation of the Hebrew, Aramaic, and Greek textual traditions which are relevant for the study of references to the Old Testament in Matthew is still unrivalled', but he sees Gundry's strong reliance on allusions to the Old Testament as his Achilles' heel, 'for the text form of allusions which rarely consist of more than two or three words is necessarily elusive! Where a writer does not indicate explicitly that he is quoting Scripture, there must be at least a good possibility that he is drawing on his memory.' Senior, 'Lure of the Formula Quotations', p. 92, agrees: the impact of Gundry's study is blunted in that 'some of his conclusions were based on an examination of the

the formula quotations. While he agrees with Stendahl about the mixed text form in the formula quotations, he differs in his assertion that the text form of the formula quotations is found in all parts of the Synoptic Gospels.[30] Gundry insists that Matthew's adherence to the LXX found in the quotations which are shared with Mark is out of line with the other Synoptic quotations and allusions which show evidence of the same 'mixed textual tradition' of the formula quotations.[31] He further asserts that the origin of this text form is Matthew the apostle, who 'was his own targumist and drew on a knowledge of the Hebrew, Aramaic, and Greek textual traditions of the Old Testament'.[32] Corollary to this suggestion is Gundry's explanation that Matthew the apostle took notes during Jesus' earthly ministry, recording events, sayings, and perhaps even Jesus' own interpretation of the Old Testament.[33]

While Gundry does not refer to Strecker's work, Richard McConnell in his *Law and Prophecy in Matthew's Gospel* directly debates Strecker.[34] Although McConnell concedes that Matthew may have drawn some of the formula quotations from a collection of quotations, he 'does not exclude the possibility that Matthew altered these quotations further, for his own purposes'.[35] In contrast to Strecker, he insists that Matthew has selected these quotations largely from the Old Testament and that Matthew has exercised an interpretative authority in adapting them to his own theological interpretation of the ministry and identity of Jesus.[36]

biblical allusions; the fragility of drawing inferences about the text type from a few words or phrases made Gundry's conclusions less decisive'.

30. Gundry, *Use of the Old Testament*, pp. 155-59.

31. Gundry, *Use of the Old Testament*, p. 150.

32. Gundry, *Use of the Old Testament*, p. 172.

33. Gundry, *Use of the Old Testament*, pp. 181-85.

34. Richard S. McConnell, *Law and Prophecy in Matthew's Gospel: The Authority and Use of the Old Testament in the Gospel of Saint Matthew* (Basel: Friedrich Reinhardt, 1969), pp. 101-41. Gundry does not refer to Strecker, because Gundry completed his work in 1961, and Gundry is not cited in McConnell, whose work was completed in 1964 but published in 1969.

35. McConnell, *Law and Prophecy*, p. 135. Both Stendahl, *School of St Matthew*, pp. 214-17, and Gundry, *Use of the Old Testament*, pp. 163-66, had already argued against *testimonia* as a source for the formula quotations in Matthew. Luz, *Matthew 1–7*, p. 160, also questions the usefulness of the hypothesis: 'One cannot really imagine a collection of proof passages which would contain our formula quotations. What else should quotations like Hos. 11.1 (= 2.15), Jer. 31.15 (= 2.18), Zech. 9.9 (= 21.5) or 11.13 (= 27.9) prove than precisely the stories in which they now appear? The great majority of the formula quotations...can, in my opinion, have been handed down only in connection with those narratives in which they are found today.'

36. McConnell, *Law and Prophecy*, pp. 136-37. For the context's influence on the wording of the quotation and the corresponding theological emphasis, see McConnell's (pp. 121-25) treatment of Mt. 12.18-21.

Although similar in its conclusions to McConnell, *Die Erfüllungszitate des Matthäus-Evangeliums* by Wilhelm Rothfuchs is 'more detailed and more theologically perceptive'.[37] Rothfuchs attempts to demonstrate how the 'fulfillment quotations', as Rothfuchs has labeled them, fit into Matthew's theology by means of redaction criticism. While agreeing with Stendahl that the quotations contain elements from all the Old Testament text forms, he differs from both Stendahl and Strecker in his assessment that the Evangelist has been responsible for adapting the formula quotations to their context.[38] Rothfuchs also disagrees with Stendahl concerning the purpose of the formula quotations; according to Rothfuchs, 'The fulfillment quotations in Matthew and particularly their introductory formula are not interested in the interpretation of the specific words of the prophet but in the interpretation of the transmitted story of Jesus'.[39] Rothfuchs discusses the reason for the uneven distribution of the formula quotations.[40] The first four quotations in Matthew 1–2 orient the reader to the main themes of Jesus' mission, while the next four quotations in Matthew 4–13, all from Isaiah, relate the ministry of Jesus to the lost sheep of Israel. Rothfuchs further assigns Mt. 21.4-5 and 27.9-10 to traditional material which already included the Old Testament citations, suggesting an even more radical grouping of the formula quotations toward the beginning of the Gospel of Matthew.[41]

An important review of the works by Gundry, McConnell, and Rothfuchs appeared in Frans Van Segbroeck's 'Les citations d'accomplissement dans l'évangile selon Matthieu d'après trois ouvrages récents'.[42] Van Segbroeck tests the conclusions of Stendahl, and, to a lesser extent, Strecker, on the basis of the contributions by Gundry, McConnell, and Rothfuchs. The conclusion of Stendahl about a mixed text form in the formula quotations has generally been accepted, whereas his hypothesis about Matthew's use of *pesher* interpretation and Strecker's hypothesis about Matthew taking the formula quotations from a *Zitatensammlung* have not generally been accepted.[43] Van Segbroeck rejects Stendahl's notion of a school as too exclusive and unilateral, but he favors the view of McConnell and Rothfuchs that the formula quotations are closely connected to their context and reflect the intention and

37. Graham Stanton, 'The Origin and Purpose of Matthew's Gospel: Matthean Scholarship from 1945–80', *ANRW* 25.3 (1931), pp. 1889-951.

38. Rothfuchs, *Erfüllungszitate*, p. 89, concludes: 'The relationship between the citations and their contexts is characterized by a reciprocal influence'.

39. Rothfuchs, *Erfüllungszitate*, p. 180.

40. Rothfuchs, *Erfüllungszitate*, pp. 97-103.

41. Rothfuchs, *Erfüllungszitate*, p. 103.

42. Frans Van Segbroeck, 'Les citations d'accomplissement dans l'évangile selon Matthieu d'après trois ouvrages récents', in M. Didier (ed.), *L'Évangile selon Matthieu: Rédaction et théologie* (BETL, 29; Gembloux: Duculot, 1972), pp. 107-30.

43. Van Segbroeck, 'Les citations d'accomplissement', pp. 128-29.

theology of Matthew.[44] An important contribution which Van Segbroeck himself makes to the study of the formula quotations relates to their distribution in the Gospel of Matthew. In his discussion of Rothfuchs's observation that Matthew has used the four Isaiah citations in Matthew 4–13 to call attention to the ministry of Jesus to the lost sheep of the house of Israel, Van Segbroeck adds that this section in Matthew is also concerned about the failure of that ministry.[45] Both the ministry of Jesus to Israel and Israel's opposition to his ministry explain Matthew's repeated reference to Isaiah.

In *The Formula Quotations in the Infancy Narratives of Matthew*, George Soares Prabhu extensively examines the issues related to the formula quotations in general before his extended treatment of the formula quotations in the infancy narrative. He provides a detailed analysis of the introductory formula, and he reconsiders the origin of the fulfillment formula and the text form of the formula quotations.[46] Soares Prabhu argues that both the introductory formula and the formula quotations are the work of Matthew; the variations in the introductory formula reveal intentional changes 'which neatly adapt each formula to its context in the Gospel', whereas the citations 'are free targumic translations made from the original Hebrew by Matthew, in view of the context into which he has inserted them'.[47] For Soares Prabhu, this rules out the likelihood that either a school or a testimony book could explain the text type of the formula quotations. Soares Prabhu also illustrates the dialectical influence between the Matthean context and the formula quotation (against Strecker), suggesting that the quotation 'influences the external form (vocabulary) of the finished narrative, while the context (or rather the tradition it embodies) determines its sense'.[48]

44. Van Segbroeck, 'Les citations d'accomplissement', pp. 129-30.
45. Van Segbroeck, 'Les citations d'accomplissement', p. 126. This is seen especially in the citation of Isa. 6.9-10 in Mt. 13.10-17. However, Senior, 'Lure of the Formula Quotations', p. 95, questions whether Rothfuchs and Van Segbroeck adequately explain the distribution of the formula quotations: 'If Matthew was capable of adding Isaian quotations to interpret a substantial portion of Jesus' public ministry in chapters 4 to 13, why could he not do so for the rest of the gospel, including the Passion Narrative in which the issue of scriptural fulfillment would seem to be most acutely posed? And if Matthew's more radical reworking of his sources in chapters 1–13 provides part of the answer for the presence of the formula quotations in the first half of the gospel, how can one explain the seemingly errant quotations in 21,4-5 and 27,9-10? Even if one concedes that the Old Testament quotations were traditionally connected to these two stories, this does not explain why Matthew would introduce his fulfillment formula at these points and no other.'
46. Soares Prabhu, *Formula Quotations*, pp. 45-106.
47. Soares Prabhu, *Formula Quotations*, pp. 48, 104. Unlike Gundry, however, Soares Prabhu (pp. 74-75) does not think that Matthew is the apostle.
48. Soares Prabhu, *Formula Quotations*, p. 160.

Although contributions to the study of the formula quotations in Matthew since that of Soares Prabhu have been fewer and less substantial, most scholars continue to emphasize the role of the evangelist in the selection and modification of the formula quotations.[49] Raymond Brown, in *The Birth of the Messiah*, adds a caution to the reminder of Stendahl about the multiple textual traditions in the first century: 'when we add to these the possibility of a free rendering by the evangelist himself, the avenue of deciding what citation is Matthean and what is pre-Matthean on the basis of wording becomes uncertain'.[50] Challenging the conclusion that the LXX was Matthew's Bible, Graham Stanton argues that 'Matthew's primary allegiance is to the textual form of the quotations in his sources rather than to the LXX as such'.[51] For Stanton (as well as Brown) this allows for the likelihood that Matthew himself is responsible for choosing and adapting many of the formula quotations, especially where the quotation and context are clearly modified for one another.[52] W.D. Davies and Dale Allison express this position regarding the formula quotations even more pointedly: 'All presumption is that they are Matthew's own work, created as he composed his gospel'; for them the mixed textual form of the citations is evidence that Matthew has drawn on his own knowledge of Hebrew.[53]

Another emphasis among more recent scholarship has been the recognition that the study of the formula quotations may have caused the neglect of other important aspects of the use of the Old Testament in Matthew. Both Stanton and Ulrich Luz call for the study of the formula quotations in connection with the other references Matthew makes to the Old Testament without his unique formula.[54] In 'The Lure of the Formula Quotations', Donald Senior more

---

49. Among the minority is Luz, *Matthew 1–7*, pp. 159-60, who argues against the hypothesis of a testimony book but wants to lessen the contribution of the evangelist Matthew to the wording of the formula quotations; according to Luz, Matthew is a 'conservative tradent and interpreter', who is obligated to the wording of the oral tradition handed down to him, an oral tradition that contained not only the formula quotations but also the stories associated with them.

50. Brown, *Birth of the Messiah*, p. 103.

51. Stanton, 'Matthew', p. 214.

52. Brown, *Birth of the Messiah*, p. 103, says: 'If one maintains that sometimes Matthew introduces as a formula citation a passage that was already known in Christian usage, one would expect that he would reproduce the familiar wording, a wording that may or may not reflect the LXX, depending on when and where the citation entered into circulation. On the other hand, when Matthew himself was the first to see the possibilities of an Old Testament fulfillment, he would presumably choose or even adapt a wording that would best fit his purposes.'

53. Davies and Allison, *Matthew*, I, p. 45. See also, III, pp. 575-76.

54. Stanton, 'Matthew', p. 205; Luz, *Matthew 1–7*, p. 157. An example of one such study is the treatment of Matthew's citations from Isaiah by Craig L. Blomberg, 'Interpreting Old Testament Prophetic Literature in Matthew: Double Fulfillment', *TJ* NS 23 (2002), pp. 17-33.

candidly contends that 'the formula quotations have been something of a "siren song", with attention to peculiar features of the formula quotations skewing a fuller appreciation of the role of the Old Testament in Matthew's narrative'.[55] To make his point, Senior appeals to the frequent and transparent use of the Old Testament in Matthew's Passion Narrative, which contains only two formula quotations but numerous other references to the Old Testament. These references include programmatic statements, direct quotations, allusions, and narrative elements inspired by Old Testament passages.[56] A recent study which follows a procedure similar to the one outlined by Senior is Michael Knowles, *Jeremiah in Matthew's Gospel: The Rejected-Prophet Motif in Matthaean Redaction*.[57] The work reproduces Knowles's doctoral dissertation done under the supervision of Richard Longenecker; it follows Longenecker's procedure of starting with explicit quotations and only then moving to allusions and biblical themes.[58] If for no other reason, the work is significant in that it illustrates a new way of studying the use of the Old Testament in Matthew's Gospel, a way which may effectively help the student of Matthew to navigate beyond the enchanting song of the formula quotations.

Zechariah in Matthew's Gospel
This investigation proposes the study of another prophetic book with a notable influence on the Gospel of Matthew, namely, Zechariah. Two of the ten so-called formula quotations (21.5; 27.9-10) and one explicit citation (26.31) come from Zechariah; moreover, two of these are the only explicit citations of the Old Testament in Matthew's Passion Narrative, which is generally understood to begin at Mt. 26.1.[59] In fact, only Isaiah among prophetic books is quoted in Matthew more often than Zechariah. The NA27 and the UBS4 list eight explicit citations from Isaiah; the only other books cited in Matthew more often than Zechariah are Deuteronomy (13*x*), Psalms (8*x*),

---

55. Senior, 'Lure of the Formula Quotations', p. 90. Senior alludes to Homer's *Odyssey* 12.37-54, where the goddess Circe instructs Odysseus, as he returns home to Ithaca after the war with Troy, on how to protect himself and his men from the mythical sisters (Σειρῆνες) who enticed seamen with their enchanting songs.

56. Senior, 'Lure of the Formula Quotations', pp. 108-14. In the fourth category of narrative elements, Senior (p. 107) includes both 'typology' and 'structural citations'; the latter occur 'where Old Testament passages or episodes provide the basic structure or inspiration for a narrative or parts of a narrative'.

57. Michael Knowles, *Jeremiah in Matthew's Gospel: The Rejected-Prophet Motif in Matthaean Redaction* (JSNTSup, 68; Sheffield: Sheffield Academic Press, 1993).

58. Richard N. Longenecker, *Biblical Exegesis in the Apostolic Period* (Grand Rapids: Eerdmans, 2nd edn, 1999), pp. xvi-xvii.

59. Raymond E. Brown, *The Death of the Messiah: A Commentary on the Passion Narratives in the Four Gospels* (ABRL; New York: Doubleday, 1994), p. 145, has written about Zech. 9–14: 'As a single Old Testament passage, next to Ps. 22, it offers the most extensive background for the passion'.

Exodus (6*x*), and Leviticus (5*x*). Matthew cites Zechariah more often than the much longer books of Genesis (2*x*), Jeremiah (1*x*), and Numbers (1*x*) and more often than any other of the Minor Prophets except Hosea (3*x*), although Matthew apparently does not contain any allusions to Hosea.[60] In addition to the explicit citations, one could count as many as 16 potential allusions to Zechariah.[61]

However, the use of Zechariah in the Gospel of Matthew has not been fully described. In a recent article, 'Jesus and Zechariah's Messianic Hope', Craig Evans remarks, 'The scholarly literature that has investigated the extent, if any, of Zechariah's influence on Jesus is modest. Much of the discussion has focused on the formal usage of Zechariah, perhaps with the result of diverting attention away from the parallels between Jesus' behavior and themes in this prophetic book.'[62] For Evans, this modest literature consists of only six works.[63] Since Evans's interest is more narrowly connected with 'the possibility that the theology of the prophet Zechariah may have informed Jesus' understanding of his mission to Jerusalem',[64] at least seven more works which deal with the use of Zechariah in the New Testament should probably be added to this short list.[65] Whereas each of these 13 works contributes to

---

60. Daniel and Micah (2*x* each); Jonah and Malachi (1*x* each).

61. The NA27 and the UBS4 list the following as allusions to Zechariah (references in the parentheses are to Zechariah) 5.33 (8.17); 9.4 (8.17); 9.36 (10.2); 11.21-22 (9.2-4); 19.26 (8.6); 21.1 (14.4); 21.12 (14.21); 23.23 (7.9); 23.35 (1.1); 24.30 (12.10, 14); 24.31 (2.6, 10); 24.36 (14.7); 25.31 (14.5); 26.15 (11.12); 26.28 (9.11); 26.56 (13.7).

62. Craig A. Evans, 'Jesus and Zechariah's Messianic Hope', in Bruce Chilton and Craig A. Evans (eds.), *Authenticating the Activities of Jesus* (NTTS, 28.2; Leiden: E.J. Brill, 1999), pp. 373-88 (380).

63. F.F. Bruce, 'The Book of Zechariah and the Passion Narratives', *BJRL* 43 (1960–61), pp. 336-53; *idem*, *New Testament Development of Old Testament Themes* (Grand Rapids: Eerdmans, 1968), pp. 100-14; Craig F. Evans, 'I Will Go before You into Galilee', *JTS* NS 5 (1954), pp. 3-18; R.T. France, *Jesus and the Old Testament: His Application of Old Testament Passages to Himself and His Mission* (London: Tyndale, 1971), pp. 103-10; Robert M. Grant, 'The Coming of the Kingdom', *JBL* 67 (1948), pp. 297-303; Seyoon Kim, 'Jesus—The Son of God, the Stone, the Son of Man, and the Servant: The Role of Zechariah in the Self-Identification of Jesus', in Otto Betz and Gerald F. Hawthorne (eds.), *Tradition and Interpretation in the New Testament: Essays in Honor of E. Earle Ellis for His Sixtieth Birthday* (Grand Rapids: Eerdmans, 1987), pp. 134-48.

64. C.A. Evans, 'Jesus and Zechariah's Messianic Hope', p. 386.

65. Mark C. Black, 'The Rejected and Slain Messiah who is Coming with his Angels: The Messianic Exegesis of Zechariah 9–14 in the Passion Narratives' (PhD dissertation, Emory University, 1990); Dodd, *According to the Scriptures*, pp. 64-67; Ian M. Duguid, 'Messianic Themes in Zechariah 9–14', in Philip E. Satterthwaite, Richard S. Hess and Gordon J. Wenham (eds.), *The Lord's Anointed: Interpretation of Old Testament Messianic Texts* (THS; Grand Rapids: Baker Book House, 1995), pp. 265-80; Paul Foster, 'The Use of Zechariah in Matthew's Gospel', in Christopher M. Tuckett (ed.), *The Book of Zechariah and its Influence* (Burlington, VT: Ashgate, 2003), pp. 65-85; Barnabas Lindars,

the present study, in actuality only one of them focuses on an understanding of Matthew's use of Zechariah. In general they treat the use of Zechariah from the perspective of all four gospels; in particular they concentrate on Zechariah 9–14 in the Passion Narrative from the assumption of the two source hypothesis, an assumption which has likely caused Matthew's use of Zechariah to be neglected.[66]

For example, one might consider the unpublished dissertation by Mark Black, 'The Rejected and Slain Messiah who is Coming with his Angels: The Messianic Exegesis of Zechariah 9–14 in the Passion Narratives'. As the title reveals, the work deals exclusively with Zechariah 9–14 as found in the Passion Narratives of all four gospels. It seeks to highlight the prophetic importance of Zechariah 9–14 for the death and coming of Jesus; it also seeks to demonstrate that 'the early Christians may have discovered within Zechariah 9–14 a narrative sequence upon which they drew in shaping the passion narratives'.[67] This latter point draws upon and seeks to substantiate the work of C.H. Dodd's *According to the Scriptures* in relation to Zechariah 9–14 as one of the *testimonia* used by early Christians. The two largest sections of the work follow an approach similar to that of David Juel,[68] describing the early Jewish and Christian messianic interpretation of texts from Zechariah 9–14. The section on early Christian interpretation, however, clearly favors the gospels of Mark and John, even though Black lists more quotations and allusions from Matthew than any of the other gospels.[69]

Another example is the only one of the 13 works mentioned above that focuses on Matthew's use of Zechariah. The study by Paul Foster, 'The Use of Zechariah in Matthew', unfortunately and unnecessarily minimizes the use of Zechariah in Matthew because of Foster's assumptions, methodology, and analysis. Since Foster assumes that Matthew has used Mark, he does not allow for Matthew to recognize, use, or expand upon material from Zechariah that may have been present in the Markan source.[70] By treating the potential

---

New Testament Apologetic: The Doctrinal Significance of the Old Testament Quotations (Philadelphia: Westminster Press, 1961), pp. 110-34; Joel Marcus, 'The Old Testament and the Death of Jesus: The Role of Scripture in the Gospel Passion Narratives', in John T. Carroll and Joel B. Green (eds.), *The Death of Jesus in Early Christianity* (Peabody, MA: Hendrickson, 1995), pp. 218-20; Moo, *Old Testament in the Passion Narratives*, pp. 173-224.

66. This is ostensibly the case for the works by M.C. Black, Bruce, C.A. Evans, C.F. Evans, Foster, France, Grant, Lindars, Marcus, and Moo, though less so for Dodd, Duguid, and Kim.

67. Black, 'Rejected and Slain Messiah', p. 8.

68. David Juel, *Messianic Exegesis: Christological Interpretation of the Old Testament in Early Christianity* (Philadelphia: Fortress Press, 1988).

69. Black, 'Rejected and Slain Messiah', p. 6, lists twelve quotations and allusions from Matthew, five from Mark, two from Luke, and seven from John.

70. Foster, 'Use of Zechariah in Matthew', pp. 67-68, 70-71.

allusions to Zechariah before his discussion of citations, Foster does not use the clear and significant use of Zechariah in Matthew by citation to corroborate any potential use by allusion.[71] Furthermore, Foster dismisses certain uses of Zechariah in Matthew by generalizing about Old Testament concepts and discounting the verbal, conceptual, and contextual correspondence between specific texts in Matthew and Zechariah.[72]

Therefore, this investigation proposes the study of the use of Zechariah in the Gospel of Matthew. It examines the explicit citations from Zechariah, assessing the continuity or discontinuity between early Jewish and early Christian interpretations of these passages and describing the distinctive interpretations of these texts in the context of Matthew's Gospel. It considers the probable presence and intention of both textual and conceptual allusions to Zechariah. It also describes the thematic and theological function of Matthew's use of Zechariah through a literary and exegetical analysis of themes derived from and related to the Zechariah material which contributes to Matthew's portrayal of Jesus and his mission.

Research Methodology

The research methodology for this project began with collating the quotations and allusions listed in the standard editions of the Greek New Testament, namely, the NA27 and the UBS4. Additionally, two other works which catalog quotations and allusions in Matthew were consulted: Wilhelm Dittmar's, *Vetus Testamentum in Novo*, and Davies and Allison's, *The Gospel according to Saint Matthew*. The resulting compilation includes three explicit citations (21.5; 26.31; 27.9-10) and 18 allusions. While the latter two sources concur with only five of the 16 allusions from the NA27 and the UBS4 (19.26; 24.30, 31; 26.15, 28),[73] Davies and Allison add two allusions not listed in either the NA27 or the UBS4 (26.64 referring to Zech. 12.10, and 27.51-53 referring to Zech. 14.5). Thus, these 21 references provide the material for analysis in this study.

71. Foster, 'Use of Zechariah in Matthew', pp. 66-80.
72. A good example of this occurs in Foster, 'Use of Zechariah in Matthew', p. 70, where he discusses the possible allusion to Zech. 9.11 in Mt. 26.28. He calls the verbal connection between the texts an 'interesting parallel'. He then asserts that 'covenant blood' is not unfamiliar in the Old Testament and suggests that the synoptic tradition draws on this 'wider body of concepts', in which 'blood' and 'covenant' are often closely linked, rather than a specific text. But, in fact, are 'blood' and 'covenant' often closely linked in the Old Testament? For instance, the two concepts do not evidently appear in the same pericope in Leviticus, and their closest proximity is Lev. 2.13 and 3.2. Moreover, the use of the specific phrase 'the blood of the covenant', which occurs only twice in the Old Testament (Exod. 24.8; Zech. 9.11), should probably be regarded as qualitatively different from the mere occurrence of the word 'blood' in a covenant context.
73. For a listing of the 16 allusions from the NA27 and the UBS4, see n. 61.

To examine the explicit citations from Zechariah, this investigation utilizes the comparative exegetical process proposed by Craig Evans in his *Noncanonical Writings and New Testament Interpretation*.[74] His approach focuses on the question of how the early Jews and Christians understood Old Testament passages which they quote in their respective literature. It examines the occurrence of Old Testament passages throughout the ancient versions and other cognate literature, namely, the Old Testament Apocrypha and Pseudepigrapha, the Dead Sea Scrolls, various versions of the Old Testament, the writings of Philo and Josephus, the Targumim, rabbinic literature, the New Testament Apocrypha and Pseudepigrapha, and the writings of the Early Church Fathers and Gnostics. To guide such an assessment of the function of Old Testament citations in the New Testament, Evans offers the following seven questions:

1.   What Old Testament text (or combination of texts) is being cited?
2.   Which text-type does the quotation follow, and how does that contribute to its meaning?
3.   Does the Old Testament text relate to a wider tradition or theology in the Old Testament?
4.   How did various Jewish and Christian interpreters understand the Old Testament text?
5.   How does the New Testament quotation relate to the various Jewish and Christian interpretations?
6.   How does the function of the quotation compare with others in the same New Testament writing?
7.   How does the quotation contribute to the meaning of the passage in which it is found?[75]

These seven questions, then, serve to guide the study of explicit quotations from Zechariah.

In order to confirm the presence and clarify the intention of allusions to Zechariah, this study uses the methodology proposed by Richard Hays in his *Echoes of Scripture in the Letters of Paul*.[76] Not only has Hays employed the approach in his study of Paul's use of the Old Testament, but also his

74.   Craig A. Evans, *Noncanonical Writings and New Testament Interpretation* (Peabody, MA: Hendrickson, 1992), pp. 6-7. Evans provides a comprehensive example of the approach in his *To See and Not Perceive: Isaiah 6.9-10 in Early Jewish and Christian Interpretation* (JSOTSup, 64; Sheffield: Sheffield Academic Press, 1989).

75.   C.A. Evans, *Noncanonical Writings*, p. 7.

76.   Richard B. Hays, *Echoes of Scripture in the Letters of Paul* (New Haven: Yale University Press, 1989), pp. 29-31; see also *idem*, 'Criteria for Identifying Allusions and Echoes of the Text of Isaiah in the Letters of Paul' (paper presented at the Isaiah 53 and Christian Origins Conference, Baylor University, Waco, TX, February 1996).

work has provided a model for several studies on Matthew's use of the Old Testament.[77] His criteria for discerning the presence of allusions can be expressed in the following seven questions:

1. Is the Old Testament source available to the writer and/or his readers?
2. How explicit or 'loud' is the allusion; that is, does the allusion have a degree of verbal repetition or formal prominence?
3. How often does the writer allude to the same Old Testament passage?
4. How well does the allusion fit the theme of the New Testament passage?
5. Could the writer have intended the effect of the alleged allusion?
6. Have other readers in the history of interpretation 'heard' the same allusion?
7. Does the proposed intertextual reading enhance the reading of the passage?

This methodology proposed by Hays has received some criticism from Longenecker and J. Christiaan Beker,[78] both of whom prefer the procedure followed by Michael Fishbane in his *Biblical Interpretation in Ancient Israel*. In their estimation, Fishbane provides clearer controls and constraints for the study of biblical allusions with his three methodological criteria: (1) the presence of 'technical formulae' used to set off explicit citations; (2) the comparison of 'parallel texts *within* the MT, or *between* the MT and its principal versions' (or, in the words of Longenecker, 'multiple attested features'); and (3) the 'dense occurrence' of biblical terms, 'often thoroughly reorganized and transposed', which are found elsewhere in another text.[79] It should be noted, however, that Fishbane limits his study of inner-biblical exegesis to the Hebrew Bible. In this regard, Hays has countered Fishbane's proposal by considering the New Testament as important for understanding the function of Scripture among the various interpretative communities which make use

77. David B. Capes, 'Intertextual Echoes in the Matthean Baptismal Narrative', *BBR* 9 (1999), pp. 37-49; Clay Alan Ham, 'The Last Supper in Matthew', *BBR* 10.1 (2000), pp. 53-69; and Knowles, *Jeremiah in Matthew's Gospel*, pp. 162-222.

78. Longenecker, *Biblical Exegesis*, pp. xv-xvii; J. Christiaan Beker, 'Echoes and Intertextuality: On the Role of Scripture in Paul's Theology', in Craig A. Evans and James A. Sanders (eds.), *Paul and the Scriptures of Israel* (JSNTSup, 83; SSEJC, 1; Sheffield: Sheffield Academic Press, 1993), pp. 64-65. For a more recent critique of the criteria offered by Hays for determining the presence of allusions, especially in the Pauline corpus, see Porter, 'Use of the Old Testament in the New Testament', pp. 82-85.

79. Michael Fishbane, *Biblical Interpretation in Ancient Israel* (Oxford: Clarendon Press, 1985), pp. 42-43, 291; Longenecker, *Biblical Exegesis*, p. xvi. An alternative but less precise procedure for identifying allusions is suggested in Moo, *Old Testament in the Passion Narratives*, p. 20; he considers the appropriateness of context, the use of the Old Testament text elsewhere, and the author's characteristic style.

of the Hebrew Bible. Furthermore, since Hays's criteria are more comprehensive and distinctive, it seems difficult to understand how they provide any less clear direction than Fishbane's. Thus, Hays's seven criteria, which can be succinctly summarized as availability, volume, recurrence, thematic coherence, historical plausibility, history of interpretation, and satisfaction, will be used to guide the study of allusions to Zechariah in Matthew's Gospel.

Research Proposal

This work is arranged into three chapters. Chapter 1, entitled 'The Quotations from Zechariah in Matthew's Gospel', examines the three explicit citations from Zechariah in the Gospel of Matthew (Mt. 21.5; 26.31; 27.9-10). Using a comparative exegetical methodology, the chapter assesses the continuity or discontinuity between early Jewish and early Christian interpretations of these three citations from Zechariah and describes the distinctive interpretations of these texts in the context of Matthew's Gospel. As is appropriate for each text, the chapter uses the seven methodological questions for analyzing the function of Old Testament citations in the New Testament to guide the specific analysis of these three explicit citations. The discussion of each quotation is not primarily concerned with the use and categorization of hermeneutical techniques but rather the contribution of the Zechariah text to Matthew and its theological presentation.

Chapter 2, entitled 'The Allusions to Zechariah in Matthew's Gospel', considers the probable presence and intention of both textual and conceptual allusions to Zechariah in the Gospel of Matthew. The compilation of allusions from the NA27, the UBS4, Dittmar, and Davies and Allison includes 18 texts, which are divided into two sections. Five of these are found in Matthew before the Passion Narrative (Mt. 5.33; 9.4, 36; 11.21-22; 19.26). Thirteen of them are found in Matthew's Passion Narrative and the material directly preceding it (Mt. 21.1, 12; 23.23, 35; 24.30, 31, 36; 25.31; 26.15, 28, 56, 64; 27.51-53). As is appropriate for each text, the chapter uses the seven methodological criteria for discerning the presence of Old Testament allusions in the New Testament to guide the specific analysis of these 18 allusions. In the case of composite references, the discussion seeks to determine whether the allusion to Zechariah is primary, and it attempts to clarify the unique contribution of the reference to Zechariah.

Chapter 3, entitled 'The Theological Use of Zechariah in Matthew's Gospel', describes the thematic and theological function of Matthew's use of Zechariah. Through a literary and exegetical analysis of themes derived from and related to the Zechariah material, the chapter describes how Matthew has made use of Zechariah in the portrayal of Jesus and his mission. In several instances, Jesus' actions and words correspond with important themes in Zechariah, namely, the presentation of the Davidic king and the rejection of the divinely appointed shepherd. Together these themes portray Zechariah's predominate messianic image, 'the shepherd-king', an image which is most influential upon the use of Zechariah in the Gospels in general and in Matthew in particular. Of special interest for this study, then, is the Gospel of Matthew's presentation of Jesus as coming king and rejected shepherd.

1

THE QUOTATIONS FROM ZECHARIAH IN
MATTHEW'S GOSPEL

This chapter examines the three explicit citations from Zechariah in Matthew (Mt. 21.5; 26.31; 27.9-10). Using a comparative exegetical methodology,[1] the chapter assesses the continuity or discontinuity between early Jewish and early Christian interpretations of the citations from Zechariah and the distinctive interpretation of these texts in the context of Matthew's Gospel. As is appropriate for each text, the chapter uses the seven methodological questions for analyzing the function of Old Testament citations in the New Testament to guide the specific analysis of these three explicit citations. The discussion of each quotation is not primarily concerned with the use and categorization of hermeneutical techniques but rather the contribution of the texts from Zechariah to Matthew and its theological presentation.

Of the three explicit citations from Zechariah in the Gospel of Matthew, two appear among the so-called formula quotations: Mt. 21.5 and 27.9-10. These texts, in fact, are the last two of the formula quotations and are found within the material leading up to Matthew's Passion Narrative (Mt. 21–25) and the Passion Narrative itself (Mt. 26–27). They provide the beginning for this study.

Matthew 21.5

In the three Synoptic Gospels, only Mt. 21.5[2] explicitly[3] refers to Jesus' entry into Jerusalem as the prophetic fulfillment of Zech. 9.9:

---

1. C.A. Evans, *Noncanonical Writings*, p. 7; see pp. 15-18, above, for a discussion of this research methodology.

2. The Gospel of John also cites a portion of Zech. 9.9 in Jn 12.15: μὴ φοβοῦ, θυγάτηρ Σιών· ἰδοὺ ὁ βασιλεύς σου ἔρχεται, καθήμενος ἐπὶ πῶλον ὄνου. The use of the citation in Jn 12.15 is discussed below, pp. 43-44.

3. The citation is introduced by the characteristic Matthean formula: τοῦτο δὲ γέγονεν ἵνα πληρωθῇ τὸ ῥηθὲν διὰ τοῦ προφήτου λέγοντος (Mt. 21.4).

εἴπατε τῇ θυγατρὶ Σιών·
ἰδοὺ ὁ βασιλεύς σου ἔρχεταί σοι
πραῢς καὶ ἐπιβεβηκὼς ἐπὶ ὄνον
καὶ ἐπὶ πῶλον υἱὸν ὑποζυγίου.

Tell the daughter of Zion,
  Look your king is coming to you,
humble, and mounted on a donkey,
  and on a colt, the foal of a donkey.[4]

The text of Zech. 9.9 in the MT is as follows.[5]

גִּילִי מְאֹד בַּת־צִיּוֹן הָרִיעִי בַּת יְרוּשָׁלַם
הִנֵּה מַלְכֵּךְ יָבוֹא לָךְ צַדִּיק וְנוֹשָׁע הוּא
עָנִי וְרֹכֵב עַל־חֲמוֹר וְעַל־עַיִר בֶּן־אֲתֹנוֹת:

Rejoice greatly, O daughter Zion!
  Shout aloud, O daughter Jerusalem!
Lo, your king comes to you;
  triumphant and victorious is he,
humble and riding on a donkey,
  on a colt, the foal of a donkey.

A comparison of the citation in Mt. 21.5 with Zech. 9.9 in the MT, however, reveals that the citation is both conflated and abbreviated.[6] While the
MT of Zech. 9.9 begins with a double imperative, הָרִיעִי...גִּילִי מְאֹד, Mt. 21.5
begins with a single imperative, εἴπατε, and one that does not correspond
with either imperative in Zech. 9.9. In addition, the two vocative construct
phrases in Zech. 9.9, בַּת־צִיּוֹן...בַּת יְרוּשָׁלַם, become a single dative phrase in

---

4. The Greek text of the New Testament used throughout is the NA27. All English
citations from the Hebrew Bible/Old Testament and the New Testament are taken from
the NRSV, unless noted otherwise.

5. The text of the Hebrew Bible/Old Testament used throughout is *BHS*.

6. E. Earle Ellis, *The Old Testament in Early Christianity: Canon and Interpretation
in the Light of Modern Research* (Grand Rapids: Baker Book House, 1991), p. 91, lists
Mt. 21.5 (Isa. 62.11 + Zech. 9.9) as one example of conflated quotations 'that often have
appended to one text a snippet from another'. Many note the presence of both Isa. 62.11
and Zech. 9.9 in Mt. 21.5, including Stendahl, *School of St Matthew*, p. 119; Strecker, *Der
Weg der Gerechtigkeit*, p. 72; Gundry, *Use of the Old Testament*, p. 120; McConnell,
Law and Prophecy, p. 126; Rothfuchs, *Erfüllungszitate*, p. 80; Gleason L. Archer and
G.C. Chirichigno, *Old Testament Quotations in the New Testament: A Complete Survey*
(Chicago: Moody, 1983), p. 131; Longenecker, *Biblical Exegesis*, p. 132; Wim Weren,
'Jesus' Entry into Jerusalem: Matthew 21,1-17 in the Light of the Hebrew Bible and the
Septuagint', in Christopher M. Tuckett (ed.), *The Scriptures in the Gospels* (BETL, 131;
(Leuven: Leuven University Press, 1997), pp. 117-41 (119); Jean Miller, *Les Citations
d'accomplissement dans L'Évangile de Matthieu: Quand Dieu se rend présent en toute
humanité* (AnBib, 140; Rome: Editrice Pontifico Istituto Biblico, 1999), p. 224; Davies
and Allison, *Matthew*, III, p. 118; Foster, 'Use of Zechariah in Matthew's Gospel', p. 74.

Mt. 21.5, τῇ θυγατρὶ Σιών. Thus, Matthew's εἴπατε τῇ θυγατρὶ Σιών would render אִמְרוּ לְבַת־צִיּוֹן, a clause which appears in the MT only in Isa. 62.11.[7] In fact, the wording of the clause in Mt. 21.5 is identical to the LXX rendering of Isa. 62.11.[8]

The rest of Mt. 21.5 does cite Zech. 9.9. The first part of the second line of Zech. 9.9, הִנֵּה מַלְכֵּךְ יָבוֹא לָךְ, is rendered in Mt. 21.5 as ἰδοὺ ὁ βασιλεύς σου ἔρχεταί σοι; this wording corresponds exactly to the LXX. While Mt. 21.5 omits the second part of the second line in Zech. 9.9, צַדִּיק וְנוֹשָׁע הוּא, the citation construes the third line in Zech. 9.9, עָנִי וְרֹכֵב עַל־חֲמוֹר וְעַל־עַיִר בֶּן־אֲתֹנוֹת, as πραΰς καὶ ἐπιβεβηκὼς ἐπὶ ὄνον καὶ ἐπὶ πῶλον υἱὸν ὑποζυγίου. In comparison, the LXX of Zech. 9.9 reads πραΰς καὶ ἐπιβε-βηκὼς ἐπὶ ὑποζύγιον καὶ πῶλον νέον. The first four words of the phrase in Matthew are identical to the LXX's translation of the MT. It is generally assumed[9] that Matthew and the LXX understand עָנָו (meaning 'humble' or 'meek') for עָנִי (meaning 'poor', 'needy', or 'afflicted') as they use πραΰς instead of πτωχός which is found in Symmachus and Quinta.[10] A clear distinction between the noun עָנָו and the adjective עָנִי, however, is complicated by both orthographic and semantic difficulties.[11]

The last six words of the citation in Mt. 21.5, ἐπὶ ὄνον καὶ ἐπὶ πῶλον υἱὸν ὑποζυγίου, more accurately translate the MT than does the LXX, which reads ἐπὶ ὑποζύγιον καί πῶλον νέον. Matthew has described the donkey with terminology closer to the MT: ὄνον for חֲמוֹר, which is the most common

---

7.   The only other Old Testament text in which בַּת־צִיּוֹן appears as the object of the prep. לְ is Mic. 1.13, a text which bears little resemblance to the context of Zech. 9.9 or Mt. 21.5. The phrase בַּת־צִיּוֹן does not follow the verb אָמַר in any other Old Testament text than Isa. 62.11.

8.   The text of the LXX used throughout is Alfred Rahlfs (ed.), *Septuaginta* (Stuttgart: Deutsche Bibelgesellschaft, 1979).

9.   Gundry, *Use of the Old Testament*, p. 120; Archer and Chirichigno, *Old Testament Quotations*, p. 131.

10.   Theodotion reads ἐπακούων instead of πραΰς or πτωχός. Almost 50x, the LXX uses ἐπακούω to translate עָנָה, which means 'to answer, respond'. Since עָנָה is another word formed from the root ענה, perhaps Theodotion has confused the root meaning 'answer' with the root meaning 'humble' or 'afflicted'.

11.   William J. Dumbrell, 'עָנִי', in *NIDOTTE*, III, pp. 454-64 (454-56). The Hebrew letters ו and י apparently were easily confused, particularly with the pl. forms of עָנָו and עָנִי; for example, Ps. 9.19; Isa. 32.7. Even though the LXX typically translates עָנִי with πτωχός (Lev. 19.10; 23.22; 2 Sam. 22.28; Job 29.12; 34.28; 36.6; Prov. 14.21; Isa. 3.14, 15; 41.17; 58.7; Ezek. 16.49; 18.12; 22.29; Hab. 3.14 and numerous times in the Psalms), 6x it uses πραΰς for עָנָו (Num. 12.3; Pss. 25.9 [2x]; 34.2; 37.11; 76.9.). Occasionally the LXX uses πτωχός for עָנָו (Ps. 69.33 [68.33 LXX]; Isa. 32.7; 61.1) and πραΰς for עָנִי (Job 24.4; Isa. 26.6; Zeph. 3.12; Zech. 9.9). According to Wolfgang Bauder, 'πραΰς', in *NIDNTT*, II, pp. 256-59 (257), these renderings suggest that the Greek and Hebrew terms may indeed have wider and overlapping connotations.

word for donkey in the Old Testament, πῶλον for עַיִר, which means young
male donkey or colt, υἱόν for בֵּן, which may designate the young of an animal or its foal, and ὑποζυγίου for אָתוֹן, which refers to a female donkey.[12]
Furthermore, Mt. 21.5 even reproduces the double preposition (with ἐπὶ for
עַל) and the explanatory waw (with καὶ for וְ)[13] which are present in the MT of
Zech. 9.9.

Zechariah 9.9
Zechariah 9 pictures the coming of the king to Jerusalem (9.9-10) in the
midst of Yahweh's conquest of Israel's enemies (9.1-8)[14] and Yahweh's
restoration of the people (9.11-17). While Zech. 9.9 announces the king's
procession, Zech. 9.10 proclaims the end of military conflict and the beginning of peace among the nations. These two verses begin with a call to
'rejoice greatly' and 'shout aloud' at the arrival of the king.[15] The first of
these words, גִיל, describes a joyful response to favorable circumstances,
often with enthusiastic and spontaneous shouts and often as the result of
divine intervention and fulfillment.[16] The second word, רוּעַ, may refer to a

12. Stendahl, *School of St Matthew*, p. 119, says that Matthew has rendered the MT
'with the literalness of Aquila'. None of the Greek versions or recensions agree with Matthew's wording: ἐπὶ ὑποζύγιον καὶ πῶλον νέον (LXX); ἐπὶ ὄνου, καὶ πώλου υἱοῦ
ὀνάδων (Aquila); ἐπὶ ὄνον, καὶ πῶλον υἱὸν ὀνάδος (Symmachus); ἐπὶ ὄνον, καὶ
πῶλον υἱὸν ὄνου (Theodotion); and ἐπὶ ὑποζύγιον, καὶ πῶλον υἱὸν ὄνων (Quinta).
13. 'Frequently *waw copulativum* is also *explanatory*', according to GKC 484
§154aN, which lists the following examples: Gen. 4.4; Exod. 24.12; 25.12; Isa. 57.11; Jer.
17.10; Amos 3.11; 4.10; Zech. 9.9. So also *IBHS*, p. 652: 'Waw may stand before clauses
which serve to clarify or specify the sense of the preceding clause'. The phenomenon also
occurs in the New Testament, where, in the words of Daniel B. Wallace, *Greek Grammar
Beyond the Basics: An Exegetical Syntax of the New Testament* (Grand Rapids: Zondervan, 1996), p. 670, καί may be used as an 'ascensive conjunction' which 'expresses a
final addition or *point of focus*. It is often translated *even*'. See also BDAG, p. 495; BDF,
pp. 228-29 §442.9.
14. Paul D. Hanson, *The Dawn of Apocalyptic* (Philadelphia: Fortress Press, 1975),
pp. 316-19, argues that Zech. 9 does not describe any historical battles but rather uses
common prophetic language and localities to depict Yahweh's deliverance of the people.
15. Both גִיל and רוּעַ appear with moderate frequency, but they are used less as
imperatives and together as such only here. They each appear 45x in the Old Testament.
The *qal* impv. of גִיל is found (8x) in Pss. 2.11; 32.11; Isa. 49.13; 65.18; 66.10; Joel 2.21,
23; Zech. 9.9; the *hiphil* impv. of רוּעַ is found (14x) in Josh. 6.10, 16; Pss. 47.2; 66.1;
81.2; 98.4, 6; 100.1; Isa. 44.23; Jer. 50.15; Hos. 5.8; Joel 2.1; Zeph. 3.14; Zech. 9.9.
16. Carol L. Meyers and Eric M. Meyers, *Zechariah 9–14* (AB, 25C; New York:
Doubleday, 1993), p. 121; cf. Pss. 9.14; 14.7; 21.1; 31.7; 32.11; 96.11; 118.24; Isa. 25.9;
49.13; 65.18; 66.10; Joel 2.21, 23.
The adv. מְאֹד marks an abundance of degree or quantity. Here it heightens the call to
rejoice at the arrival of the king. It appears five other times in Zechariah. In Zech. 9.2
it describes the great skill with which Tyre had fortified itself and accumulated wealth.

loud shout that begins a battle, celebrates a triumph, affirms the selection of a king, or addresses exuberant praise to God.[17] Together the words call for a celebration, 'honoring Yahweh with enthusiasm that reaches beyond words'.[18]

The one summoned to rejoice and shout is addressed as 'Daughter Zion... Daughter Jerusalem'. The designations employ a common convention in Hebrew poetry, referring to a place personified as a daughter. Although the idiom is used occasionally for other cities, it is used most frequently, as here, for Zion/Jerusalem.[19] Apart from Zech. 9.9, both 'Daughter Zion' and 'Daughter Jerusalem' appear in the same text only five times (2 Kgs 19.21; Isa. 37.22; Lam. 2.13; Mic. 4.8; Zeph. 3.14). The last of these texts, Zeph. 3.14, provides an important textual antecedent to Zech. 9.9:

> Sing aloud, O daughter Zion;
>   shout, O Israel!
> Rejoice and exult with all your heart,
>   O daughter Jerusalem!

The setting for such exultation is the presence of Yahweh as king after the victory over Israel's enemies. The presence of 'shout' with 'Daughter Zion' in Zech. 9.9 also evokes an earlier reference in Zech. 2.10 (2.14 MT): 'Sing and rejoice, O daughter Zion! For lo, I will come and dwell in your midst, says the LORD.' As in Zeph. 3.14, this text summons 'Daughter Zion' to 'sing and rejoice' at Yahweh's promise to 'come and dwell' in their midst.[20] Both Zeph. 3.14 and Zech. 2.10 (2.14 MT) envision the enthronement of Yahweh

---

In Zech. 9.5 it notes the great agony which Gaza will experience at the loss of her king. In Zech. 14.4 it refers to the great valley formed when the Mount of Olives splits in half. In Zech. 14.14 it marks the great quantities of gold, silver, and clothing collected by Judah from the surrounding nations.

17.   Cf. Num. 10.9; Josh. 6.5, 10, 16, 20; 1 Sam. 10.24; 17.52; Ezra 3.11; Pss. 41.11; 47.1; 66.1; 81.1; 95.1-2; 98.4, 6; Isa. 8.9; 42.13; 44.13; Jer. 50.15.

18.   Carroll Stuhlmueller, *Rebuilding with Hope: A Commentary on the Books of Haggai and Zechariah* (ITC; Grand Rapids: Eerdmans, 1988), p. 124.

19.   Other cities include Babylon (Ps. 137.8), Sidon (Isa. 23.12), Tarshish (Isa. 23.10), and Tyre (Ps. 45.12). 'Daughter Zion' appears 26x: 2 Kgs 19.21; Ps. 9.14 (9.15 MT); Isa. 1.8; 10.32; 16.1; 37.22; 52.2; 62.11; Jer. 4.31; 6.2, 23; Lam. 1.6; 2.1, 4, 8, 10, 13, 18; 4.22; Mic. 1.13; 4.8, 10, 13; Zeph. 3.14; Zech. 2.10 (2.14 MT); 9.9. 'Daughter Jerusalem' appears 7x: 2 Kgs 19.21; Isa. 37.22; Lam. 2.13, 15; Mic. 4.8; Zeph. 3.14; Zech. 9.9. Joyce G. Baldwin, *Haggai, Zechariah, Malachi: An Introduction and Commentary* (TOTC, 24; Downers Grove, IL: Intervarsity Press, 1982), 165, notes that 'daughter' usually 'occurs in contexts which speak of a broken relationship...; the contrast in this verse is striking' (cf. Isa. 1.8; Jer. 4.31; 6.2; Lam. 2.1).

20.   While the *futurum instans* (see GKC 360 §116p; *IBHS*, p. 627; cf. Jer. 1.15; 8.17; Amos 6.14; Hab. 1.6; Zech. 2.9 [2.14 MT]) may possess an ominous force as it warns of Yahweh's intended punitive actions, here the ptc. following כִּי הִנְנִי apparently intensifies the certainty of Yahweh's coming in the future (cf. Isa. 65.17, 18; Jer. 30.10; 46.27; Zech. 3.8).

as king in Zion as the reason for exultation.[21] By allusion, Zech. 9.9 indicates that the arrival of the king deserves the same celebration as that of Yahweh's presence among the people.[22]

After Yahweh conquers Israel's enemies (Zech. 9.1-8), the king enters Jerusalem. Although nothing is said of the king's participation in Yahweh's conquest, the king emerges as one whose reign will bring peace (Zech. 9.10). He is recognized as king of Daughter Zion/Daughter Jerusalem by the possessive feminine singular suffix (מַלְכֵּךְ). However, the specific identity of the king in Zech. 9.9 is more difficult.[23] In the Old Testament, מֶלֶךְ generally

---

21. On the enthronement of Yahweh as king in Zion, see Pss. 48; 95; 97; Isa. 52.7-10. The use of שָׁכַן in Zech. 2.10-11 (2.14-15 MT) and in Zech. 8.3 may echo Exod. 25.8; 29.45-46.

22. David L. Petersen, *Zechariah 9–14 and Malachi: A Commentary* (OTL; Louisville, KY: Westminster/John Knox Press, 1995), pp. 57-58.

23. The basic itinerary of locations listed in Zech. 9.1-8 and the mention of the sons of Greece in Zech. 9.13 have suggested to some that the 'king' of Zech. 9.9 is none other than Alexander the Great. For example, see Matthias Delcor, 'Les allusions à Alexandre le Grand dans Zach 9.1-8', *VT* 1 (1951), pp. 110-24 (123-24), and Joseph Blenkinsopp, *A History of Prophecy in Israel* (Louisville, KY: Westminster/John Knox Press, rev. edn, 1996), p. 231. However, Marvin A. Sweeney, *The Twelve Prophets* (BerOl; 2 vols.; Collegeville, MN: Liturgical Press, 2000), II, p. 664, rejects the identification of the king with Alexander the Great because the itinerary of the conquest in Zech. 9.1-8 does not correspond with that of Alexander. For the same reason, he rejects such an identification with any historical Davidic monarch. Reflecting on the depiction of Yahweh as king in Isaiah (Isa. 65–66) following references to a Davidic monarch (Isa. 9.1-6; 11.1-16) and a Persian monarch (Isa. 44.24-28; 45.1-7), Sweeney does suggest that Zech. 9.9 may initially refer to Darius I, who fought to restore order through his empire with campaigns against the Greeks in the early fifth century. Sweeney also sees a similar progression of kingship in Zechariah: first a Davidic monarch (Zech. 4; 6; 12–13), second a Persian king (Zech. 9), and third Yahweh as king (Zech. 14). Since Isa. 44.28; 45.1, 13 do in fact name the Persian king, Cyrus, one may see this threefold progression more clearly in Isaiah. However, Darius appears only in Zech. 1.1, 7; 7.1 as a chronological indicator for three prophetic messages; he is not named in Zech. 9–14, and his campaigns in the region do not correspond to the itinerary of Zech. 9.1-8.

Following Petersen, *Zechariah 9–14*, pp. 58-59, Adrian Leske, 'Context and Meaning of Zechariah 9.9', *CBQ* 62 (2000), pp. 663-78, has argued for the 'corporate' character of kingship in Zech. 9.9, similar to that of Isa. 55.1-5 (cf. Isa. 42.6; 49.6-8), explaining 'king' as a cipher referring to Yahweh's faithful people. In the midst of a postexilic struggle between three different messianic ideologies (the promised leadership of a Davidic descendant, the primary leadership of the high priest, and the exclusive leadership of Yahweh as king over the faithful people), Zechariah, like Isaiah, has relinquished a traditional royal messianism in favor of a representative kingship. Through a democratization of kingship, the Davidic covenant is transferred not to one of David's descendant but to the faithful people of Yahweh. This collective messianism is seen particularly in the parallels among the descriptions of earlier Davidic kings, Servant Israel, the 'afflicted and lowly' exiles, and the king in Zech. 9.9. While Leske's proposal is compelling, the corporate concept of kingship should nonetheless retain the singular identity of the 'king' in whose person

refers to the king of Israel, Judah, or some other nation, to the Davidic king, especially in messianic predictions, or to Yahweh as king of Israel. Other occurrences of מֶלֶךְ in Zechariah clearly illustrate its reference to a nation's king (Zech. 7.1; 9.5; 11.6; 14.5, 10) or to Yahweh as the universally worshiped king (Zech. 14.9, 16, 17). The political reality of a Judean province under Persian rule during the early postexilic period may explain the tendency to circumvent any direct reference to a future Davidic monarch. Such royal passages as Zech. 3.8; 4.6-10; 6.12 are thus cast in terms which avoid the notions of power imagery and political independence.[24] Such texts do, however, present 'the people's faith in the mysterious arrival of a new David',[25] especially by referring to 'my servant the Branch'.[26] Similarly, while Zech. 9.9 markedly deviates from the military language of the preceding and following passages, it possesses a messianic aura as it announces the arrival of the king of Zion/Jerusalem. Moreover, Zech. 9.9 and 2.10 (2.14 MT) use the same exclamation and verb. The presence of 'lo'[27] and 'comes' with 'shout' and 'Daughter Zion' in both texts suggests a strong connection between them. Clearly, Zech. 2.10 (2.14 MT) identifies the one who comes and dwells in the midst of Zion as Yahweh. The similarities between these two passages then may suggest that Zech. 9.9 also anticipates the eschatological appearance of Yahweh as king over Zion and ultimately all the earth (Zech. 14.9-21).

From the announcement of the king's arrival, the passage now focuses on the king's character. The coming king is first described as 'triumphant'. This designation (צַדִּיק) may refer to the king's just actions with regard to the administration of government and justice, or it may refer to the king's vindication by Yahweh.[28] If the former sense suits this context, the passage may connect with descriptions of the rightful heir to the Davidic throne, such as Jer. 23.5: 'The days are surely coming, says the LORD, when I will raise up for David a righteous Branch, and he shall reign as king and deal wisely, and shall execute justice and righteousness in the land'.[29] In this regard, צַדִּיק

those faithful to Yahweh are incorporated. If one were to adopt the notion of corporate kingship in Zech. 9.9, it should be necessary to emphasize both the individual and corporate dimensions of the king/people.

24. Meyers and Meyers, *Zechariah 9–14*, p. 124.

25. Stuhlmueller, *Rebuilding with Hope*, p. 124; cf. Pss. 2; 110; Isa. 9.1-7; Mic. 5.2-5.

26. Zech. 3.8; cf. Zech. 6.12; Jer. 23.5; 33.15.

27. The interjection הִנֵּה underlines the significance of the statement it introduces. Of the 63x it appears in the Minor Prophets, 23 occur in Zechariah. In general, the word either makes vivid a visionary element (1.8, 11, 18 [2.1 MT]; 2.1 [2.5 MT], 3 [2.7 MT]; 4.2; 5.1, 7, 9; 6.1, 12) or introduces a future prediction (2.9 [2.13 MT], 10 [2.14 MT]; 3.8, 9; 8.7; 9.4, 9; 11.6, 16; 12.2; 14.1).

28. BDB, p. 843.

29. This sense is understood in the translation 'just' (see KJV, NKJV, NASB) and 'legitimate' in the New English Translation (NET).

suggests that the king meets the standard of righteousness and is thus fully qualified to assume the Davidic throne. This conceptual link with Jer. 23.5 and also Jer. 33.15 is strengthened by the appearance of the word 'shoot' (צֶמַח) as an expression of dynastic legitimacy in Zech. 3.8 and 6.12.[30] If the latter sense suits the context of Zech. 9.9, the passage may connect with descriptions of the vindication of the Suffering Servant, as in Isa. 53.11b-12a:

> The righteous one, my servant, shall make many righteous,
>   and he shall bear their iniquities.
> Therefore I will allot him a portion with the great,
>   and divide the spoil with the strong.[31]

As in Isa. 50.7-9 where vindication is granted to the Servant, so the king in Zech. 9.9 receives deliverance but not through military means. This association with the Servant is further intimated through the occurrence of צַדִּיק with the next word describing the king, יָשָׁע.[32]

The second description of the coming king is נוֹשָׁע, translated as 'victorious' in the NRSV. The *niphal* participle, however, is passive, not active as it is usually rendered in the Greek and other ancient translations.[33] Only one other Old Testament passage, Ps. 33.16, contains the *niphal* participle,[34] where it is translated 'saved': 'A king is not saved by his great army: a warrior is not delivered by his great strength'. The parallel is striking, because both Ps. 33.16-17 and Zech. 9.9-10 emphasize the deliverance of the king without military means; both passages subvert militaristic expectations through their pronouncements about the 'war horse'.[35] Thus, the translations 'victorious' (NRSV and RSV) and 'having salvation' (KJV and NIV),[36] which have likely

---

30. Meyers and Meyers, *Zechariah 9–14*, pp. 125-26.

31. For a similar use of צַדִּיק in Isaiah, see 3.10; 26.7; 57.1, and the corresponding ptc. in 50.8. In addition, the Psalms often affirm that the righteous receive vindication (Pss. 7.9; 11.3, 5, 7; 14.5; 34.15, 19, 21; 37.16-17, 25, 39; 55.22; 58.10-11; 75.10; 92.12; 112.6; 146.8).

32. Righteousness and salvation appear together in Isa. 45.8; 46.13; 51.4-5; 61.10.

33. According to *IBHS*, p. 620, 'the participles of the reflexive or passive stems, especially the *niphal*, correspond occasionally to an English *-ible/-able* term'; in Zech. 9.9 the ptc., 'conventionally rendered "victorious", is difficult; it may have the sense "saveable, (worthy) of being saved"'. *BHS* lists at least four ancient translations with an active rendering of נוֹשָׁע: LXX σῴζων = Syr. *(w)prwq'* = Tg. *(w)prjq* = Vulg. *salvator*.

34. In addition to the two *niphal* participles, יָשָׁע appears 19x in the *niphal* stem (Num. 10.9; Deut. 33.29; 2 Sam. 22.4; Pss. 18.4; 80.4, 8, 20; 119.117; Prov. 28.18; Isa. 30.15; 45.17, 22; 64.4; Jer. 4.14; 8.20; 17.14; 24.6; 30.7; 33.16).

35. Mark Hahlen, 'The Background and Use of Equine Imagery in Zechariah', *SCJ* 3 (2000), pp. 243-60 (255-56).

36. Based on a repointing of the ptc. as a pf. verb, the translation 'having salvation' was proposed by the twelfth-century Hebrew grammarian, David Kimchi, *Commentary upon the Prophecies of Zechariah* (trans. A.M. Caul; London: James Duncan, 1837), p. 87.

been influenced from the surrounding battle context (especially Zech. 9.1-8, 13-17), may not convey well the passive sense of the king's deliverance, presumably by Yahweh. Moreover, this description may contrast a passage evoked by the calling of Daughter Zion to shout (Zeph. 3.14); Zeph. 3.17 describes Yahweh with the active form יוֹשִׁיעַ, as 'a warrior who gives victory'. In Zech. 9.9, the king does not bring victory; he is 'saved' by the Yahweh's deliverance, and his status depends on Yahweh's action.[37]

The third word which identifies the coming king is 'humble'. The question here is whether עָנִי has the connotation of affliction or humiliation. Typically, עָנִי refers to the poor, needy, afflicted, or oppressed.[38] The use of the word for one wrongfully afflicted in Zech. 7.10; 11.7, 11 may suggest a similar nuance here. This alternative is also made attractive by the portrayal of the Servant as one 'afflicted' in Isa. 53.4, 7, although the word used in Isaiah 53 is עָנָה rather than עָנִי. Nonetheless, the immediate context may not require עָנִי to mean 'afflicted' in Zech. 9.9. If it is not understood as such, עָנִי would mean 'humble' or 'lowly'.[39] The use is not widely attested; examples include 2 Sam. 22.28; Ps. 18.27 (18.28 MT); Isa. 66.2; and Zeph. 3.12. The following clause, which refers to the king riding on a donkey, may favor this more general sense,[40] which evidently stands behind the rendering πραΰς in the LXX and Mt. 21.5.[41]

His character depicted as 'humble', so also is the king's arrival portrayed; he comes 'riding on a donkey, on a colt, the foal of a donkey'. Each of these three phrases more narrowly describes the king's mount, for the construction suggests not that the king rides on more than one donkey but that the king rides on a particular kind of donkey. The word חֲמוֹר denotes a male donkey used for riding, farming, or bearing a load; the word עַיִר, a young male

---

37. Baldwin, *Haggai, Zechariah, Malachi*, p. 165; Meyers and Meyers, *Zechariah 9–14*, p. 127. Cf. Isa. 45.17: 'But Israel is saved by the LORD with everlasting salvation'.

38. It does so numerous times in the Psalms (9.18; 12.5; 22.24; 25.16; 35.10; 37.14; 40.17; 68.10; 70.5; 72.4, 12; 74.21; 82.3; 86.1; 109.22; 140.12) and Isaiah (3.14-15; 10.2; 14.32; 26.6; 32.7; 41.17; 49.13; 54.11; 58.7).

39. The notion of humility before God is more often expressed with the word עָנָו, as in Num. 12.3 where Moses is described as 'very humble, more so than anyone else on the face of the earth'.

40. Thomas Edward McComiskey, *Zechariah*, in *The Minor Prophets: An Exegetical and Expository Commentary*. III. *Zephaniah, Haggai, Zechariah, and Malachi* (Grand Rapids: Baker Book House, 1998), p. 1166. According to Stuhlmueller, *Rebuilding with Hope*, p. 125, the description of king riding on donkey not only favors the more general meaning of humble but also rejects the 'ostentatious splendor of preexilic kings, condemned by the prophets (Jer. 17.25)'.

41. This is so, unless the LXX and Matthew have read עָנִי as עָנָו, a supposition about which one cannot be certain. On the confusion between עָנָו and עָנִי, see the discussion on p. 22, above.

donkey, perhaps still wild.[42] The phrase בֶּן־אֲתֹנוֹת refers to the young foal of a female donkey.[43] For a king to ride a donkey is not unprecedented in the ancient Near East.[44] However, the use of horses by the Persians may have incited some of the prophetic scorn for a misplaced trust in the war horse.[45] Such a military mount would thus be inharmonious with the king's mission of peace in Zech. 9.10; moreover, 'riding on a donkey' further elucidates the king's character of humility.[46] The use of a lowly animal counters any power imagery associated with political domination and underscores the meaning of עָנִי. His riding on a young donkey may also portray the king's legitimate reign, if the description reapplies the dynastic promise to Judah in Gen. 49.10-11:[47]

> The scepter shall not depart from Judah,
>> nor the ruler's staff from between his feet,
> until tribute comes to him;
>> and the obedience of the peoples is his.
> Binding his foal to the vine
>> and his donkey's colt to the choice vine,
> he washes his garments in wine
>> and his robe in the blood of grapes.

Zechariah 9.9 may draw on the language of Gen. 49.11, since two of three terms for 'donkey' in Zech. 9.9 are used in Gen. 49.11 (עִירֹה or [עִירֹו] and בְּנִי אֲתֹנוֹ). If Zech. 9.9 has so reworked the blessing of Gen. 49.10-11, it affirms the expectation of the legitimate Davidic heir.[48] This expectation,

---

42. For חֲמוֹר, cf. Gen. 12.16; 30.43; 42.26; Exod. 4.20; 9.3; 13.13; 20.17; Josh. 9.4; 1 Sam. 8.16; 16.20; 25.18; 2 Sam. 16.2; 1 Kgs 13.13; Neh. 13.15; Isa. 32.20; Jer. 22.19; Zech. 14.15. For עַיִר, cf. Gen. 32.15; Judg. 10.4; 12.14; Job 11.12; Isa. 30.6, 24.

43. For אָתוֹן, cf. Gen. 12.16; 32.15; 49.11; Num. 22.21; Judg. 5.10; 1 Sam. 9.3; 2 Kgs 4.22; Job 1.3. According to *IBHS*, p. 122, the plural אֲתֹנוֹת is 'a kind of generalization whereby a whole *species of animal* is designated'; according to GKC 400 §124o, the pl. form is occasionally used for an indefinite sg. (cf. Deut. 17.5).

44. For an overview of the ancient Near Eastern evidence of human kings riding donkeys, especially from the second millennium BCE at Ur and Mari, see E. Lipiński, 'Recherches sur le livre de Zacharie', *VT* 20 (1970), pp. 25-55 (50-53); cf. Judg. 5.10; 10.4; 12.14; 2 Sam. 16.2; 1 Kgs 1.33. However, *ANET*, p. 238 refers to 330 princes taken prisoner and forced to ride on donkeys, after their horses were taken from them.

45. Hahlen, 'Equine Imagery in Zechariah', p. 247; cf. Isa. 2.7; 31.1; Mic. 5.10; Hag. 2.22; Zech. 9.10. For biblical evidence of the Persians' affinity for horses, see Est. 6.6-11; 8.9-12.

46. K&D, X, p. 335.

47. So Fishbane, *Biblical Interpretation in Ancient Israel*, pp. 501-502; Meyers and Meyers, *Zechariah 9–14*, p. 129; Sweeney, *Twelve Prophets*, p. 663.

48. The third line of Gen. 49.10 is quite difficult. Although rendered 'until tribute comes to him' in the NRSV, it may also be translated 'until he comes to whom it belongs' as in the NIV.

however, contains a radically altered portrayal of the coming of Zion's king as one who does not trust in human might or the implements of war but one who is humble.

Zechariah 9.9 in Jewish and Christian Interpretation
Dead Sea Scrolls. Evidence for the use of Zech. 9.9 in the Dead Sea Scrolls and Old Testament Pseudepigrapha is meager at best and nonexistent at worst. While the book of Zechariah is among the biblical scrolls found in the Judean Desert, the text of *The Greek Minor Prophets Scroll* (8Hev 1 B2) unfortunately cuts off at Zech. 9.5.[49] Furthermore, none of the Dead Sea Scrolls appear to cite Zech. 9.9. Still, some have attempted to identify Zech. 9.9 as the source of the language in the *War Scroll*.[50] In 1QM XII, the sectarians anticipate their participation in the defeat of the wicked, and the cry in 1QM XII, 13 anticipates the procession of captives and spoils from defeated nations into Jerusalem:

> Rejoice, Sion, passionately!
> Shine with jubilation, Jerusalem!
> Exult, all the cities of Judah![51]

49. Emanuel Tov, *The Greek Minor Prophets Scroll from Nahal Hever (8HevXIIgr)* (DJD, 8; Oxford: Clarendon Press, 1990), p. 77; Martin G. Abegg, Peter W. Flint and Eugene C. Ulrich (eds.), *The Dead Sea Scrolls Bible: The Oldest Known Bible* (San Francisco: HarperSanFrancisco, 1999), p. 474.

50. Jan de Waard, *A Comparative Study of the Old Testament Text in the Dead Sea Scrolls and in the New Testament* (STDJ, 4; Leiden: E.J. Brill, 1965), p. 72. The *War Scroll* (or *Milhamah*), one of the original seven scrolls, describes a forty-year war between the sons of light and the sons of darkness. The forces of good are led by archangel Michael against the forces of evil and the prince of darkness Belial in this final eschatological war. The document seems intended to prepare the sectarians with instructions for this pre-ordained war, in which evil is ultimately and finally destroyed (see 1QM I, 10). The work contains three major sections: instructions on the organization and tactics of the war (1QM I-IX), a collection of prayers and blessings to be recited during the war (1QM X-XII), and a description of the war against the Kittim or the people ruling the world (1QM XIV-XIX). Suggested dates of composition range from the second half of second century BCE to the middle of the first century BCE. Based on linguistic considerations, Devorah Dimant in Michael E. Stone (ed.), *Jewish Writings of the Second Temple Period: Apocrypha, Pseudepigrapha, Qumran Sectarian Writings, Philo, Josephus* (CRINT, 2.2; Assen: Van Gorcum, 1984), p. 516, favors an earlier date, while Geza Vermes, *The Complete Dead Sea Scrolls in English* (New York: Penguin Books, 1997), p. 163, points to the descriptions of weapons and war tactics as evidence of a time nearer the middle of the first century BCE.

51. Unless otherwise noted, English citations from the Dead Sea Scrolls are taken from Florentino García Martínez, *The Dead Sea Scrolls Translated: The Qumran Texts in English* (trans. Wilfred G.E. Watson; Grand Rapids: Eerdmans, 2nd edn, 1996).

1QM XIX, 5 contains basically the same expression at the complete destruction of the Kittim and the forces of Belial. Both Zech. 9.9 and the two 1QM
texts share the words Zion (צִיּוֹן) and greatly (מְאֹד, cf. 1QM מוֹאֲדָה and
מֵאָדָה); however, this alone does not confirm Zech. 9.9 as a source for the
expressions in 1QM, since similar exhortations occur with some frequency in
the Old Testament.[52] France is likely correct in his assessment of the texts in
1QM: the passages are 'best seen as an echo of a general Old Testament
idiom, and specific reference to Zechariah 9.9, appropriate though this would
be in a battle-hymn looking forward to eschatological victory, is not likely'.[53]

Among the Old Testament commentaries is 4QCommGen A (or 4Q252).
Within the blessing of Judah, 4QCommGen A V, 3-4 (49.10) asserts that
legitimate royal power belongs to the descendants of David rather than rulers
who are not descendants of David (to repudiate the Hasmonean kings of the
first century BCE).[54] 'Until the messiah of justice comes, the branch of David.
For to him and to his descendants has been given the covenant of royalty
over his people for all everlasting generations'. Allegro points to a close
relationship between Gen. 49.10-11 and Zech. 9.9, and suggests a parallel
between עַד בּוֹא מְשִׁיחַ הַצֶּדֶק of 4Q252 and מַלְכֵּךְ יָבוֹא לָךְ צַדִּיק וְנוֹשָׁע
הוּא of Zech. 9.9.[55] While it is likely that 4QCommGen A did comment on
Gen. 49.11, unfortunately the text only comments on Gen. 49.10 and does not
mention a donkey. While the Dead Sea sectarians who evidently interpreted
Gen. 49.10 in relation to the Messiah may also have regarded Zech. 9.9 similarly, neither this fragment nor any other extant text clearly alludes to Zech.
9.9.[56]

Old Testament Pseudepigrapha. Near the end of the second century BCE, the
Testaments of the Twelve Patriarchs was written by a Pharisee who admired
John Hyrcanus and recognized his Levite family as the legitimate dynasty.
However, later Christian interpolations of *Testaments* recast this perspective
to argue that the Messiah would come from the tribe of Judah.[57] *Testament of*

---

52. For example Pss. 14.7; 32.11; 48.11; 81.1; 95.1; 98.4; Isa. 12.6; 44.23; 52.9; 54.1;
66.10; Jer. 20.13; 31.7; Lam. 4.21; Joel 2.21, 23; Zeph. 3.14; Zech. 2.10.
53. France, *Jesus and the Old Testament*, p. 175.
54. Vermes, *Complete Dead Sea Scrolls in English*, p. 460.
55. J.M. Allegro, 'Further Messianic References in Qumran Literature', *JBL* 75
(1956), pp. 174-75.
56. France, *Jesus and the Old Testament*, p. 176.
57. C.A. Evans, *Noncanonical Writings*, p. 28. Several critical studies have attempted
to remove these Christian interpolations; among these are R.H. Charles, *The Greek
Versions of the Testaments of the Twelve Patriarchs* (Oxford: Clarendon Press, 1908;
repr., Oxford: Clarendon Press, 1960), pp. xlviii-li; Marinus de Jonge, 'Christian Influence in the Testaments of the Twelve Patriarchs', in *idem* (ed.), *Studies on the Testaments
of the Twelve Patriarchs: Text and Interpretation* (SVTP, 3; Leiden: E.J. Brill, 1975),

Judah 24.1 reads: 'And after this there shall arise for you a Star from Jacob in peace. And a man shall arise from my posterity like the Sun of righteousness, walking with the sons of men in gentleness and righteousness, and in him will be found no sin'.[58] The text does bring together the attributes of peace, gentleness, and righteousness, all three of which are present in Zech. 9.9-10; however, other texts, such as Num. 24.17, Ps. 45.4, or Isa. 53.9, are more likely to stand behind *T. Jud.* 24.1.[59]

1 Enoch records the Jewish hope of a heavenly ruler to judge the enemies of the people of God. The work, a collection of writings ascribed pseudonymously to the patriarch Enoch, is actually a composite of distinct sections written by different authors beginning in the second century BCE. One section not found among the fragments at Qumran, *The Similitudes* (*1 En.* 37–71), contains a passage, which like *T. Jud.* 24.1 above, may also be a 'near echo' of Zech. 9.10 as it combines righteousness and peace.[60] *1 Enoch* 71.14-15 reads:

> Then an angel came to me and greeted me and said to me, 'You, son of man, who art born in righteousness and upon whom righteousness had dwelt, the righteousness of the Antecedent of Time will not forsake you'. He added and

pp. 193-246. In the *Testaments of the Twelve Patriarchs*, messianic expectation associates the Messiah with both Levi and Judah (*T. Sim.* 7.1-3; *T. Jos.* 19.11). According to J.J. Collins, 'Testaments', in Stone (ed.), *Jewish Writings of the Second Temple Period*, pp. 325-56 (339), this incorporation of an earlier expectation of two Messiahs, as seen in Dead Sea Scrolls (e.g. 1QS IX, 11; 1QSa II, 11-22; cf. Zech. 4.14), may be a reaction against the consolidation of power by the Hasmonean priest-kings.

58.   All citations from the Old Testament Pseudipigrapha are from *OTP*. Other pseudepigraphic texts combine similar listings of such virtues; for example, *T. Dan* 6.9: 'For he is true and patient, lowly and humble, exemplifying by his actions the Law of God'.

59.   France, *Jesus and the Old Testament*, p. 183; cf. CD VII, 11-20.

60.   France, *Jesus and the Old Testament*, p. 183. The dating of *The Similitudes* is difficult. Because the section does not appear among the Aramaic fragments of *1 Enoch* found at Qumran, J.T. Milik alleges a date of 260–270 CE in 'Problèmes de la Littérature Hénochique à la Lumière des Fragments Araméens de Qumrân', *HTR* 64 (1971), pp. 333-78 (377). In his *The Books of Enoch* (Oxford: Clarendon Press, 1976), pp. 91-92, Milik calls *1 Enoch* 'a Christian Greek composition...which draws its inspiration from the writings of the New Testament'. Previously, R.H. Charles in *APOT*, p. 171, had suggested a date of either 94–79 or 70–64 BC by identifying the kings and mighty with the later Maccabean princes and their Sadducean supporters (the Pharisees found support with Alexandra from 79–70 BC) and by noting that Rome was not yet known as a world power before 64 BCE. More recently scholarship, such as *OTP*, I, p. 7 and C.A. Evans, *Noncanonical Writings*, p. 23, have seen *Similitudes* as a Jewish composition dating from the middle of the first century CE. The *Similitudes*, where the phrase 'Son of Man' appears in a manner not unlike the gospels, is of special interest to the title's background. For a recent survey of this background, see Clay Alan Ham, 'The Title "Son of Man" in the Gospel of John', *SCJ* 1 (1998), pp. 67-84 (74-76).

said to me, 'He shall proclaim peace to you in the name of the world that is to become. For from here proceeds peace since the creation of the world, and so it shall be unto you forever and ever and ever.'

Perhaps the closest parallel is found in the *Psalms of Solomon*, a collection of 18 psalms originally written in Hebrew. The *Psalms of Solomon* was probably composed in the middle of the first century BCE in response to the recent Roman takeover of Palestine by Pompey in 63 BCE. The author of the *Psalms* also criticizes various Jewish groups, including the Sadducees, and renounces support for the Hasmonean dynasty. One important section describes the coming of the Davidic Messiah/King (*Pss. Sol.* 17.32-35):

> And he will be a righteous king over them, taught by God.
> There will be no unrighteousness among them in his days,
>   for all shall be holy,
>   and their king shall be the Lord Messiah.
> (For) he will not rely on horse and rider and bow,
>   nor will he collect gold and silver for war.
> Nor will he build up hope in a multitude for a day of war.
> The Lord himself is his king,
>   the hope of the one who has a strong hope in God.
> He shall be compassionate to all the nations
>   (who) reverently (stand) before him.

The king is described as righteous and compassionate, although compassionate translates the future indicative verb ἐλεήσει (cf. 'humble' from the adjective πραΰς in Zech. 9.9). The text also asserts that the king will not depend on the normal instruments of war, namely, 'horse and rider and bow' (ἵππον καὶ ἀναβάτην καὶ τόξον). This concept is similar to the one in Zech. 9.10, which includes two of these three items (ἵππον...τόξον):

> He will cut off the chariot from Ephraim
>   and the war-horse from Jerusalem;
> and the battle bow shall be cut off,
>   and he shall command peace to the nations;
> his dominion shall be from sea to sea,
>   and from the River to the ends of the earth.

In addition, both *Pss. Sol.* 17.35 and Zech. 9.10 extend the king's rule 'to all the nations'. This combination of the attributes of kingship and righteousness with the repudiation of military might may recall Zech. 9.10,[61] even if *Psalms of Solomon* 17 does not describe the arrival of the king as humble and riding on a donkey as does Zech. 9.9.[62]

---

61. France, *Jesus and the Old Testament*, p. 183.

62. The *Psalms of Solomon* in particular and the Old Testament Pseudepigrapha in general do not associate humility with the Messiah/king nor a donkey with his coming.

A pseudepigraphic work that clearly refers to Zech. 9.9 is the *Sibylline Oracles*; however, it also undoubtedly follows Matthew's Gospel.[63] Although *Sibylline Oracle* 8 may preserve some Jewish material, its final form shows clear Christian redaction.[64] Lines 217-50 are an acrostic poem that spells out Ιησους Χριστος Θεου Υιος Σωτηρ Σταυρος, and the theme of the larger section of ll. 217-500 is the incarnation and earthly ministry of Jesus Christ. *Sibylline Oracle* 8.324 refers specifically to Jesus' entry into Jerusalem.

> Rejoice, holy daughter Sion, who have suffered much.
> Your king himself comes in, mounted on a foal,
> appearing gentle to all so that he may lift our yoke
> of slavery, hard to bear, which lies on our neck
> and undo the godless ordinances and constraining bonds.

The use of the terms πραΰς and ἐπιβαίνω (rather than καθίζω, which is found in Jn 12.15) suggests that the redactor of the passage follows Matthew. In addition, the appearance of ζυγός, alongside πραΰς, may be an implicit reference to Mt. 11.29-30, and the presence of χαῖρε (and the vocative θύγατερ Σιών) may indicate the redactor knows the LXX text of Zech. 9.9, as Matthew's wording, εἴπατε τῇ θυγατρὶ Σιών, follows Isa. 62.11.[65]

Rabbinic Literature. Zechariah 9.9 is evidently not clearly cited in the Mishnah or other rabbinic writings from the Tannaic period (50 BCE to 200 CE), although it appears in several of the rabbinic writings of the Amoraic period (220–500 CE).[66] The Babylonian Talmud, which combines the Mish-

---

For πραΰς, see *Jos. Asen.* 8.8; 15.8; *Sib. Or.* 4.159; for ὄνος, see *T. Job* 9.6; 16.3; Artap. 9.25.2, 3.

63.   The *Sibylline Oracles* consist of fourteen books written from the second century BCE to the seventh century CE. Although such oracles were largely a pagan phenomenon in the ancient world (the mythical 'Sibyls' were generally depicted as older women who pronounced prophecies in poetic form), both Jews and Christians used them to express their religious and political views. According to J.J. Collins, 'The Sibylline Oracles', in Stone (ed.), *Jewish Writings of the Second Temple Period*, pp. 357-82 (380), the Christian adaption of these oracles arose from their desire to demonstrate 'that even the pagan Sibyl prophesied about Christ'.

64.   According to Collins, in *OTP*, I, p. 416, *Sib. Or.* 8.1-216 dates from 175–195 CE, and 8.217-500 dates from a time earlier than Lactantius (c. 240–c. 320 CE), who quotes extensively from it (although 8.217-500 may possibly have been written closer to 190 than to 300 CE).

65.   Édouard Massaux, *The Influence of the Gospel of Saint Matthew on Christian Literature Before Saint Irenaeus* (ed. Arthur J. Bellinzoni; trans. Norman J. Belval and Suzanne Hecht; NGS, 5; 3 vols.; Macon: Mercer University Press, 1990–93), II, p. 91.

66.   Other works among the Middle Age Midrashim (c. 640–900 CE) use Zech. 9.9 in ways similar to the earlier Amoraic literature. Overwhelmingly these texts emphasize the coming of the Messiah as one humble and riding on a donkey; for example, *Deut. Rab.* 4.11 (on Deut. 12.20), *Midr. Ps. 60 §3* (on Ps. 60.10), and *Pesiq. R.* 34.1-2. Other texts

nah with interpretive expansions called Gemara, explicitly cites Zech. 9.9 in three texts in two of its 36 tractates. The first citation is from *Berakot*, a tractate concerning benedictions; the text is from *b. Ber.* 56b: 'If one sees an ass in a dream, he may hope for salvation, as it says, *Behold thy king cometh unto thee; he is triumphant and victorious, lowly and riding upon an ass*'.[67] *Sanhedrin*, which deals primarily with criminal law and capital punishment, includes two of the citations. The second text, *b. Sanh.* 98a, reads:

> R. Alexandri said: R. Joshua b. Levi pointed out a contradiction. It is written, *in its time* [will the Messiah come], whilst it is also written, *I [the Lord] will hasten it!*—If they are worthy, I will hasten it: if not, [he will come] at the due time. R. Alexandri said: R. Joshua opposed two verses: it is written, *And behold, one like the son of man came with the clouds of heaven*; whilst [elsewhere] it is written, *[behold, thy king cometh unto thee…] lowly, and riding upon an ass!*—If they are meritorious, [he will come] *with the clouds of heaven*; if not, *lowly and riding upon an ass.*

The third text is *b. Sanh.* 99a; it reads:

> R. Hillel said: There shall be no Messiah for Israel, because they have already enjoyed him in the days of Hezekiah. R. Joseph said: May God forgive him [for saying so]. Now, when did Hezekiah flourish? During the first Temple. Yet Zechariah, prophesying in the days of the second, proclaimed, *Rejoice greatly, O daughter of Zion; shout, O daughter of Jerusalem; behold thy king cometh unto thee! he is just and having salvation; lowly, and riding upon an ass, and upon a colt the foal of an ass.*

All three of these texts from the Babylonian Talmud apply Zech. 9.9 to the Messiah.[68] The donkey indicates that the coming Messiah brings salvation in

interpret passages in the Pentateuch that mention donkeys ridden by Abraham or Moses as foreshadowing the arrival of the Messiah on a donkey; for example, *Eccl. Rab.* 1.9 §1 and *Pirqe R. El.* §31. Rarely is Zech. 9.9 cited without reference to the Messiah's riding on a donkey; for example, *Exod. Rab.* 30.24 (on Exod. 21.1) relates the future coming of the king to the merit of Israel (cf. *b. Sanh.* 98a) and *Song Rab.* 1.4 §1-2 stresses the joy that Jerusalem will experience at the coming of her King, mentioning only the words 'triumphant' and 'victorious'.

Approximate dates for the rabbinic writings and the various rabbis are drawn from Herbert Danby, *The Mishnah* (Oxford: Oxford University Press, 1933), pp. 799-800; C.A. Evans, *Noncanonical Writings*, pp. 115-38; C.G. Montefiore and H. Loewe, *A Rabbinic Anthology* (New York: Schocken Books, 1974), pp. 700-708; and Shmuel Safrai (ed.), *The Literature of the Sages*. I. *Oral Tora, Halakha, Mishna, Tosefta, Talmud, External Tractates* (CRINT, 2.3; Assen: Van Gorcum, 1987), pp. 236-38.

67.   English citations from the Babylonian Talmud are taken from Isidore Epstein (ed.), *The Babylonian Talmud* (18 vols.; London: Soncino, 1978).

68.   Of these three passages, the earliest may be *b. Ber.* 56b. The saying is attributed to 'our Rabbis', a phrase which, according to Montefiore and Loewe, *Rabbinic Anthology*, p. 739, may indicate a tradition of the Tannaic period that was not incorporated in the

b. Ber. 56b. Zechariah 9.9 is seen as validation for the future coming of the Messiah in spite of R. Hillel's earlier denial in *b. Sanh.* 99a. More intriguing is *b. Sanh.* 98a, which juxtaposes Zech. 9.9 with Dan 7.13. The proposed contradiction concerns the manner in which the Messiah will come, that is, on the clouds of heaven (Dan. 7.13) or riding on a donkey (Zech. 9.9). The resolution offered relates to whether the people are worthy. If they are worthy, the Messiah will come on the clouds, as in Dan. 7.13. If not, the Messiah will come riding on a donkey, as in Zech. 9.9, thus emphasizing the coming of the Messiah 'more in terms of abasement than exaltation'.[69]

Among the Amoraic midrashic literature, *Genesis Rabbah* contains three passages that connect Zech. 9.9 with Gen. 32.6 and 49.11.[70] The first text is *Gen. Rab.* 75.6 (on Gen. 32.6):

> AND I HAVE AN OX, AND AN ASS, etc. R. Judah said: From one ox many oxen came forth, and from one ass many asses came forth. R. Nehemiah said: This is the common idiom: an ass, a camel. The Rabbis maintained: Ox is an allusion to the one anointed for battle, as it says, *His firstling bullock, majesty is his*; Ass refers to the royal Messiah, for it says of him, *Lowly, and riding upon an ass.*

This comment on Gen. 32.5 (32.6 MT) sees donkey as a reference to the Messiah. The second text is *Gen. Rab.* 98.9 (on Gen. 49.11):

> R. Judah, R. Nehemiah, and the Rabbis discuss this verse. R. Judah explained it:... The Rabbis interpreted: 'I', [said God], 'am bound to the vine and the choice vine' [Israel]. HIS FOAL AND HIS COLT intimate: when he will come of whom it is written, *Lowly and riding upon an ass, even upon a colt the foal of an ass.*

The third text is *Gen. Rab.* 99.8 (on Gen. 49.11):

> BINDING HIS FOAL UNTO THE VINE. This alludes to him who will gather together all Israel who are called a vine, as it says, *Thou didst pluck up a vine out of Egypt.* AND HIS ASS'S COLT UNTO THE CHOICE VINE alludes to him of whom it is written, *Lowly, and riding upon an ass, even upon a colt the foal of an ass.*

Both passages on Gen. 49.11 offer a messianic interpretation of the phrase 'He will tether his donkey to a vine'.

Mishnah. The two passages from *Sanhedrin* are Amoraic, as R. Joshua b. Levi is Amoraic first generation (220–250 CE) and R. Joseph is Amoraic third generation (290–320 CE).

69.   Michael S. Moore and Michael L. Brown, 'חֲמוֹר', in *NIDOTTE*, II, pp. 173-74 (173).

70.   While *Genesis Rabbah* dates to c. 425–450 CE, it does include both Tannaic and Amoraic material. The three texts cited here may indeed contain Tannaic traditions, as R. Judah and R. Nehemiah are Tannaic fourth generation (140–75 CE). All English citations from *Midrash Rabbah* are taken from H. Freedman and Maurice Simon (eds.), *Midrash Rabbah* (10 vols.; New York: Soncino, 3rd edn, 1983).

Early Church Fathers. Several writings among the Early Church Fathers of the second century CE use Zech. 9.9. The first of these is Justin Martyr (c. 100–c. 165 CE), who died in Rome as a martyr during the reign of Emperor Marcus Aurelius (161–80 CE). He wrote *Apologia i* (*First Apology*) and *Apologia ii* (*Second Apology*), both of which comprise an erudite defense of Christianity against the charges of atheism and sedition. Although addressed to Emperor Antoninus Pius (138–161 CE), Justin intended that both works be read by the educated public. In them, he develops the theme of the divine plan of salvation, fulfilled in Christ the Word.

Part of Justin's exposition and demonstration of Christianity in *Apologia i* concerns the fulfillment of Old Testament prophecy in the life and ministry of Jesus Christ. For example, in *1 Apol.* 32, Justin argues that Christ was predicted by Moses and particularly so in the text of Gen. 49.10-11. He contends that the removal of Jewish rule over Judea by the Romans is evidence that Jesus Christ has come as the one 'for whom the kingdom was reserved'. Moreover, he connects the binding of his foal to the vine as 'a significant symbol of the things that were to happen to Christ, and of what He was to do. For the foal of an ass stood bound to a vine at the entrance of a village, and He ordered His acquaintances to bring it to Him then; and when it was brought, He mounted and sat upon it, and entered Jerusalem' (*1 Apol.* 32.6).[71] In their accounts of Jesus' entry into Jerusalem, none of the gospels mentions a donkey tied to a vine; Mk 11.4 says only that the disciples 'found a colt tied near a door, outside in the street'. Even though the source of this information is unknown,[72] clearly Justin stresses this particular fulfillment of the prophecy. In so doing, he brings together Gen. 49.10-11 and Zech. 9.9.[73]

In a later section of the same work, Justin discusses several other prophecies fulfilled in the life of Christ, namely, Isa. 9.6; 65.2; Ps. 22.16, 18; and Zech. 9.9. Here Justin uses Zech. 9.9 to emphasize the manner in which Jesus entered Jerusalem—riding on a donkey:

---

71. Commenting further on Gen. 49.11, Justin also pictures the washing of his robe in the blood of grapes as a prediction of Jesus' passion and his 'cleansing by His blood those who believe on Him'; the robe is seen as those who believe. Unless otherwise noted, English citations from the Early Church Fathers are taken from *ANF*, while Greek citations come from Migne, *Patrologia graeca*.

72. Massaux, *Influence of the Gospel of Saint Matthew*, III, p. 42, suggests that Justin may have relied on a popular story about the donkey being tied to a vine, unless Justin has added the information in order to connect Gen. 49.11 with Zech. 9.9.

73. According to Meyers and Meyers, *Zechariah 9–14*, p. 131, Justin is evidently the first ancient author to link Zech. 9.9 (and Mt. 21.5 and Jn 12.5) with Gen. 49.11. Such a connection is made later in both Jewish writings, for example, *Gen. Rab.* 99.8 (on Gen. 49.11), and Christian writings, for example, Clement of Alexandria, *Paed.* i.5.15.

> And we will cite the prophetic utterances of another prophet, Zephaniah, to the effect that He was foretold expressly as to sit upon the foal of an ass and to enter Jerusalem. The words are these: 'Rejoice greatly, O daughter of Zion; shout, O daughter of Jerusalem: behold, thy King cometh unto thee; lowly, and riding upon an ass, and upon a colt the foal of an ass'. (*1 Apol.* 35.10-11)

While Justin has incorrectly attributed the citation to the prophet Zephaniah, the first part of the citation coincides with the LXX text of Zech. 9.9: Χαῖρε σφόδρα, θύγατερ Σιών, κήρυσσε, θύγατερ Ιερουσαλημ· ἰδοὺ ὁ βασιλεύς σου ἔρχεταί σοι. However, the second part of the citation may follow Mt. 21.5, in that it omits δίκαιος καὶ σῴζων αὐτός and describes Jesus' riding ἐπὶ πῶλον ὄνον υἱὸν ὑποζυγίου. While the LXX uses two words to depict the donkey, ὑποζύγιον and πῶλος, both Justin and Matthew add a third word ὄνος. Since Justin has asserted that Jesus was to enter Jerusalem sitting 'upon the foal of an ass' (ἐπὶ πῶλον ὄνου), he has possibly followed the wording of Matthew to make the prediction correspond more clearly with his affirmation about its fulfillment.[74]

In another work entitled *Dialogus cum Tryphone* (*Dialogue with Trypho*), Justin also uses Zech. 9.9 in two passages. In this work Justin narrates a supposed conversation with a prominent rabbi. The work quotes extensively from the Old Testament in an effort to demonstrate Christian truth in the Old Testament and in the life of Jesus. Both *Dial.* 53.2-4 and 88.6 occur in a long section on the fulfillment of Old Testament scriptures in the life of Jesus as a demonstration that he is the Christ. Specifically, *Dial.* 53.2-4 argues that Zechariah and the patriarch Jacob had predicted that Jesus Christ would ride into Jerusalem on a donkey.[75] In this passage Justin seems to follow the account in Matthew.[76] He refers to and insists on the presence of two animals (ὄνον δὲ τινα...σὺν πώλῳ αὐτῆς). This allows Justin to bring alongside Zech. 9.9 the prophecy from Gen. 49.11, which also mentions two animals: 'Now, that the Spirit of prophecy, as well as the patriarch Jacob, mentioned both an ass and its foal...' (τὸ δὲ καὶ ὄνον ὑποζύγιον ἤδη μετὰ τοῦ πώλου αὐτῆς). While he has already connected Zech. 9.9 and Gen. 49.11 in *1 Apol.* 32.6, in that text Justin accentuates the binding of the donkey to the vine, but here he stresses the actuality of two animals. However, Justin does not appeal to the two animals in this text as a mere fulfillment of prophecy; he allegorizes them as symbols for the Jews and the Gentiles.

---

74. Massaux, *Influence of the Gospel of Saint Matthew*, III, p. 37.

75. Justin underscores the humility of Jesus in *Dial.* 53.3 with the addition of the word 'lowly' (καὶ πραὺς καὶ πτωχός) to his citation from Zech. 9.9.

76. Moreover, Massaux, *Influence of the Gospel of Saint Matthew*, III, p. 58, suggests that Justin follows a written text 'because of the presence of many Matthean words: ὄνος, πῶλος, κώμη, βηθσφαγή, εἰσέρχομαι, εἰς 'Ιεροσόλυμα, ὁ κύριος, and τοὺς μαθητὰς ἀγαγεῖν'.

Irenaeus (c. 140–c. 202 CE) was appointed bishop of Lyon in 177 CE. As a child, he had heard the preaching of Polycarp, a disciple of John the Apostle (or possibly John the Presbyter?). Best known for his opposition against Gnosticism, Irenaeus wrote his *Adversus haereses* (*Against Heresies*) around 180 CE. In it he offers both an exposition of the heretical beliefs of the Gnostics and a presentation of orthodox doctrines, including a defense of Christ's incarnation and resurrection. In three passages (*Haer*. 3.19.2; 4.33.1; 4.33.12) he includes a statement that Jesus 'sat upon the foal of an ass' in a list of phenomena fulfilled by Jesus in order to establish both his human and divine nature.

In a lesser known work entitled *Epideixis tou apostolikou kerygmatos* (*Demonstration of the Apostolic Preaching*), Irenaeus does not confute heretics but confirms Christians with a demonstration of the truth of the gospel by means of the Old Testament prophecies. In *Epid*. 65 Irenaeus simply refers to the fulfillment of Isa. 62.11 by attribution and of Zech. 9.9 by citation in the manner of Jesus' entry into Jerusalem:

> And the manner of His entry into Jerusalem, which was the capital of Judaea, where also was His royal seat and the temple of God, the prophet Isaiah declares: *Say ye to the daughter of Sion, Behold a king cometh unto thee meek and sitting upon an ass, a colt the foal of an ass.* For, sitting on an ass's colt, so He entered into Jerusalem, the multitudes strewing and putting down for Him their garments. And by *the daughter of Sion* he means Jerusalem.[77]

Zechariah 9.9 in the New Testament
The New Testament cites Zech. 9.9 in only two texts: Mt. 21.5 and Jn 12.15. Neither Mark nor Luke use the prophetic passage in their accounts of the entry into Jerusalem.

Matthew 21.5. The citation of Zech. 9.9 is introduced with Matthew's characteristic formula: τοῦτο δὲ γέγονεν ἵνα πληρωθῇ τὸ ῥηθὲν διὰ τοῦ προφήτου λέγοντος.[78] These introductory formulas generally point to something said previously, in which case τοῦτο would refer to Jesus' command to the two disciples to obtain the donkey and her colt.[79] However, the formula, which has been inserted into the middle of the narrative (cf. Isa. 7.14 in Mt. 1.23), may be taken proleptically, that is, as pointing forward,

---

77. The text is taken from Irenaeus, *The Demonstration of the Apostolic Preaching* (trans. J. Armitage Robinson; New York: Macmillan, 1920).

78. On the introductory formula in general, see pp. 3-5, above. Robert H. Gundry, *Matthew: A Commentary on His Literary and Theological Art* (Grand Rapids: Eerdmans, 1982), p. 408, suggests that the name of the prophet has been omitted in this instance, since 'the essential part of the quotation comes from a minor prophet'. Still a few MSS add 'Zechariah' or 'Isaiah'. See pp. 21-23 on the specific wording of Matthew's citation.

79. Gundry, *Matthew*, p. 408.

since it primarily concerns the actions recorded in Mt. 21.6-11, namely, Jesus' riding into Jerusalem on a donkey.

The first four words of the citation, εἴπατε τῇ θυγατρὶ Σιών, likely come from Isa. 62.11, in which Yahweh makes a universal proclamation ('to the end of the earth'[80]) that salvation is coming to Daughter Zion. Since 'salvation' comes as if personalized ('his reward is with him, and his recompense before him'), it is not surprising that later versions make it overtly so (e.g. the LXX, Syriac, Vulgate, and Targum read 'your Savior', as do the NIV and NLT). Such an understanding is probably implicit within the pronouncement: the coming of Zion's salvation is the arrival of Yahweh. Both the clear verbal dependence upon Isa. 40.10 and the possible contextual connection with Isa. 63.1-6 support this. The last section of Isa. 62.11 comes almost entirely from Isa. 40.10, in which Yahweh comes to Zion/Jerusalem in power and with reward. Isaiah 63.1-6 identifies a figure who approaches from Bozrah, the capital of Israel's constant enemy Edom, as Yahweh whose garments are blood-spattered from the defeat of the nations and as the one who brings vengeance and redemption.

Ostensibly this modification alters the use of Zech. 9.9 in Mt. 21.5 from invitation to proclamation. In this way the modification may reflect Matthew's knowledge of Jerusalem's negative response to Jesus' entry (Mt. 21.10) and the eventual rejection of Jesus by the Jews. Such an awareness is evident in the Parable of the Wicked Tenants (Mt. 21.33-44), which understands that God has presently rejected Israel, and in the remainder of the gospel, which does not show Israel 'rejoicing'.[81] The use of Isa. 62.11 may express Matthew's 'evangelistic challenge to unconverted Israel',[82] identified here as θύγατερ Σιών, an idiom for Jerusalem and its inhabitants that occurs in the New Testament only here and in Jn 12.15. Furthermore, the juxtaposed texts may suggest that Zech. 9.9 be read in light of Isa. 62.11: 'God's kingship in Zion (Isa. 62,11) is realised when the messianic king, who will rule in God's name, enters the city (Zech. 9,9)'.[83]

After introducing the citation with words from Isa. 62.11, the citation takes up the wording of Zech. 9.9: ἰδοὺ ὁ βασιλεύς σου ἔρχεταί σοι. Βασιλεύς, which occurs 22 times in Matthew, often, as here, refers to the Messianic king.[84] Still, Matthew surprisingly omits Zechariah's description of the king as righteous and saved (δίκαιος καὶ σῴζων αὐτός as rendered in the LXX). Both words are common in Matthew: δίκαιος occurs 17 times, and σῴζω,

80. Cf. Isa. 11.12; 49.6, Ps. 72.8; Zech. 9.10.
81. Willard M. Swartley, *Israel's Scripture Traditions and the Synoptic Gospels: Story Shaping Story* (Peabody, MA: Hendrickson, 1994), p. 173.
82. Gundry, *Matthew*, p. 408; cf. Mt. 10.6; 15.24.
83. Weren, 'Jesus' Entry into Jerusalem', p. 126.
84. Mt. 2.2; 21.5; 25.34, 40; 27.11, 29, 37, 42.

15 times. Generally δίκαιος refers to those considered 'good' in distinction from those deemed as 'wicked' or 'evil';[85] however, it relates only once to Jesus, when Pilate's wife warns Pilate: 'Have nothing to do with that innocent man' (Mt. 27.19). Matthew's use of σῴζω commonly identifies Jesus as one capable of 'saving others'.[86] Thus, neither word would have been incongruous with Matthew's description of Jesus elsewhere.[87] Their absence may be inappropriate in the present context of the Jews' rejection of Jesus,[88] or their absence may be Matthew's way of underlining their appropriateness.

The omission further highlights how Matthew does depict the manner of Jesus' coming with the adjective πραΰς. Of the four times the word is used in the New Testament, three are in Matthew (Mt. 5.5; 11.29; 21.5; 1 Pet. 3.4).[89] In Mt. 11.29 both πραΰς and the adjective ταπεινός ('humble, lowly, poor') are applied to Jesus. In the LXX these two adjectives are found together in such prophetic texts as Isa. 26.6 and Zech. 3.12; moreover, the LXX translates עָנִי with ταπεινός in Isa. 14.32; 49.13; 54.11; 66.2; and Jer. 22.16. The association of these two adjectives, πραΰς and ταπεινός, in Matthew and the LXX may provide an alternative explanation for Matthew's agreement with the LXX, Targum, Peshitta, and Aquila in translating עָנִי with πραΰς.[90]

Matthew further describes the manner of Jesus' entry into Jerusalem as riding[91] on a donkey. The last part of Matthew's citation from Zech. 9.9, ὄνον καὶ ἐπὶ πῶλον υἱὸν ὑποζυγίου, departs from the wording of the LXX and thereby exhibits a closer rendering of the MT. This phenomenon need not be combined, however, with the mention of two animals in Mt. 21.2 (καὶ εὐθέως εὑρήσετε ὄνον δεδεμένην καὶ πῶλον μετ' αὐτῆς)[92] as a way of making a dubious judgment of Matthew's account, that is to say, that

---

85. Mt. 5.45; 9.13; 10.41; 13.17, 43, 49; 23.28, 29, 35; 25.37, 46.

86. Mt. 1.21; 8.25; 14.30; 27.40, 42.

87. In the words of Stendahl, *School of St Matthew*, p. 199, 'the omission of the adjectives δίκαιος and σῴζων is surprising, since those words...would constitute the very epitome of Matthew's Christology'.

88. Gundry, *Matthew*, pp. 408-409.

89. BDAG 861 defines πραΰς as pertaining to 'not being overly impressed by a sense of one's self-importance, gentle, humble, considerate, meek in the older favorable sense'.

90. Gundry, *Matthew*, p. 409, accounts for the wording textually: 'Matthew agrees with the LXX, Targum, Peshitta, and Aquila in taking עָנִי "humble" (MT), as עָנָו "meek". Since copyists often confused י and ו, the latter probably appeared in the Hebrew text used by Matthew'.

91. In the New Testament, ἐπιβαίνω generally means to get on board or embark (Acts 21.2, 4; 27.2) or to set foot in (Acts 20.18; 25.1); only here does it mean to mount or ride.

92. Cf. Mt. 21.7: ἤγαγον τὴν ὄνον καὶ τὸν πῶλον καὶ ἐπέθηκαν ἐπ' αὐτῶν τὰ ἱμάτια, καὶ ἐπεκάθισεν ἐπάνω αὐτῶν. While the anarthrous ὄνον in Mt. 21.5 may apply to either a male or female donkey, its occurrence in Mt. 21.2, 7 clearly refers to a female donkey. In Mt. 21.2 it agrees with the fem. ptc., and in Mt. 21.7 it follows a fem. art.

Matthew has added an extra animal to fit his misunderstanding of Zech. 9.9.[93] Since Matthew translates the MT more closely than does the LXX, Matthew presumably would have understood the Hebrew parallelism (and gender) that identifies the donkey as a young colt.[94] Some scholars point to a particular tradition behind the phrase 'a colt that has never been ridden' in Mk 11.2 as the reason for Matthew mentioning the colt and its mother.[95] Therefore, by noting the presence of two animals, Matthew has plainly pointed out that Jesus rode on the unbroken *colt*, not its *mother* (whose presence may still have been needed to calm the young colt).[96] Another possibility suggests that in Mt. 21.5, Matthew may indeed have had two animals in mind. The mention of two donkeys, however, does not result from a misreading of Zech. 9.9, rather from an interpretive reading of Zech. 9.9 in light of Gen. 49.11, where two donkeys are clearly depicted (δεσμεύων πρὸς ἄμπελον τὸν πῶλον αὐτοῦ καὶ τῇ ἕλικι τὸν πῶλον τῆς ὄνου αὐτοῦ).[97] Mt. 21.2, 5, 7 and Gen. 49.11 thus make the same distinction between the colt and its mother. An additional conceptional correspondence between the texts is 'binding' (δεσμεύων, a derivative of δέω) in Gen. 49.11 and 'tied' (δεδεμένην) in Mt. 21.2. If so, Mt. 21.5 also identifies Jesus as the legitimate Davidic heir, one whom the crowds appropriately acclaim with 'Hosanna to the Son of David!' (Mt. 21.9).

93.   For example, Rudolf Bultmann, *The History of the Synoptic Tradition* (trans. John Marsh; Oxford: Basil Blackwell, 1968), pp. 261-62, sees this as evidence that the entire account is written up as a fulfillment of Zech. 9.9. Yet Roman Bartnicki, 'Das Zitat von Zach 9.9-10 und die Tiere im Bericht von Matthäus über dem Einzug Jesu in Jerusalem', *NovT* 18 (1976), pp. 161-66 (161-65), discusses several options for understanding Matthew's two animals, including allegory, doublet, literal fulfillment, and rabbinical interpretation, but he prefers the proposal that in Mt. 21.5 ὄνον should be taken as masc. and in reference to the same animal as πῶλον.

94.   Gundry, *Use of the Old Testament*, p. 198; Soares Prabhu, *Formula Quotations*, pp. 158-59; see the discussions above, pp. 23, 28-30.

95.   Stendahl, *School of St Matthew*, p. 200; Lindars, *New Testament Apologetic*, p. 114; Longenecker, *Biblical Exegesis*, pp. 148-49.

96.   D.A. Carson, *Matthew*, in Frank E. Gaebelein (ed.), *Expositor's Bible Commentary*. XIII. *Matthew, Mark, Luke* (Grand Rapids: Zondervan, 1984), pp. 1-599 (438); Craig S. Keener, *A Commentary on the Gospel of Matthew* (Grand Rapids: Eerdmans, 1999), p. 492, adds: 'At the same time, in view of his doubling of other figures in his narratives, this may simply be Matthew's way of underlining the importance of the event (8.28; 9.27; 20.30)'.

97.   Weren, 'Jesus' Entry into Jerusalem', pp. 132-33. Cf. David Instone-Brewer, 'The Two Asses of Zechariah 9.9 in Matthew 21', *TynBul* 54 (2003), pp. 87-98, who suggests that Matthew assumes, as did the rabbinic Judaism of first century Palestine, that the Old Testament does not contain parallelism; therefore, Matthew would not see a fulfillment of the Zechariah text unless Jesus rode on two donkeys.

John 12.15. The citation of Zech. 9.9 in Jn 12.15 is introduced by καθώς ἐστιν γεγραμμένον (cf. Jn 6.31). The citation itself is more abbreviated than in Mt. 21.5, and its wording departs from both the MT and the LXX: μὴ φοβοῦ, θυγάτηρ Σιών· ἰδοὺ ὁ βασιλεύς σου ἔρχεται, καθήμενος ἐπὶ πῶλον ὄνου. The opening prohibition 'do not be afraid' differs from both Zechariah's double imperative, 'Rejoice greatly...shout aloud', and Matthew's modification, 'Tell'. The prohibition μὴ φοβοῦ and its plural form μὴ φοβεῖσθε appear with some frequency in the LXX, especially in Isaiah.[98] However, in none of these instances does either occur with 'daughter of Zion'; only in Zeph. 3.14-17 do 'Daughter Zion' and 'do not be afraid' appear together.[99] Zephaniah 3.14-17 not only provides an important textual antecedent to Zech. 9.9,[100] but it also contains the phrase 'the king of Israel', a prominent appellation in Jn 12.13. In this way, Jn 12.15 may be an example of a conflated citation, prefixing a phrase from Zeph. 3.16 to Zech. 9.9. The remainder of the citation comes from Zech. 9.9 but differs from Mt. 21.5. It includes the main statement, ἰδοὺ ὁ βασιλεύς σου ἔρχεται minus the dative σοι, omits πραΰς, states that Jesus is 'sitting' (καθήμενος), on a donkey's colt, and identifies the donkey with only one description, πῶλον ὄνου.[101]

These factors (the prohibition against being afraid, the omission of 'humble', and the presentation of Jesus 'sitting' on a donkey) suggest a greater interest with Jesus as king than with his entry into Jerusalem.[102] This notion also draws support from the absence of any procession in Jn 12.12-19. That 'Jesus found a young donkey and sat on it' (Jn 12.14) seems to fulfill sufficiently the prophecy of kingship. Important for John (and also Zechariah) is the nature of this kingship; it is not nationalistic, as the response of the crowd would seem to indicate,[103] but universal (cf. Zech. 9.10; Jn 11.51-52; 12.19-20, 32). Thus, John uses the citation from Zech. 9.9 (and Zeph. 3.16) to

98. Isa. 35.4; 40.9; 41.10, 13; 43.1, 5; 44.2; 51.7; 54.4.

99. Here Jn 12.15 translates more closely the MT (אַל־תִּירְאִי צִיּוֹן) than does the LXX (θάρσει Σιών). Given the earlier reference to 'Hosanna' in Jn 12.13, the prohibition 'do not be afraid' may be similar to 'rejoice' in Zeph. 3.14 and Zech. 9.9; cf. Joel 2.21-23.

100. See the earlier discussion of Zeph. 3.14-17 and Zech. 9.9 above, pp. 24-25.

101. Freed, *Old Testament Quotations*, p. 79, sees in the description (πῶλον ὄνου) the possibility of influence from Gen. 49.11, which contains the same two words.

102. Freed, *Old Testament Quotations*, p. 75.

103. Jn 12.13. That the crowd meets Jesus with palm branches in the spirit of the Maccabean victory following the defeat of Antiochus IV by Judas (2 Macc. 10.7; cf. Simon's victory in 1 Macc. 13.51) may suggest a nationalistic temper to their acclamations of Jesus, according to William R. Farmer, 'The Palm Branches in John 12.13', *JTS* 3 (1952–53), pp. 62-66 (63). Soares Prabhu, *Formula Quotations*, p. 138, also sees Jesus' actions as a 'correction of the spontaneous, politically coloured ovation of the crowd'.

reassure Jerusalem that as king of Israel Jesus is the universal king, who is Yahweh in their midst.[104]

Summary

Matthew 21.5 has conflated two Old Testament texts (Isa. 62.11 and Zech. 9.9); it has followed the LXX rendering of the MT for the most part but has drawn some elements from the MT.[105] The citation begins with Isa. 62.11; these four introductory words, εἴπατε τῇ θυγατρὶ Σιών, are identical to the LXX (= MT). The main citation comes from Zech. 9.9; of these 16 words, the first ten words, ἰδοὺ ὁ βασιλεύς σου ἔρχεταί σοι πραῢς καὶ ἐπιβεβηκὼς ἐπὶ, are also identical to the LXX. They translate well the MT with the possible exception of πραῢς, in which case Matthew has followed the LXX over the MT. Matthew's omission of one line from Zech. 9.9, וְנוֹשָׁע הוּא צַדִּיק, may further emphasize πραῢς. The last six words, ὄνον καὶ ἐπὶ πῶλον υἱὸν ὑποζυγίου, depart from the wording of the LXX and more closely render the MT.

Zechariah 9.9 announces the king's procession into Jerusalem, calling for the inhabitants of Jerusalem to celebrate the king's arrival as they would Yahweh's presence among them. After Yahweh conquers Israel's enemies (Zech. 9.1-8), the king enters Jerusalem for the purpose of bringing peace and salvation to the nations under the king's universal reign (Zech. 9.10-17; cf. Ps. 72.1-11). This arrival of the Davidic king anticipates the eschatological appearance of Yahweh as king over Zion and ultimately all the earth (cf. Zeph. 3.14; Zech. 2.10 [2.14 MT]; 14.9, 16-17). The king is described as 'triumphant' and 'victorious', that is, the king is fully qualified to assume the Davidic throne and has received deliverance without military means. The king is also described as 'humble'[106] and rides into Jerusalem on a donkey's colt, thereby portraying the king's legitimate reign (cf. Gen. 49.10-11).

The Jewish writings from the Second Temple period rarely use Zech. 9.9. The biblical scroll among the discoveries in the Judean Desert cuts off at Zech. 9.5. The Dead Sea sectarians interpreted Gen. 49.10 as relating to the legitimate royal power of the descendant of David, but no clear connection of Gen. 49.10 with Zech. 9.9 can be discerned. A few texts in the Old Testament

---

104. Raymond E. Brown, *The Gospel according to John (i–xii)* (AB, 29; Garden City, NY: Doubleday, 1966), p. 462.

105. Gundry, *Use of the Old Testament*, p. 149, lists Mt. 4.15-16; 5.33; 8.17; 12.18-21; 13.35; 21.5 among the formal citations unique to Matthew showing a mixture of Septuagintal and non-Septuagintal features.

106. Rex A. Mason, 'The Relation of Zech. 9–14 to Proto-Zechariah', *ZAW* 88 (1976), pp. 227-39 (236), notes that the qualities of the king—triumphant, victorious, and humble—are all 'paralleled by qualities assigned to the king in the Psalms' and especially to 'the Suffering Servant of Second Isaiah'.

Pseudepigrapha ascribe righteousness, peace, and gentleness to the one coming as messiah (*T. Jud.* 24.1), king (*Pss. Sol.* 17.32-35), and cosmic ruler (*1 En.* 71.14-15), but these texts do not describe his coming on a donkey.[107] Written well after the time of the New Testament, *Sib. Or.* 8.324 does describe the king's coming on a donkey; however, the text shows that its Christian redactor likely knew both the texts of Matthew and Zechariah.

Zechariah 9.9 is not directly cited in the Mishnah or other rabbinic writings from the Tannaic period. It does, however, appear in a few texts from the Amoraic period. In each instance the application of Zech. 9.9 is messianic, and these texts especially emphasize the lowliness of the Messiah's coming, in that 'humble and riding on a donkey' is the portion of Zech. 9.9 most frequently cited.[108] While *b. Sanh.* 98a accepts that the Messiah may come on the clouds of heaven as envisioned in Dan. 7.13, the text also affirms that the Messiah's riding on a donkey would indicate that people are not worthy of the Messiah's coming. *Genesis Rabbah* 98.9 (on Gen. 49.11) and *Gen. Rab.* 99.8 (on Gen. 49.11) connect Zech. 9.9 with a messianic interpretation of the donkey tethered to the vine in Gen. 49.11, as is evidenced in other Christian writings.[109]

The early Church Fathers use Zech. 9.9 as part of their overriding concern to demonstrate the fulfillment of Old Testament prophecy in the life and ministry of Jesus Christ and thereby to prove his divinity (especially Justin, *1 Apol.* 32.6; 35.10-11; *Dial.* 53.2-4; 88.6; Irenaeus, *Haer.* 3.19.2; 4.33.1, 12; *Epid.* 65). To a lesser extent, Justin underscores the humility/lowliness of Jesus' entry into Jerusalem, because he uses both πραΰς and πτωχός in his citation of Zech. 9.9 in *Dial.* 53.3. Justin (*1 Apol.* 32.6) also connects Zech. 9.9 with Gen. 49.10-11 to show that Jesus is the one 'for whom the kingdom was reserved'; indeed, Justin argues that the removal of Jewish rule of Judea by the Romans signals Jesus' legitimate rule. In this passage Justin probably follows the wording of Matthew in order to establish the presence of two animals as a fulfillment of the prophecy and to construe those two donkeys as allegorical symbols for Jews and Gentiles.

In the New Testament only Matthew and John cite Zech. 9.9. Both use the citation to make explicit the meaning implied in Jesus' action of entering

---

107. France, *Jesus and the Old Testament*, p. 183, observes that the motif of the donkey does not occur in the texts of the Old Testament Pseudepigrapha.

108. France, *Jesus and the Old Testament*, p. 189, supports this conclusion: 'The early rabbinic application of Zechariah 9.9, then, is to the expected coming of the Messiah ben David, the royal Messiah, and its particular use is to stress the lowliness of his coming'.

109. Justin Martyr, *1 Apol.* 32.6, and Clement of Alexandria, *Paed.* i.5.15, also make this connection between Zech. 9.9 and Gen. 49.11. While the texts cited above from *Genesis Rabbah* may contain Tannaic traditions that are roughly contemporary with Justin and Clement, *Apologia i* and *Paedagogus* were written more than two hundred years before *Genesis Rabbah*.

Jerusalem on a donkey; both use the citation to draw attention to the kingship of Jesus and its lowly nature.[110] In Jn 12.15 the citation begins with a phrase based on Zeph. 3.16 prefixed to it ('do not be afraid, daughter of Zion'), omits all three descriptions of the king from Zech. 9.9, even 'humble', and presents Jesus as one 'sitting' on a donkey's colt. Thus, John uses the citation to reassure Jerusalem that as king of Israel, Jesus is the universal king, who is Yahweh in their midst. In Mt. 21.5 the citation follows Matthew's characteristic formula; it either refers to the authoritative command to obtain the donkey or to the action of Jesus riding into Jerusalem on a donkey. The citation actually begins with a modification based on Isa. 62.11 ('Tell the daughter of Zion'), which speaks about the coming of Zion's salvation in the arrival of Yahweh. Rather than inviting Israel to rejoice, this alteration makes the citation a proclamation to Israel, announcing Jesus as king of Israel, who, according to the Gospel of Matthew, has rejected Jesus. The wording used from Zech. 9.9 omits the description of the king as 'triumphant and victorious', either to exclude something inappropriate to the context, to underline the importance of the characteristics omitted, or to highlight the character of Jesus as humble. This humble character is further emphasized by Matthew's portrayal of Jesus riding on a donkey's colt, which, read in view of Gen. 49.11, may identify Jesus as the legitimate Davidic heir.

Therefore, Matthew concurs with both the Jewish rabbis and the early Church Fathers in their understanding of Zech. 9.9 as messianic and with their primary application of the text to emphasize the lowliness of the Messiah's coming. Certainly, Matthew's concern for demonstrating the fulfillment of this Old Testament prophecy in the life and ministry of Jesus Christ is shared by the early Church Fathers, but this marks the inevitable difference from the rabbis in his application of it. While the rabbis looked forward to a future fulfillment of Zech. 9.9, Matthew saw its fulfillment already in Jesus's entry into Jerusalem.[111] Like *Gen. Rab.* 99.8 (on Gen. 49.11) and Justin Martyr, *1 Apol.* 32.6, Matthew may also connect Zech. 9.9 with a messianic interpretation of the donkey tethered to the vine in Gen. 49.11. If so, Matthew, like Justin, sees Jesus' entry into Jerusalem on a donkey (or two donkeys) as a clear sign of Jesus' legitimate rule as a descendant of Judah, the Son of David.

Matthew and John show some similarities in their use of Zech. 9.9. Both stress the kingship of Jesus and its humble nature. With the omission of 'triumphant and victorious', both emphasize the assertion that the coming king is humble (πραΰς). With their distinct alterations of the beginning of the citation, both gospels apparently correct any undue nationalistic expectations surrounding Jesus' entry into Jerusalem. Both affirm that the kingship of Jesus extends beyond Jerusalem to include 'the ends of the earth' (Zech. 9.10).

110. France, *Jesus and the Old Testament*, p. 197.
111. France, *Jesus and the Old Testament*, p. 197.

In fulfillment of Zech. 9.9, Matthew presents Jesus riding into Jerusalem on a donkey—a deliberate action, rich in symbolic value, speaking 'more powerfully than words could have done of a royal claim'.[112] In so doing, the symbolic parable serves as Jesus' 'confession' to illustrate 'the character of his messiahship—its modesty'.[113] Moreover, Matthew's application of Zech. 9.9 (and the particular Old Testament texts to which it relates) may also indicate that 'the various activities displayed by God in Zech. 9 are now transferred to Jesus'.[114] Thus, Matthew presents Jesus as the coming king, who brings salvation to the nations.

Matthew 27.9-10

Of the four gospels, only Mt. 27.9-10 explicitly[115] refers to Judas's death after his betrayal of Jesus as the prophetic fulfillment Zech. 11.12-13:

καὶ ἔλαβον τὰ τριάκοντα ἀργύρια, τὴν τιμὴν τοῦ τετιμημένου ὃν ἐτιμήσαντο ἀπὸ υἱῶν 'Ισραήλ, καὶ ἔδωκαν αὐτὰ εἰς τὸν ἀγρὸν τοῦ κεραμέως, καθὰ συνέταξέν μοι κύριος.

And they took the thirty pieces of silver, the price of the one on whom a price had been set, on whom some of the people of Israel had set a price, and they gave them for the potter's field, as the Lord commanded me.

The text of Zech. 11.12-13 in the MT is as follows:

וָאֹמַר אֲלֵיהֶם אִם־טוֹב בְּעֵינֵיכֶם הָבוּ שְׂכָרִי וְאִם־לֹא חֲדָלוּ וַיִּשְׁקְלוּ
אֶת־שְׂכָרִי שְׁלֹשִׁים כָּסֶף: וַיֹּאמֶר יְהוָה אֵלַי הַשְׁלִיכֵהוּ אֶל־הַיּוֹצֵר
אֶדֶר הַיְקָר אֲשֶׁר יָקַרְתִּי מֵעֲלֵיהֶם וָאֶקְחָה שְׁלֹשִׁים הַכֶּסֶף וָאַשְׁלִיךְ אֹתוֹ
בֵּית יְהוָה אֶל־הַיּוֹצֵר:

I then said to them, 'If it seems right to you, give me my wages; but if not, keep them'. So they weighed out as my wages thirty shekels of silver. Then the LORD said to me, 'Throw it into the treasury'—this lordly price at which I was valued by them. So I took the thirty shekels of silver and threw them into the treasury in the house of the LORD.

A comparison of the citation in Mt. 27.9-10 with Zech. 11.12-13 in the MT reveals that the citation has been substantially modified.[116] The citation

112. N.T. Wright, *Christian Origins and the Question of God*. II. *Jesus and the Victory of God* (Minneapolis: Fortress Press, 1996), p. 490.

113. Frederick Dale Bruner, *Matthew* (2 vols.; Dallas: Word Books, 1987–90), II, p. 748.

114. Weren, 'Jesus' Entry into Jerusalem', p. 128.

115. The citation is introduced by the characteristic Matthean formula with minor modification: τότε ἐπληρώθη τὸ ῥηθὲν διὰ 'Ιερεμίου τοῦ προφήτου λέγοντος.

116. Significant portions of Zech. 11.12-13 are omitted from Matthew's citation. These include: 'I then said to them, "If it seems right to you, give me my wages; but if not,

departs from both the MT and the LXX, but it is closer to the MT than the LXX.[117] In Mt. 27.9, the citation begins with καὶ ἔλαβον τὰ τριάκοντα ἀργύρια; the clause is closest to the wording near the end of Zech. 11.13, וָאֶקְחָה שְׁלֹשִׁים הַכֶּסֶף, and the mention of שְׁלֹשִׁים הַכֶּסֶף in Zech. 11.12.[118] The difference between the two texts is slight; Mt. 27.9 has a third person plural verb, ἔλαβον, while Zech. 11.13 has a first person singular verb, וָאֶקְחָה. This change in person and number arises from the preceding narrative in Matthew, since Judas has already received the thirty pieces of silver from the chief priests (Mt. 26.14-15) and has already returned them by throwing them into the temple (Mt. 27.3-5). Thus, Matthew has altered the wording to accommodate the purchase of the potter's field with the thirty pieces of silver (Mt. 27.7).

The rest of Mt. 27.9, τὴν τιμὴν τοῦ τετιμημένου ὃν ἐτιμήσαντο ἀπὸ υἱῶν Ἰσραήλ, parallels an earlier part of Zech. 11.13, אֶדֶר הַיְקָר אֲשֶׁר יָקַרְתִּי מֵעֲלֵיהֶם. Matthew's rendering differs in several respects.[119] The noun אֶדֶר, meaning 'glory, magnificence',[120] is omitted, and 'price' is qualified instead by the participial phrase τοῦ τετιμημένου. The preposition with masculine plural suffix (מֵעֲלֵיהֶם) is rendered as ἀπὸ υἱῶν Ἰσραήλ ('some of the people of Israel'), which becomes the third person subject of the verb ἐτιμήσαντο (the MT has the first person singular יָקַרְתִּי). In view of the contexts of Mt. 27.3-10 and Zech. 11.4-14, these changes may identify more clearly the

---

keep them"' (וָאֹמַר אֲלֵיהֶם אִם־טוֹב בְּעֵינֵיכֶם הָבוּ שְׂכָרִי וְאִם־לֹא חֲדָלוּ), 'so they weighed out as my wages' (וַיִּשְׁקְלוּ אֶת־שְׂכָרִי), and 'throw it into the treasury' (הַשְׁלִיכֵהוּ אֶל־הַיּוֹצֵר).

117. In the words of Stendahl, *School of St Matthew*, p. 124: 'The relation to the LXX in this quotation is therefore very slight, and its form is definitely dependent on Matthew's interpretation of the Hebrew text'.

118. Matthew's attributive phrase, τὰ τριάκοντα ἀργύρια, uses the neut. pl. form of ἀργύριον, while the LXX, Aquila, and Symmachus, translate the MT's const. phrase, שְׁלֹשִׁים הַכֶּסֶף, with the phrase, τοὺς τριάκοντα ἀργυροῦς, using the masc. pl. ἀργυροῦς. Matthew prefers the neut. pl. ἀργύρια, consistently with negative connotations, in 25.18, 27; 26.15; 27.3, 5, 6, 9; 28.12, 15 over forms of ἄργυρος, which appears only in Mt. 10.9, and ἀργυροῦς, which does not appear. In the LXX, Zech. 6.11; 9.3; 13.9; 14.14 have the sg. ἀργύριον, while ἀργυροῦς is used in Zech. 11.12-13; the pl. of ἀργύριον does not appear in the New Testament outside of Matthew.

119. The LXX has significant differences from the MT (εἰ δόκιμόν ἐστιν ὃν τρόπον ἐδοκιμάσθην ὑπὲρ αὐτῶν), which follow its rendering of 'potter' (יוֹצֵר) as 'furnace' (χωνευτήριον; cf. LXX 2 Kgdms 8.51; Wis. 3.6; Mal. 3.2). Like the LXX, Symmachus also has χωνευτήριον, but Aquila is closer to the MT with πλάστης, which generally means one who molds with clay or wax (cf. Rom. 9.20-21). Aquila also uses πλάστης for יוֹצֵר in Isa. 64.8 (64.7 MT). Furthermore, the three Greek translations suggest that the pricing was not accomplished by 'them', namely, 'the flock doomed to slaughter', but it was done 'for their sakes' (ὑπὲρ αὐτῶν).

120. BDB, p. 12; the word appears elsewhere in the MT only in Mic. 2.8, where it means 'robe', 'cloak', or 'mantle'.

person priced (that is, Jesus as the shepherd) and those who did the pricing (that is, the people of Israel as the sheep merchants).

Matthew 27.10 begins with a statement having little in common with Zech. 11.12-13: καὶ ἔδωκαν αὐτὰ εἰς τὸν ἀγρὸν τοῦ κεραμέως. Perhaps the closest comparable wording is the last clause of Zech. 11.13, וָאַשְׁלִיךְ אֹתוֹ בֵּית יְהוָה אֶל־הַיּוֹצֵר, but if so Matthew has made considerable changes. The phrase בֵּית יְהוָה is omitted (although it is likely implied earlier in Mt. 27.5: ῥίψας τὰ ἀργύρια εἰς τὸν ναὸν); the singular אֹתוֹ becomes the plural αὐτὰ to agree with Matthew's earlier reference to ἀργύρια. The verb ἔδωκαν replaces אַשְׁלִיךְ, since Judas has already thrown the pieces of silver into the temple in Mt. 27.5, and the citation now focuses on the use of the money for the purchase of the potter's field. What is more, the potter's 'field' finds no conceptual antecedent in Zech. 11.12-13 or its context, where the silver is thrown to the 'potter'. Instead, the attribution of the citation to Jeremiah may call to mind one or more of several texts in Jeremiah that do mention a potter or a potter's field, namely, Jer. 18.1-2; 19.1-13, and 32.7-9.[121]

Apparently Matthew uses κεραμεύς to translate the MT's יוֹצֵר, 'potter'. However, the Syriac Peshitta and Aramaic Targum give evidence of another reading: 'treasury', presumably rendering the Hebrew אוֹצָר.[122] This reading,

---

121. Many note the presence of both Zech. 11.12-13 and Jer. 18.1-2 and/or 32.7-9 in Mt. 27.9-10, including Dittmar, *Vetus Testamentum in Novo*, pp. 66-67; Stendahl, *School of St Matthew*, p. 122; Strecker, *Der Weg der Gerechtigkeit*, p. 77; McConnell, *Law and Prophecy*, p. 132; Longenecker, *Biblical Exegesis*, p. 133; Archer and Chirichigno, *Old Testament Quotations in the New Testament*, p. 163. Others argue for an allusion to Jer. 19.1-13 instead of either Jer. 18.1-2 or 32.7-9, including Gundry, *Use of the Old Testament*, pp. 124-25, Martinus J.J. Menken, 'The References to Jeremiah in the Gospel according to Matthew (Mt. 2.17; 16.14; 27.9)', *ETL* 60 (1984), pp. 5-24 (10-11); *idem*, 'The Old Testament Quotation in Matthew 27,9-10: Textual Form and Context', *Bib* 83 (2002), pp. 305-28 (316-17); Knowles, *Jeremiah in Matthew's Gospel*, pp. 69-77; Miller, *Les Citations d'accomplissement*, pp. 266-71. Davies and Allison, *Matthew*, III, 569-70, 574-75, and Herbert Frankemölle, *Matthäus: Kommentar* (2 vols.; Düsseldorf: Patmos, 1994–97), II, p. 474, suggest that Matthew may refer to all three texts from Jeremiah, while K&D, X, pp. 375-77, apparently argues against any reference to Jeremiah in Mt. 27.9-10. Michael Quesnel, 'Les citations de Jérémie dans l'évangile selon saint Matthieu', *EstBib* 47 (1989), pp. 513-27 (523-24), proposes Lam. 4.1-2, 13 as an alternative text from 'Jeremiah' that may stand behind Mt. 27.9-10.

122. Similar to 'treasury' in the Syr. Peshitta is *Tg.* Zech. 11.12-13, which reads: 'And I said to them, "If it is good in your eyes *fulfil my will*; and if not, refrain". *And some people fulfilled my will.* And the Lord said to me, "*Write a record of their deeds on a writing tablet and* cast it into *the Sanctuary, into the care of an official*, because *my fear was precious in their eyes*". *So I wrote a record of their deeds on a writing tablet and* cast it into the *Sanctuary* of the Lord, into *the care of the chief official*'. The English text of the *Minor Prophets Targum* is taken from Kevin Cathcart and Robert P. Gordon, *The Targum of the Minor Prophets* (ArBib, 14; Wilmington, DE: Michael Glazier, 1989). According to Cathcart and Gordon, *Targum of the Minor Prophets*, p. 214, the text has drastically

'treasury', is followed by the RSV, NRSV, NAB, and NJPS. The word κορβανᾶς in Mt. 27.6 may suggest that Matthew is aware of both traditions: 'potter' in the MT and 'treasury' in the Peshitta/Targum.[123] Any decision about such an awareness is also complicated by the possibility that Matthew may have known about the existence of a temple foundry, in which case יוֹצֵר in the MT would have been sufficient to suggest a connection with the temple.[124] Against this view that Matthew knows both traditions (the MT and the Peshitta/Targum), however, stands Matthew's own narrative (Mt. 27.5-6), which appears to distinguish between where Judas throws the pieces of silver (εἰς τὸν ναόν) and where the chief priests could not lawfully put them (εἰς τὸν κορβανᾶν).[125]

The citation in Mt. 27.10 ends with the words καθὰ συνέταξέν μοι κύριος. The clause may be understood as construing the opening words of Zech. 11.13: וַיֹּאמֶר יְהוָה אֵלַי.[126] Both texts have in common the words 'Lord' (יְהוָה/κύριος) and 'to me' (אֵלַי/μοι). However, συντάσσω, meaning 'direct, instruct, order', is generally a stronger word than אָמַר, although אָמַר may also be translated 'command'.[127] The presence of the comparative conjunction καθά with συντάσσω may indicate that the citation does not follow

revised 'give me my wages' to 'fulfill my will', since the speaker in *Tg.* is Yahweh and Yahweh's due is obedience (cf. the use of שָׁמַר in Zech. 11.11, which can mean to keep covenant or observe commands). Consequently, the text interprets שְׁלֹשִׁים הַכֶּסֶף as a record of the deeds of the people who do the will of Yahweh and thereby obliterates the MT's reference to the thirty pieces of silver. Some degree of correspondence exists between this interpretation and those given in *b. Ḥull* 92a and *Gen. Rab.* 98.9 (on Gen. 49.11), discussed below, pp. 58-59.

The reading אוֹצָר in Zech. 11.13 does appear in Kennicott MS 530 (Benjamin Kennicott, *Vetus Testamentum Hebraicum, cum variis lectionibus* [Oxonii: E typographeo Clarendoniano, 1776–80], II, p. 299; and Johannis B. de Rossi, *Variae lectiones Veteris Testamenti* [Parma: Ex Regio typographeo, 1784–88; repr., Amsterdam: Philo, 1969], II, p. 216), but it probably does not merit consideration as a witness to a unique textual tradition, according to Dominique Barthélemy, *Critique textuelle de l'Ancien Testament* (OBO, 50; 3 vols.; Fribourg Suisse: Éditions Universitaires, 1982–92), III, p. 993.

123. Julius Wellhausen, *Das Evangelium Matthaei*, 2nd edn, in *Evangelienkommentare* (Berlin: Georg Reimer, 1904–1914; repr., Berlin: W. de Gruyter, 1987), p. 137; Charles C. Torrey, 'The Foundry of the Second Temple at Jerusalem', *JBL* 55 (1936), pp. 247-60 (253); F.F. Bruce, *New Testament Development of Old Testament Themes*, p. 110.

124. Cathcart and Gordon, *Targum of the Minor Prophets*, p. 215. For a discussion of Torrey's argument for understanding יוֹצֵר as a technical term for 'founder', see pp. 55-57.

125. Gundry, *Use of the Old Testament*, p. 123.

126. K&D, X, p. 374; Stendahl, *School of St Matthew*, p. 123; Moo, *Old Testament in the Passion Narratives*, p. 197; Donald Senior, 'The Fate of the Betrayer: A Redactional Study of Matt. XXVII, 3-10', *ETL* 48 (1972), p. 372-426 (390).

127. BDB, p. 56; e.g. 2 Chron. 14.4; 29.21, 27; Neh. 13.22; Est. 1.10, 17; 9.14; Ps. 106.34.

the wording of Zech. 11.13 but rather Exod. 9.12, according to the suggestion of some scholars.[128]

Zechariah 11.12-13

Zechariah 11.4-17, one of the more enigmatic passages in the Old Testament, is best understood as a symbolic prophetic action.[129] Probably to establish the prophet's credibility against rival leaders (most likely false prophets),[130] Yahweh instructs the prophet to act as shepherd for the 'flock doomed for slaughter', that is, the postexilic Judahites. After tending the sheep for some time, the shepherd decides to quit acting as a shepherd for the people, so he breaks his two staffs. This action possesses a certain 'retrospective character',[131] which explains the people's present situation in view of their past, as the staff named Favor pertains to the breaking of the Mosaic covenant, which is evidenced in Judah's exile, and the staff named Unity pertains to the continuing national division between Israel and Judah. Those watching, the sheep merchants,[132] desire to rid themselves of the shepherd, and apparently

---

128. Dittmar, *Vetus Testamentum in Novo*, pp. 66-67; Archer and Chirichigno, *Old Testament Quotations in the New Testament*, p. 161; yet, Gärtner, 'Habakkuk Commentary', p. 17, points to Zech. 11.11: כִּי דְבַר־יְהוָה הוּא ('that it was the word of the LORD').

129. Sweeney, *Twelve Prophets*, p. 681; Meyers and Meyers, *Zechariah 9–14*, p. 299, describe a symbolic prophetic action as conveying an abstract message signified by some physical activity. Other Old Testament examples of symbolic prophetic action include Isa. 20.1-6; Jer. 13.1-11; 19.1-13; 27.1–28.17; 32.6-15; Ezek. 4.1-17; 5.1-12; 12.1-25; 24.15-27. Similar is P.D. Hanson, *Dawn of Apocalyptic*, pp. 337-41, who labels the text as commissioning narrative, in which Yahweh instructs a prophet to take some particular action; nonetheless, not all actions in Zech. 11.4-17 are called forth by divine commission (e.g. the breaking of both staffs).

130. Meyers and Meyers, *Zechariah 9–14*, p. 297. Hanson, *Dawn of Apocalyptic*, p. 344, also relates the claims of such rival leaders to Ezekiel's vision in Ezek. 37.16-28. On the contrasts between Ezek. 37 and Zech. 11, see Ralph L. Smith, *Micah–Malachi* (WBC, 32; Waco, TX: Word Books, 1984), p. 271; Stuhlmueller, *Rebuilding with Hope*, pp. 138-39; and Katrina J.A. Larkin, *The Eschatology of Second Zechariah: A Study of the Formation of a Mantological Wisdom Anthology* (CBET, 6; Kampen: Kok Pharos, 1994), pp. 118-23.

131. Meyers and Meyers, *Zechariah 9–14*, p. 303.

132. The NIV translates the MT as 'afflicted of the flock' in Zech. 11.7, 11 (cf. כֵּן עֲנִיֵּי הַצֹּאן in 4QpIsa^c 21 II, 7, πτωχοί in Aquila, KJV, NASB, and NLT); however, the NRSV reads 'sheep merchants' (cf. RSV, JB), following the LXX (εἰς τὴν Χαναανῖτιν) and with that combining the two words in the MT (לָכֵן עֲנִיֵּי) into one (לִכְנַעֲנִיֵּי), meaning 'to the Canaanites' or 'to the traders'. For other examples of 'Canaan' meaning 'merchant' or 'trader', cf. כְּנַעַן in Ezek. 16.29; 17.4; Hos. 12.8 (12.7 MT); Zeph. 1.11 and כְּנַעֲנִי in Job 41.6 (40.30 MT); Prov. 31.24; and esp. Zech. 14.21. See Thomas J. Finley, 'The Sheep Merchants of Zechariah 11', *GTJ* 3 (1982), pp. 51-65, for a detailed defense of 'sheep merchants'.

they recognize the prophet's action in breaking the first staff as illustrating the will of Yahweh.

Between the breaking of the two staffs, the prophet asks for a wage for his service as shepherd over the flock in Zech. 11.12. The phrases 'if it seems right to you' and 'but if not' begin with the hypothetical particle אִם and call for the sheep merchants to offer a qualitative judgment of the shepherd's work.[133] Either action (giving a wage or keeping it) would signal the termination of the shepherd's work, though 'keeping the wage' would be more emphatic. Instead, they weigh out a 'severance' pay of thirty pieces of silver. The request and payment are ironic, in that the prophetic action of breaking the staff Favor is acknowledged as true and the true prophet requests a wage for his work as a prophet.[134] Moreover, the prophet is paid in spite of his negative message about the annulment of the covenant; that is, those who pay the shepherd 'confirm the terrible decree by participation in a symbolic acceptance of it'.[135]

In response to the shepherd's request for payment, the sheep merchants weigh out a wage of thirty pieces of silver. The word שָׁקַל means 'to weigh out' (generally silver) as a payment for purchase (Gen. 23.16; Isa. 46.6; Jer. 32.9-10) or for penalty (Exod. 22.17 [22.16 MT]; 1 Kgs 20.39). Evidently the practice of weighing out silver continued into the postexilic period, even though the Persians had already introduced the use of stamped coinage.[136] The word שָׂכָר means 'wages for work';[137] the corresponding verb form (שָׂכַר) is used once for payment of a priest-prophet in Judg. 18.4. The weighing of the wage is unmistakably seen as payment for the prophet with the accusative marker and the first singular suffix (אֶת־שְׂכָרִי).

The wage itself is denoted as שְׁלֹשִׁים כָּסֶף or 'thirty of silver'. In combination with the verb שָׁקַל, the amount is often translated, as in the NRSV, 'thirty shekels of silver'; otherwise, it is simply rendered 'thirty pieces of silver', as in the NIV. Both English translations undoubtedly name equal amounts of

---

133. The phrase אִם־טוֹב בְּעֵינֵיכֶם, a form of a familiar formula in the Old Testament, expresses someone's approval or disapproval (see Gen. 16.6; 20.15; Josh. 9.25; Judg. 10.15; 19.24; 1 Sam. 1.23; 11.10; 14.36, 40; 2 Sam. 15.26; 19.38; 24.22; 2 Kgs 10.5; Est. 8.5, 8; Jer. 26.14; 40.4); it may also relate to Yahweh's evaluation of an event or behavior (see Deut. 6.18; 12.28; 1 Sam. 3.18; 2 Sam. 10.12; 2 Kgs 20.3; 1 Chron. 19.13; 2 Chron. 14.2 [14.1 MT]; Mal. 2.17).

134. True prophets do not receive payment for their prophecies (cf. Amaziah's dismissal of the prophet Amos in Amos 7.12-13), while false prophets generally make favorable prophecies in order to receive payment (cf. 1 Kgs 22.1-28, where only Micaiah prophesies against Ahab, in contrast to four hundred prophets who predict success for the king).

135. Meyers and Meyers, *Zechariah 9–14*, p. 273.

136. Baldwin, *Haggai, Zechariah, Malachi*, p. 184.

137. *HALOT*, p. 1331; cf. Zech. 8.10 for the only other use of שָׂכָר in Zechariah.

silver, since the Hebrew שֶׁקֶל refers to the standard weight of silver or gold and thus identifies a specified monetary value.[138] However, what remains ambiguous about the wage is its value. Is the amount substantial or despicable? The biblical material may indicate that the amount is a sizable or an appropriate payment for the shepherd's wage.[139] In Exod. 21.32, thirty shekels of silver (כֶּסֶף שְׁלֹשִׁים שְׁקָלִים) is given as the value for restitution for the death of a slave,[140] and, in Neh. 5.15, forty shekels of silver is seen as a burdensome tax (presumably *per annum*) exacted by Persian governors during the exile.[141] In contrast, the extrabiblical origin of the phrase may suggest that 'thirty shekels of silver' is a trivial amount and, as such, an expression of ignomy. Erica Reiner suggests that when the Sumerian phrase 'thirty pieces of silver' reappears in Hebrew and other ancient Near Eastern languages, the phrase retains its literal meaning ('thirty') but loses its idiomatic meaning ('half' or 'fraction'). The transcriptional ambiguity has arisen since the cuneiform sign in the Sumerian numbering system that represents the number 'thirty' may also be read as 'half'. Thus, the ancient texts in which 'thirty shekels' appears, including Zech. 11.12-13, interpret the idiom correctly as a trifling amount, while rendering it in their own language 'with the incompatible literal equivalent "thirty shekels"'.[142]

A parenthetical statement in Zech. 11.13 also describes the wages paid to the shepherd: 'this lordly price at which I was valued by them'. The statement reflects the estimation of the shepherd's work by the sheep merchants in 11.12. The *qal* verb יָקַר generally means 'to be precious or highly valued';

138. According to *HALOT*, p. 1643, the word denotes a weight further specified by 'the nature of the substance weighed' or 'a prevailing standard of measurement'.

139. Commentators who see the amount as substantial or appropriate, include Baldwin, *Haggai, Zechariah, Malachi*, p. 184; Sweeney, *Twelve Prophets*, p. 681; and Meyers and Meyers, *Zechariah 9–14*, pp. 275-76.

140. The *Code of Hammurabi* 206-208 (*ANET*, p. 175) distinguishes the value of life according to a person's status; the fine for the accidental death of a member of the aristocracy is one-half mina of silver (about twenty-five shekels), whereas the fine for the accidental death of a common person is one-third mina of silver (about seventeen shekels).

141. In other instances a similar amount is paid: thirty shekels of silver is required for a female to make a special vow, and males are required to pay fifty shekels of silver (Lev. 27.4); fifty shekels of silver per homer of barley seed (i.e. perhaps about four acres) is required to dedicate any inherited landholding (Lev. 27.16); for fifty shekels of silver David purchased a threshing floor and oxen (2 Sam. 24.24); King Menahem of Israel exacts fifty shekels of silver from the rich to keep King Pul of Assyria from attacking (2 Kgs 15.20); seventeen shekels of silver are given for the purchase of a field by Hanamel (Jer. 32.9); and Hosea pays fifteen shekels of silver, plus barley and wine, for his wife's redemption (Hos. 3.2).

142. Erica Reiner, 'Thirty Pieces of Silver', *JAOS* 88 (1968), pp. 186-90 (189-90). K&D, X, p. 368; Petersen, *Zechariah 9–14*, p. 97, and Lipiński, 'Recherches sur le livre de Zacharie', pp. 53-55, also see the amount as paltry.

yet the word in this context appears to be used sarcastically in combination with the noun forms יְקָר and אֶדֶר.[143] Appearing elsewhere only in Mic. 2.8 (where it means 'robe'), אֶדֶר is generally understood to mean 'glory' or 'splendor', and the word has been variously translated: 'goodly' (KJV), 'handsome' (NIV, NAB), 'magnificent' (NASB), 'noble' (NJPS), 'princely' (NKJV, REB, NJB), and 'lordly' (RSV, NRSV). Even though the word is textually and exegetically disputed,[144] אֶדֶר also seems to possess an ironic sense here,[145] a sense supported by the merchant's regard for the shepherd ('they also detested me' in Zech. 11.8) and the shepherd's refusal to keep the silver.

After the merchants rudely reward the shepherd for his service, Yahweh instructs the shepherd to throw the silver. The *hiphil* verb שָׁלַךְ means 'to throw or cast'. The word often refers to divine judgments or to the rejection of divine authority, and it may also involve the idea of contempt.[146] In Deut.

---

143. William Yarchin, 'יקר', in *NIDOTTE*, II, pp. 522-25 (523); furthermore, Yarchin submits that in several texts the word 'refers to the value of human life, particularly when a human life…is in helpless jeopardy or in need of deliverance' (cf. 1 Sam. 26.21; 2 Kgs 1.13-14; Ps. 49.8 [49.9 MT]; 72.14; Isa. 43.4). Likewise, BDB, p. 429, offers the specific meaning and sense: 'be appraised, magnificence of the price at which I was appraised (and dismissed) from them'.

144. G.W. Ahlström, 'אֶדֶר', *VT* 17 (1967), pp. 1-7, argues that אֶדֶר refers to some kind of vessel into which something is thrown, by suggesting a possible relation to the Neo-Babylonian word *adaru*. The 'something thrown' is identified by יוֹצֵר, which Ahlström takes as an alternative form of the word יֵצֶר, meaning something made by a potter (for similar phrases, cf. Gen. 37.22; Josh. 10.27; 2 Sam. 18.17; Jer. 38.6, 9; Zech. 5.8).

145. Ernst Wilhelm Hengstenberg, *Christology of the Old Testament and a Commentary on the Messianic Predictions* (trans. Theod. Meyer and James Martin; 4 vols.; Edinburgh: T. & T. Clark, 2nd edn, 1856–58; repr., Grand Rapids: Kregel, 1956), IV, p. 40; K&D, X, p. 368; BDB, p. 12; Baldwin, *Haggai, Zechariah, Malachi*, p. 185; and McComiskey, *Zechariah*, III, p. 1200. To the contrary, Sweeney, *Twelve Prophets*, p. 681, sees the description in Zech. 11.13 as showing that the shepherd considers the 'thirty shekels of silver' a significant amount; Meyers and Meyers, *Zechariah 9–14*, p. 279, see it as more than adequate.

146. Robert B. Chisholm, 'שלך', in *NIDOTTE*, IV, pp. 127-28 (127). For divine judgment, see Josh. 10.11; Neh. 9.11; Pss. 51.11 (51.13 MT); 102.10 (102.11 MT); Amos 4.3; Jon. 2.3 (2.4 MT); for rejection of divine authority, see 1 Kgs 14.9; Neh. 9.26; Pss. 2.3; 50.17; Ezek. 23.35. K&D, X, p. 369, understands the phrase 'throw to the potter' as an expression of contempt; cf. שָׁלַךְ in Gen. 37.24; Exod. 32.19; Deut. 9.17; 2 Sam. 18.17; 1 Kgs 13.24; 2 Kgs 9.25-26; 23.12; 2 Chron. 30.14; 33.15; Pss. 60.8; 71.9; 102.10; Isa. 2.20; 34.3; Jer. 7.29; 14.16; 22.19; 26.33; 38.6; Ezek. 20.7; Nah. 3.6. On the contrary, Meyers and Meyers, *Zechariah 9–14*, p. 276, assert that the verb does not 'have a negative connotation or imply contempt'; they cite 2 Chron. 24.10, where the word describes the act of depositing money into a chest. If one accepts the textual emendation of אוֹצָר for יוֹצֵר, it could be argued that שָׁלַךְ in Zech. 11.13 means 'to make a deposit', as it is translated in the NJPS: 'Deposit it in the treasury'.

9.17, 21, Moses throws down the two tablets of the covenant and throws the dust of the destroyed calf into a stream; these actions of Moses symbolizes the Israelites' idolatry, that is, their breaking of the covenant, and the enactment of Yahweh's judgment upon them. So too in Zech. 11.10-13, the shepherd represents the annulment of Yahweh's covenant with the Judahites, through the symbolic actions of breaking the staff Favor and throwing the silver.

According to the MT, Yahweh instructs the shepherd to throw the silver to the potter (הַשְׁלִיכֵהוּ אֶל־הַיּוֹצֵר), and the shepherd obeys Yahweh by carrying out the symbolic action; he takes the thirty pieces of silver and throws them into the house of Yahweh to the potter. The interpretation of this action has focused on the appropriateness of the word יוֹצֵר ('potter'). Since the text clearly indicates a context in the temple (בֵּית יְהוָה),[147] the word 'potter' appears to be problematic, as a potter's presence in the temple is dubitable. Moreover, the Peshitta and Targum give evidence of another reading, 'treasury', presumably rendering the Hebrew אוֹצָר, and the RSV, NRSV, REB, NAB, and NJPS accept this emendation of the MT (אוֹצָר for יוֹצֵר).[148]

However, Charles Torrey considers 'treasury' as an ill-founded conjectural improvement of the MT's 'potter' and argues that יוֹצֵר should be understood as a technical term for 'founder', one who melts down precious metals given to the temple.[149] Indeed, יוֹצֵר can refer to one who forms a figure out of metal, as in Exod. 32.4; Isa. 44.9, 12; and Hab. 2.18. Torrey also sees the LXX's

---

147. The noun phrase בֵּית יְהוָה is an adverbial acc. of place; cf. Josh. 6.19.

148. For אוֹצָר, see 1 Kgs 7.51; 15.18; 2 Kgs 12.19; 14.14; 16.8; 18.15; 1 Chron. 9.26; 26.20, 22, 24, 26; 28.12; 2 Chron. 5.1; Neh. 10.39; Jer. 38.11; Mal. 3.10; cf. 1 Macc. 14.46-49 for a similar precedent of depositing a record in the temple. Baldwin, *Haggai, Zechariah, Malachi*, p. 185, observes that 'the Temple treasury stored not only the tithes and precious things dedicated to the Lord (Josh. 6.24; Ezra 2.69; Neh. 7.70), but also served as a "bank" for the private individual (2 Macc. 3.10ff)'.

149. Torrey, 'Foundry of the Second Temple', pp. 256-57; Otto Eissfeldt, 'Eine Einschmelzstelle am Tempel zu Jerusalem', in *idem, Kleine Schriften* (ed. Rudolf Sellheim and Fritz Maass; Tübingen: J.C.B. Mohr [Paul Siebeck], 1962–79), pp. 107-109. Torrey assumes that a foundry was used in the Second Temple to melt down gifts of gold and silver to be stored in earthenware jars, according to the Persian practice described in Herodotus (*Hist.* 3.96), where Darius Hystaspis melts metal and stores it in earthen jars: 'This was Darius' revenue from Asia and a few parts of Libya. But as time went on he drew tribute also from the islands and the dwellers in Europe, as far as Thessaly. The tribute is stored by the king in this fashion: he melts it down and pours it into earthen vessels: when the vessel is full he breaks the earthenware away, and when he needs money coins as much as will serve his purpose.' *HALOT*, p. 429, follows Torrey's argument and lists 'caster (who melts down metal vessels and tools into ingots)' as one of the meanings for יוֹצֵר; so too W.H. Schmidt, 'יצר', in *TLOT*, II, p. 566. The NJB, which reads 'Throw it to the smelter', apparently also follows this alternative proposal. Cf. 2 Kgs 12.10-13.

χωνευτήριον ('furnace') as an expression of the same tradition, although rendered freely.[150] The suggestion is doubtful, according to Gundry, since the LXX's 'furnace' depends on 'an interpretation in which the money is tested to determine whether it is genuine' and neither 'treasury' nor 'founder' suit the context of Zechariah 11 and its symbolic action, in which a despicable sum is repudiated rather than presented as an offering.[151]

While the phrase 'in the house of the LORD' does make certain that the shepherd's action takes place in the temple, it does not necessarily follow that the phrase reinforces the emendation of the text from אוֹצָר for יוֹצֵר. Therefore, the assumption that the text originally spoke of silver thrown into the temple treasury (אוֹצָר), even though the present form of the MT reads the potter (יוֹצֵר), should be challenged. In view of the principle *lectio difficilior lectio potior*, it would furthermore be appropriate to consider why, if the text originally read אוֹצָר, it has now come to read יוֹצֵר, either accidentally or deliberately—a question that does not have a satisfactory answer.[152]

If one accepts the MT's 'potter', its sense may thus be understood: the silver is thrown to the potter, who is in the temple. The potter's presence in

---

150. Torrey, 'Foundry of the Second Temple', p. 255. However, had the LXX meant a person, it could have used χωνευτής, meaning 'caster' or 'founder'; cf. *Tg.* Zech. 11.13: 'cast it into the *Sanctuary* of the Lord, into *the care of the chief official*'. Magne Sæbø, *Sacharja 9–14: Untersuchungen von Text und Form* (WMANT, 34; Neukirchen–Vluyn: Neukirchener Verlag, 1969), suggests that the reading יוֹצֵר in the MT is a *Kompromißform*, a combination of אוֹצָר ('treasury') and perhaps יֹצֵק or צוֹרֵף ('smelter'); the first of these variants appears in the Peshitta, while the second is similar to the LXX reading.

151. Gundry, *Use of the Old Testament*, p. 123; furthermore, the conjecture by Torrey, 'Foundry of the Second Temple', p. 258, that the *Tg.* has abandoned the MT in this verse as a reaction to its use as a Christian proof-text cannot be corroborated. Matthais Delcor, 'Deux passages difficiles: Zacharie 12.11 et 11.13', *VT* 3 (1953), pp. 67-77 (73-77), does not think that Torrey adequately explains the irony of the noble price; however, Delcor links the verse with Judg. 17.4, where an 'idol of cast metal' was made from two hundred shekels of silver. By comparison thirty pieces would make only a small figurine. According to Delcor, this provides the irony for the monetary detail; furthermore, it suggests that Yahweh calls for Israel/Judah, who does not choose to have Yahweh's shepherd rule over them, to make a little god from the silver pieces. Thus, the text expresses the people's unfaithfulness through the image of idolatry (cf. Ezek. 16.17; Hos. 2.8).

152. M.P. Weitzman, *The Syriac Version of the Old Testament: An Introduction* (UCOP, 56; Cambridge: Cambridge University Press, 1999), p. 54, cautions against assuming that the Peshitta's Hebrew source or *Vorlage* differed from the majority MT; he remarks, 'As the meaning "treasury" could readily have been inferred from the context, we cannot safely infer that P's *Vorlage* actually had הָאוֹצָר rather than the majority reading of MT'. Similarly, Baldwin, *Haggai, Zechariah, Malachi*, p. 185, calls the reading 'treasury' in the Syriac 'the result of a scribe's ingenuity, accommodating the reading to what he took to be the sense', or, as illustrated in Delcor, 'Deux passages difficiles', p. 74, 'En outre, אוֹצָר paraît bien être une leçon facilitante'.

the temple is likely explained by the need for new earthen vessels used in the sacrificial ritual (e.g. Lev. 6.28). If, according to *b. Yoma* 21a and *b. Zebah* 96a, the broken sherds used in the sacrificial ritual were disposed of within the temple courtyard, the refuse heap inferred from Zech. 11.13 may have been within the temple itself. Thereby, the prophet-shepherd goes to the house of Yahweh so that his actions may be done in public and in the presence of Yahweh.[153] The shepherd's action of throwing the silver to the potter represents the sheep merchants' rejection of Yahweh (and perhaps Yahweh's rejection of them),[154] since the potter is seen as a place of rejection (not acceptance, as would be demanded by the reading 'treasury').[155]

153. K&D, X, p. 370, points out that 'the house of Jehovah came into consideration here rather as the place where the people appeared in the presence of their God, either to receive or to solicit the blessings of the covenant from Him. What took place in the temple, was done before the face of God, that God might call His people to account for it.'

154. Yahweh's rejection of the sheep merchants is suggested in the general context of Zech. 11.4-17 (e.g. in the breaking of the two staffs) and in the ambiguous referent of the first pers. verb יָקַרְתִּי ('I was valued'). The question is, does 'I' refer to the shepherd-prophet or to Yahweh? Or, said another way, is the phrase 'this lordly price at which I was valued by them' spoken by the shepherd-prophet or by Yahweh? Clearly the verbs וָאֶקְחָה ('I took') and וָאַשְׁלִיךְ ('I threw') name actions executed by the shepherd-prophet, but the possibility remains that the words spoken by Yahweh include the command to throw the silver to the potter and the parenthetical statement about the lordly price. If so, paying a wage to the shepherd may be seen as the sheep merchants' appraising Yahweh. Cf. Yahweh's rejection of the shepherds in Jer. 23.1-8 and Ezek. 34.1-31.

155. According to Eugene H. Merrill, *Haggai, Zechariah, Malachi: An Exegetical Commentary* (Chicago: Moody, 1994), pp. 298-99, 'The potters' shops were usually located near refuse pits where the sherds and other unusable or broken materials could be cast (Jer. 18.2; 19.1-2). The place of the potter, then, was not only a place of creation and beauty but one of rejection and ruin. It became a metaphor for a scrap heap.' Commenting on the Potsherd Gate in Jer. 19.2, James L. Kelso, *The Ceramic Vocabulary of the Old Testament* (BASORSup, 5-6; New Haven, CT: American Schools of Oriental Research, 1948), p. 9, writes: 'There was always considerable wastage from a kiln, and it was this discarded pottery from which the gate of potsherds derived its name'.

The ptc. יוֹצֵר naturally refers to one who forms vessels out of clay (2 Sam. 17.18; 1 Chron. 4.23; Ps. 2.9; Isa. 29.16; 30.14; 41.25; Jer. 18.2, 3, 4, 6; 19.1, 11; Lam. 4.2), but its verb form often describes the creative activity of Yahweh (Gen. 2.7, 8; Pss. 33.15; 94.9; Isa. 27.11; 43.1, 21; 44.2, 24; 45.9, 11, 18; 49.5; 64.7; Jer. 10.16; 51.19; Amos 7.1; Zech. 12.1). Sweeney, *Twelve Prophets*, p. 681, accounts for the reading 'potter' in Zech. 11.13 according to this latter sense: because יָצַר may refer to Yahweh's acts of creation, 'the MT therefore indicates that YHWH instructs the prophet to throw the money to "the creator", i.e., to YHWH in the Temple'. If the emendation 'treasury' were accepted, then its sense might be this: the shepherd donates the money in the temple as a way of redeeming his life, and thereby setting him free from further obligation to the sheep merchants. Cf. Lev. 27.1-33.

Zechariah 11.12-13 in Jewish and Christian Interpretation
Dead Sea Scrolls. The evidence for the use of Zech. 11.12-13 in the Dead
Sea Scrolls and Old Testament Pseudepigrapha is entirely nonexistent. The
biblical scrolls found in the Judean Desert contain only fragments of Zech.
11.1-2 in 4QXIIᵍ (= 4Q82) 104, 3-4. In CD B XIX, 9, the *Damascus Document* shares the phrase 'the poor of the flock' (עניי הצאן) with Zech. 11.11,
but the text (CD B XIX, 5-11) and the phrase are best considered with
Mt. 26.31 and its use of Zech. 13.7. After commenting on Isa. 29.17, 4QpIsᶜ
(= 4Q163) 21.7-8 possibly also contains a portion of Zech. 11.11: '[It was
annulled on that day, and] thus the most helpless of the flock which [was
watching me knew] [that it was in fact the word of the Lord]'. However, the
phrase depends on a tentative restoration based on the MT.[156]

Old Testament Pseudepigrapha. Unfortunately the following observation by
France about the use of Zechariah 11 in the Old Testament Pseudepigrapha is
correct: 'There is no obvious use of Zechariah 10–13 at all anywhere in this
literature. The shepherd figure, the thirty pieces of silver, and the mourning
over the one pierced are all absent'.[157] In *T. Gad* 2.3-4, written near the end
of the second century BCE, a reference to 'thirty pieces of gold' as the price
for which Joseph was sold to the Ishmaelites has no apparent relation to
Zechariah 11:

> Because of his dreams my hatred toward him increased and I wanted to gobble
> him up from among the living as an ox gobbles up grass from the ground. For
> this reason Judah and I sold him to the Ishmaelites for thirty pieces of gold; we
> hid the pieces and showed only the twenty to our brothers. Thus it was through
> greed that our plot to kill him was carried out. But the God of my fathers
> rescued him from my hands so that I might not perform a lawless deed in Israel.

Rabbinic Literature. Zechariah 11.12-13 is evidently not clearly cited in the
Mishnah or other rabbinic writings from the Tannaic period (50 BCE to 200
CE), although it appears in the rabbinic writings of the Amoraic period (220–
500 CE). Specifically, two texts, one from the Babylonian Talmud and another
from *Midrash Rabbah*, consider two conflicting interpretations of the thirty
pieces of silver in Zech. 11.12-13.[158] Both interpretations are recorded in *b.
Ḥull.* 92a:

---

156. Maurya P. Horgan, 'Isaiah Pesher 3 (4Q163 = 4QpIsac)', in James H. Charlesworth (ed.), *The Dead Sea Scrolls: Hebrew, Aramaic, and Greek Texts with English
Translations*. VIB. *Pesharim, Other Commentaries, and Related Documents* (PTSDSSP;
Louisville, KY: Westminster/John Knox Press, 2002), pp. 47-82 (66 n. 80), notes that the
restoration 'does not seem to fill the space'.

157. France, *Jesus and the Old Testament*, pp. 183-84.

158. While the Babylonian Talmud may have been written earlier than *Midrash
Rabbah*, the two texts probably record traditions from the same time period. The passage

These are the forty-five righteous men on account of whom the world continues to exist. But I know not whether thirty of them are here [in Babylon] and fifteen in the land of Israel, or thirty in the land of Israel and fifteen here [in Babylon]; but when the verse says, *And I took the thirty pieces of silver and cast them into the treasury, in the house of the Lord*, I know that thirty [righteous men] are in the land of Israel and fifteen here. Said Abaye, Most of them are to be found in the synagogue under the side chamber. *And I said to them, If ye think good, give me my hire; and if not, forbear. So they weighed out for my hire thirty pieces of silver.* Said Rab Judah, These are the thirty righteous men among the nations of the world by whose virtue the nations of the world continue to exist. Ulla said, These are the thirty commandments which the sons of Noah took upon themselves but they observe three of them, namely, (i) they do not draw up a *kethubah* document for males, (ii) they do not weigh flesh of the dead in the market, and (iii) they respect the Torah.

Genesis Rabbah 98.9 (on Gen. 49.11) also mentions both interpretations:

R. Hanin said: Israel will not require the teaching of the royal Messiah in the future, for it says, *Unto him shall* the nations *seek* (Isa. IX, 10), but not Israel. If so, for what purpose will the royal Messiah come, and what will he do? He will come to assemble the exiles of Israel and to give them [the Gentiles] thirty precepts, as it says, *And I said unto them: If ye think good, give me my hire; and if not, forbear. So they weighed for my hire thirty pieces of silver* (Zech. XI, 12). Rab said: This alludes to thirty mighty men. R. Hohanan said: It alludes to thirty precepts.

Thus, the rabbinic literature includes two interpretations of the thirty pieces of silver in Zech. 11.12-13. The monetary amount refers either to thirty commandments or thirty righteous men; that is, Israel will receive its teaching directly from God, and the Gentiles will obey thirty commandments given them by the Messiah when he comes, or thirty righteous men who respect the worship of Yahweh must always exist in the world.[159] This second interpretation regarding the thirty righteous men among the nations shows some degree of correspondence with *Tg.* Zech. 11.12-13 ('And the Lord said to me, "*Write a record of their deeds on a writing tablet and* cast it into *the Sanctuary*"'), but dependence by either *b. Ḥull* 92a or *Gen. Rab.* 98.9 on *Tg.* Zech. 11.12-13 cannot be substantiated.[160]

---

from *Ḥullin*, which means 'non-holy things' and concerns animals slaughtered for food, is Amoraic, because R. Judah and R. Ulla are both Amoraic second generation (250–90 CE). The passage from *Genesis Rabbah* may also be Amoraic, since Rab is Amoraic first generation (220–50 CE), R. Hohanan is Amoraic second generation (250–320 CE), and R. Hanin dates from a later Amoraic generation.

159. France, *Jesus and the Old Testament*, pp. 189-90; the thirty-men tradition goes back at least to R. Simeon ben Johai (Tannaic third generation 140–65 CE): 'The world possesses not less than thirty men as righteous as Abraham' (*Gen. Rab.* 35.2 [Gen. 11.12]).

160. Cathcart and Gordon, *Targum of the Minor Prophets*, p. 214.

Early Church Fathers. Zechariah 11.12-13 is apparently ignored by the Early Church Fathers of the second century CE except for Irenaeus, *Epid.* 81.7:[161]

> And again Jeremiah the prophet says: And they took the thirty pieces of silver, the price of him that was sold, whom they bought from the children of Israel; and they gave them for the potter's field, as the Lord commanded me. For Judas, being one of Christ's disciples, agreed with the Jews and covenanted with them, when he saw they desired to kill Him, because he had been reproved by Him: and he took the thirty staters of the province, and betrayed Christ unto them: and then, repenting of what he had done, he gave the silver back again to the rulers of the Jews, and hanged himself. But they, thinking it not right to cast it into their treasury, because it was the price of blood, bought with it the ground that was a certain potter's for the burial of strangers.

The text used by Irenaeus is quite similar to Mt. 27.9-10, and Irenaeus even attributes the citation to Jeremiah.[162] In the explanatory description that follows the citation, Irenaeus refers to the monetary amount as 'thirty *staters*', an alteration (στατῆρας for ἀργύρια) also appearing in several manuscripts at Mt. 26.15 (D a b q r¹ Eusᵖᵗ); a stater is a silver coin equal to four days' wages (cf. Mt. 17.27).

Zechariah 11.12-13 in the New Testament

The New Testament cites Zech. 11.12-13 only in Mt. 27.9-10, and elsewhere in the New Testament a tradition of Judas's death is recorded only in Acts 1.18-20, a passage which cites Psalms (presumably 69.25 and 109.8) for the Old Testament scriptures fulfilled in Judas's act.[163]

Matthew 27.9-10. The citation of Zech. 11.13 is introduced with Matthew's characteristic formula. However, the use and wording of the formula in Mt. 27.9, τότε ἐπληρώθη τὸ ῥηθὲν διὰ Ἰερεμίου τοῦ προφήτου λέγοντος, differs slightly from the formula found in Mt. 21.4, τοῦτο δὲ γέγονεν ἵνα πληρωθῇ τὸ ῥηθὲν διὰ τοῦ προφήτου λέγοντος. In Mt. 21.4, the formula appears in the middle of the narrative and probably points forward to the

---

161. France, *Jesus and the Old Testament*, p. 212.

162. Tertullian (c. 160–c. 225 CE) in *Marc.* 4.40, a section showing the passion of Jesus as fulfillment of Old Testament prophecy, also attributes the citation to Jeremiah: 'The very amount and the destination of the money, which on Judas' remorse was recalled *from its first purpose of a fee*, and appropriated to the purchase of a potter's field, as narrated in the Gospel of Matthew, were clearly foretold by Jeremiah: "And they took the thirty pieces of silver, the price of Him who was valued, and gave them for the potter's field"'.

163. On the two traditions of Judas's death, see Pierre Benoit, 'The Death of Judas', in *Jesus and the Gospel* (trans. Benet Weatherhead; 2 vols.; New York: Herder & Herder, 1973–74), I, pp. 189-207, who finds a greater degree of historical accuracy in Matthew's account.

actions that follow. The formula in Mt. 27.9 occurs at the end of the narrative and points to something that Matthew has already recorded, as is typical for these introductory formulas. The wording of the formula in Mt. 27.9 begins with τότε ἐπληρώθη τὸ ῥηθὲν, while in Mt. 21.4 it begins τοῦτο δὲ γέγονεν ἵνα πληρωθῇ τὸ ῥηθὲν. The wording in Mt. 27.9 corresponds precisely to the wording of the introductory formula used with the other formula quotation from Jeremiah in Mt. 2.17: τότε ἐπληρώθη τὸ ῥηθὲν διὰ ᾽Ιερεμίου τοῦ προφήτου λέγοντος. These two formula quotations from Jeremiah (Mt. 2.17; 27.9) differ significantly from the other eight formula quotations, in that they begin with the adverb τότε rather than the final conjunctions ἵνα or ὅπως (Mt. 1.22; 2.15, 23; 4.14; 8.17; 12.17; 13.35; 21.4). This substitution allows Matthew to avoid ascribing the fulfilling event (specifically, the slaughter of innocent babies by Herod and the purchase of a field with the money received from Judas's betrayal of Jesus) to a divine plan: it allows Matthew 'to indicate that the evil in question originates not so much in God's design as in human action'.[164]

Indubitably the most conspicuous issue relating to the introductory formula in Mt. 27.9 is the attribution of the citation to Jeremiah, since what Matthew quotes, except for the reference to a potter's field, comes not from Jeremiah but Zech. 11.12-13. Various solutions have been proposed, of which the best-known belongs to Jerome (c. 340–420 CE):

> This prophecy does not come from Jeremiah but from a similar passage in Zechariah, who is almost the last of the twelve prophets. Although the meaning does not differ much, Zechariah's word order and vocabulary do conflict with Matthew's quotation. In a copy of the Hebrew Scriptures given to me by a member of the Nazarene sect, I recently read an apocryphal edition of the book of Jeremiah in which this quotation from Matthew appeared word for word. Nevertheless it still seems more likely to me that Matthew took this prophecy from Zechariah, since it was the ordinary practice of the Evangelists and apostles to communicate only the meaning of texts from the Old Testament while neglecting to observe their word order.[165]

164. Menken, 'References to Jeremiah', p. 9; so too Rothfuchs, *Erfüllungszitate*, pp. 38-39; Senior, 'Fate of the Betrayer', pp. 393-95; and Gundry, *Matthew*, p. 557. Τότε occurs 90 of 160x in Matthew and, according to Stephanie L. Black, *Sentence Conjunction in the Gospel of Matthew: καί, δέ, τότε, γάρ, οὖν and Asyndeton in Narrative Discourse* (JSNTSup, 216; SNTG, 9; Sheffield: Sheffield Academic Press, 2002), p. 253, functions generally as 'a signal of "marked continuity" in Matthew's narrative framework'. In view of Matthew's typical usage in fulfillment texts, διὰ ᾽Ιερεμίου τοῦ προφήτου expresses intermediate agency with a pass. verb (cf. διά in Mt. 2.5, 15, 17, 23; 3.3; 4.14; 8.17; 12.17; 13.35; 21.4; 24.15; 27.9); divine agency is expressed with ὑπό (cf. Mt. 2.15; 22.31).

165. Jerome, *Comm. Matt.* 4.27.10 in CCSL 77.264-65; the English translation comes from Manlio Simonetti (ed.), *Matthew 14–28* (ACCS; Downers Grove, IL: Intervarsity Press, 2002), Ib, p. 275.

Indeed, Knowles lists nine proposed explanations for the attribution of the citation to Jeremiah: transcriptional error,[166] mental error, an apocryphal book of Jeremiah, a testimony source ascribed to Jeremiah, a general reference to the latter prophets by naming Jeremiah as the first book, a confused identification of Zechariah (ben Jehoida) and Jeremiah, a thematic reference to the prophetic tradition of Jeremiah, a topographical reference linking Jeremiah with the Hinnom Valley near the Potsherd Gate, or the canonical book of Jeremiah as part of a mixed citation.[167] Most of these, if not all but the last one, are improbable solutions, as demonstrated by Knowles. More likely, Matthew names Jeremiah rather than Zechariah according to the Jewish literary practice of citing the name of the more notable prophet when combining elements from more than one text.[168] Besides, the naming of Jeremiah over Zechariah draws attention to allusions to Jeremiah found in Mt. 27.3-10 (especially in the mention of a potter's field, which is not in Zech. 11.12-13) and to Matthew's interest in Jeremiah as an example of innocent suffering and as the prophet of rejection.[169]

If Matthew does intend for the reader to recognize an allusion to Jeremiah, what specific text or texts stand behind the citation? Usually one or more of three texts from Jeremiah are suggested: Jer. 18.1-2; 19.1-13; and 32.6-9. In Jer. 18.1-12, Yahweh instructs Jeremiah to go to the potter's house. While there, Jeremiah observes the reworking of a spoiled vessel into another one, and he receives an interpretation of the symbolic action: like clay in the

166. A few witnesses try to correct the reading διὰ ʼΙερεμίου in Mt. 27.9 either by substituting διὰ Ζαχαρίου (22 sy[hmg]) or διὰʼ Ησαΐου (21 1), since Isaiah is the prophet most often cited by Matthew, or by omitting the name altogether (Φ 33 a b sh[s.p] bo[ms]). In each case, however, these variant readings are correctly judged as inferior attempts to clarify the prophetic reference.

167. Knowles, *Jeremiah in Matthew's Gospel*, pp. 60-67.

168. Archer and Chirichigno, *Old Testament Quotations in the New Testament*, p. 163; cf. Mk 1.2, which is attributed to Isaiah, even though the citation consists mainly of Mal. 3.1 rather than Isa. 40.3. See Joseph A. Fitzmyer, '"4Q Testimonia" and the New Testament', in *idem*, *Essays on the Semitic Background of the New Testament* (London: Geoffrey Chapman, 1971), pp. 59-89, on composite citations in ancient Jewish literature.

169. In the words of Keener, *Matthew*, p. 657, 'by appealing to "Jeremiah" rather than to Zechariah, however, Matthew makes clear that he intends his biblically literate audience to link an analogous passage in Jeremiah...and to interpret them together'. So also Gärtner, 'Habakkuk Commentary', pp. 16-17; Lindars *New Testament Apologetic*, p. 120; Gundry, *Matthew*, pp. 556-57; Brown, *Death of the Messiah*, p. 651; and Carson, 'Matthew', p. 562.

States Marcus, in 'Old Testament and the Death of Jesus', p. 228: 'It seems more likely, however, given Matthew's special interest in Jeremiah (cf. 2.17-18; 16.14), that he is deliberately invoking the image of the Old Testament prophet, whose life was one of suffering witness to the word of God and rejection by religious authorities'. So also Senior, 'Fate of the Betrayer', pp. 397-98; Menken, 'References to Jeremiah', p. 11; and Knowles, *Jeremiah in Matthew's Gospel*, pp. 77-81.

potter's hand, Yahweh is about to shape evil against Judah unless the people repent from their evil ways. In Jer. 19.1-13, Yahweh instructs Jeremiah to buy a potter's flask and take some of the elders and senior priests to the valley of Ben-Hinnom and there to announce Yahweh's harsh judgment upon Jerusalem because of the people's infidelity and idolatry (specifically, the people have forsaken Yahweh by worshiping idols and perhaps sacrificing their own children to the god Baal). Yahweh further directs Jeremiah to announce the people's horrible fate: the valley of Ben-Hinnom will be called valley of Slaughter, Yahweh will void the plans of Judah and Jerusalem, and the people will be defeated by their enemies and will resort to cannibalism. Then Yahweh instructs Jeremiah to break the flask as a sign that Yahweh will break Jerusalem as one breaks a potter's vessel and that the city will become a mass grave, a place defiled like Topheth[170] where Molech is worshiped by human sacrifice, a place in which Yahweh no longer abides. In Jer. 32.6-15, Yahweh tells Jeremiah that his cousin Hanamel is going to ask him to purchase a field at Anathoth. When Hanamel comes to Jeremiah during the siege of Jerusalem, Jeremiah buys the field according to his right of redemption (allowing for the family inheritance to stay intact). The purchase is done as a proper public transaction (including the weighing out of 17 shekels of silver and the signing of the deeds of purchase) in the presence of witnesses. As the land and its worth are jeopardized by the presence of the Babylonian military (Jer. 32.1-5), Jeremiah's purchase illustrates his confidence in the future restoration of Judah's economy.

Which of these three texts, then, stands behind Matthew's reference to Jeremiah? More often Jer. 18.1-2 is linked with Jer. 32.6-9, since 18.1-2 does not mention a field and 32.6-9 does not mention a potter. Still, the two passages seem largely unrelated, and their specific meanings (especially Jer. 32.6-15 with its symbolic illustration of a future restoration of Judah's economy) do not correspond well with Mt. 27.3-10.[171] Jeremiah 19.1-13, however, offers the closest verbal and thematic connections with the context of Mt. 27.3-10. Both Jer. 19.1-13 and Mt. 27.3-10 include the involvement of the chief priests and elders, the association of a potter with a piece of land, locations used for burial places with names connoting bloodshed ('valley of Slaughter' and 'Field of Blood'), and judgment against the shedding of innocent blood. The importance of this last item should not go unnoticed, since the expression 'innocent blood', which is of some frequency in the Old Testament and especially in Jeremiah, appears in the New Testament only in

---

170. See also Jer. 7.32-33; 2 Kgs 23.10.

171. Gundry, *Use of the Old Testament*, p. 124; Senior, 'Fate of the Betrayer', pp. 387-88; Douglas J. Moo, 'Tradition and Old Testament in Matt. 27.3-10', in R.T. France and David Wenham (eds.), *Gospel Perspectives*. III. *Studies in Midrash and Historiography* (Sheffield: JSOT Press, 1983), pp. 157-79 (159).

Mt. 27.4.[172] By alluding to Jer. 19.1-13, Matthew discerns a parallel between Judah/Jerusalem and Judas: they are guilty of shedding/betraying innocent blood;[173] moreover, with the allusion, Matthew presents the fate of Judas as an anticipation of the fate of the Jewish leaders, who are responsible for the death of Jesus.

The citation itself begins with reference to the thirty pieces of silver: καὶ ἔλαβον τὰ τριάκοντα ἀργύρια (cf. Mt. 26.15; 27.3). The statement in Mt. 27.9 is similar to a clause near the end of Zech. 11.13 (and the mention of thirty pieces of silver in Zech. 11.12), but it differs in that the verb is third person plural (ἔλαβον) to accommodate the purchase of the potter's field by the chief priests, after the return of the silver by Judas (Mt. 27.3-7). The description of the monetary amount continues with the phrase: τὴν τιμὴν τοῦ τετιμημένου ὃν ἐτιμήσαντο ἀπὸ υἱῶν Ἰσραήλ. The word τιμή stands for 'the amount at which something is valued'[174] and is used in Matthew only in Mt. 27.6, 9. The noun is modified by its corresponding verb form, τετιμημένου, a perfect passive participle, perhaps referring to the amount for which Judas agreed to betray Jesus to the chief priests in Mt. 26.14-15.[175] The masculine singular pronoun ὃν differs from the first person singular verb 'I was valued' (יָקַרְתִּי) in Zech. 11.13, where the prophet is priced; in Mt. 27.9 it thus distinguishes the one priced from Judas and may intimate that the one priced is Jesus. Matthew identifies those who do the pricing as ἀπὸ υἱῶν Ἰσραήλ; the prepositional phrase functions as an idiom for (some of) 'the people of Israel as an ethnic entity'.[176]

---

172. Jer. 19.4 reads דָּם נְקִים in the MT and αἱμάτων ἀθῴων in the LXX, and Mt. 27.4 reads αἷμα ἀθῷον. Cf. 2 Kgs 21.16; 24.4; Ps. 106.38 (105.38 LXX); Jer. 2.34; 7.6; 22.3, 17; 26.15 (33.5 LXX). Occasionally, the LXX translates the Hebrew phrase as αἷμα ἀναίτιον in Deut. 19.10, 13; 21.8-9 or as αἷμα δίκαιον in Prov. 6.17; Joel 4.19 (3.19 NRSV). Cf. also the words spoken by Pilate in Mt. 27.24: ἀθῷός εἰμι ἀπὸ τοῦ αἵματος τούτου; and those attributed to Joseph in *Prot. Jas.* 14.1: 'I fear lest that which is in her may have sprung from the angels and I should be found delivering up innocent blood [παραδιδοὺς αἷμα ἀθῷον] to the judgment of death'. Concerning this passage, Massaux, *Influence of the Gospel of St Matthew*, II, p. 229, writes: 'In the Protevangelium of James, these words are read in a totally different context; yet their actual identity with the words in Mt., which are without parallel in the New Testament, suggest a literary reminiscence of the Matthean text'. On 'innocent blood' in Matthew, see Ham, 'Last Supper', pp. 67-68.

173. Gundry, *Use of the Old Testament*, p. 125; Carson, 'Matthew', p. 562; according to Keener, *Matthew*, p. 657, if Mt. 27.3-10 refers to Jer. 19.1-13, then Matthew uses it to evoke 'a prophecy of the impending destruction of Jerusalem'.

174. BDAG, p. 1005.

175. L&N, I, p. 576 define τιμάω in this context as 'to set a price on, estimate, value' —'to determine an amount to be used in paying for something'.

176. L&N, I, p. 131; cf. τῇ θυγατρὶ Σιών in Mt. 21.5. The phrase ἀπὸ υἱῶν Ἰσραήλ should probably be read as a partitive gen., τινές ἀπὸ υἱῶν Ἰσραήλ. The phrase υἱῶν Ἰσραήλ occurs only 14x in the New Testament (Mt. 27.9; Lk. 1.16; Acts 5.21; 7.23, 37; 9.15; 10.36; Rom. 9.27; 2 Cor. 3.7, 13; Heb. 11.22; Rev. 2.14; 7.4; 21.12).

Since Judas has already thrown the pieces of silver into the temple, the citation in Mt. 27.10 now focuses on the use of the money for the purchase of the potter's field. A few witnesses (א B²ᵛⁱᵈ W *pc* sy Eus) have the first singular verb ἔδωκα ('I gave'); the singular form resembles the MT's אֶקַּח ('I took'), but it coincides with the first singular pronoun (μοι) later in the verse and may be influenced by the account of Judas's death in Acts 1.16-18, where it seems that Judas acquired the field himself. The better reading, then, is the third plural ἔδωκαν ('they gave'). As narrated in Mt. 27.7, the chief priests use the silver to buy 'the potter's field' (τὸν ἀγρὸν τοῦ κεραμέως) as a burial place for foreigners. In Mt. 27.10 their intent is more distinctly noted with the preposition εἰς, which serves as a marker of a goal 'with the vocation, use, or end indicated'.¹⁷⁷

The chief priests purchase the field with the silver, since they cannot lawfully receive blood money into the temple treasury (οὐκ ἔξεστιν βαλεῖν αὐτὰ εἰς τὸν κορβανᾶν, ἐπεὶ τιμὴ αἵματός ἐστιν). Presumably a similar location in the temple¹⁷⁸ is described by Josephus, *J.W.* 2.175: 'On a later occasion he [Pilate] provoked a fresh uproar by expending upon the construction of an aqueduct the sacred treasure known as *Corbonas*' (Μετὰ δὲ ταῦτα ταραχὴν ἑτέραν ἐκίνει τὸν ἱερὸν θησαυρόν, καλεῖται δὲ κορβωνᾶς, εἰς καταγωγὴν ὑδάτων ἐξαναλίσκων). Matthew's use of κορβωνᾶς may suggest an awareness of both interpretations of Zech. 11.13: the MT's יוֹצֵר ('potter') and the emendation אוֹצָר ('treasury'), supported by the Peshitta and Targum and followed by the RSV, NRSV, NAB, and NJPS.¹⁷⁹ However, the LXX stands against such a possibility, in that it uses θησαυρός, but never κορβωνᾶς, to translate אוֹצָר.¹⁸⁰ Also, against the notion are Matthew's citation, which uses potter (κεραμεύς / יוֹצֵר) as the textual link for the allusion to Jeremiah,¹⁸¹ and Matthew's narrative, which says that the chief priests are not

---

177. BDAG, p. 290.

178. Cf. 'the treasury of the temple', a location specified in Mk 12.41, 43; Lk. 21.1; and Jn 8.20 with the word γαζοφυλάκιον, which probably refers to the place in the temple where people (both men and women, according to Mk 12.41-43) placed their offerings.

179. Among those who understand Matthew to know of both readings are Stendahl, *School of St Matthew*, p. 124; Lindars, *New Testament Apologetic*, p. 118; Marcus, 'Old Testament and the Death of Jesus', p. 228; Meyers and Meyers, *Zechariah 9–14*, p. 278.

180. For example, Deut. 28.12; 32.34; Josh. 6.19, 24; 3 Kgdms 7.51; 14.26; 15.18; 4 Kgdms 12.19; 14.14; 16.8; 18.15; 20.13, 15; 24.13; 1 Chron. 9.26; 26.20, 22, 24, 26; 27.25, 27, 28; 2 Chron. 5.1; 8.15; 12.9; 16.2; 25.24; 32.27; 26.18; 2 Esd. 2.69; Neh. 7.70, 71; 12.44; 13.12; Job 38.22; Pss. 32.7 (33.7 MT); 134.7 (135.7 MT); Prov. 8.21; 10.2; 15.16; 21.20; Isa. 2.7; 39.2, 4; 45.3; Jer. 10.13; 15.13; 20.5; 27.25, 37 (50.27, 37 MT); 28.13, 16 (51.13, 16 MT); Ezek. 27.24; Mic. 6.10; Joel 1.17.

181. Sjef van Tilborg, 'Matthew 27.3-10: An Intertextual Reading', in Sipke Draisma (ed.), *Intertextuality in Biblical Writings: Essays in Honour of Bas van Iersel* (Kampen: Kok, 1989), pp. 159-74 (163).

authorized to put the money into the treasury.[182] On the contrary, Judas throws the money into the temple (ῥίψας τὰ ἀργύρια εἰς τὸν ναὸν). This action implicates the temple in Jesus' death as the consummation of a history of bloodshed by Israel's religious leaders and thereby disqualifies the temple.[183] So, too, the chief priests implicate themselves in Jesus' death, when they determine to purchase a field with the money received for the betrayal of innocent blood. In purchasing the potter's field, they fulfill the citation from Zechariah attributed to Jeremiah, since Matthew sees Jeremiah as 'the prophet of the rejection of the Messiah'.[184]

Nevertheless, the purchase of the potter's field takes place according to the purpose of God, that is, καθὰ συνέταξέν μοι κύριος. The clause may recall the opening words of Zech. 11.13, וַיֹּאמֶר יְהוָה אֵלַי, or the presence of the comparative conjunction καθά with συντάσσω may indicate that the citation follows the LXX wording of a Pentateuchal formula found, among other places, in Exod. 9.12. If the clause does correspond to this wording (καθὰ συνέταξεν κύριος), then one wonders why Matthew would call attention to the sixth plague (Exod. 9.8-12).[185] More likely, Matthew has modified the phrase from Zech. 11.13 to indicate that the betrayal of Jesus and the judgment upon those responsible for Jesus' death happen according to the divine purpose. This modification uses the word συντάσσω, which appears only three times in the New Testament (Mt. 21.6; 26.19; 27.10). In the other two instances, the word refers to the command of Jesus: to secure a donkey and to prepare for Passover. Perhaps also here συντάσσω refers to the implicit directive for Judas to execute his betrayal of Jesus (Mt. 26.20-25), a directive made explicit only in the Johannine tradition (Jn 13.27).

Summary

The citation of Zech. 11.12-13 in Mt. 27.9-10 has been substantially modified, making it difficult to determine the text upon which Matthew depends. Furthermore, it is difficult to say that Matthew has followed the MT over the LXX; the citation, however, does not agree with the LXX against the MT at any point.[186] While some of Matthew's wording is similar to Zech. 11.13,

---

182. So Gundry, *Use of the Old Testament*, pp. 122-23, argues against the 'double fulfillment' of both readings in Mt. 27.3-10.

183. Swartley, *Israel's Scripture Traditions*, p. 178; cf. Mt. 23.29-36.

184. Menken, 'Jeremiah in Matthew', p. 10.

185. Gundry, *Matthew*, p. 558, offers a doubtful explanation: 'Probably the mention of a furnace in Zech. 11.13 LXX reminded Matthew of the ashes of the furnace in the account of the sixth Egyptian plague (Exod. 9.1-12)'.

186. Senior, 'Fate of the Betrayer', p. 382, asserts, 'Close alignment with either the LXX or the MT is questionable'. Davies and Allison, *Matthew*, III, p. 574, describe the citation as a 'loose rendering of MT Zech. 11.13 with LXX influence'. However, such LXX influence is minimal, since Gundry, *Use of the Old Testament*, p. 149, lists only Mt. 2.6,

Matthew has altered other portions to accommodate the citation to its narrative context (e.g. 'I took' to 'they took'). At another place Matthew makes other modifications to clarify the identity of the person priced (Jesus as the shepherd) and those who did the pricing (the people of Israel as the sheep merchants). Most notably, Matthew alters the citation so that the silver is not thrown to the potter but is given for the purchase of the potter's field. Along with the attribution of the citation to Jeremiah, the addition of the potter's 'field' may suggest that Matthew has in mind one or more of the following texts from Jeremiah, namely, 18.1-2; 19.1-13; and 32.7-9. Matthew may know both the reading from the MT ('potter') and the reading reflected in the Peshitta/Targum ('treasury'), but he distinguishes between where Judas throws the pieces of silver ('into the temple') and where the chief priests could not lawfully put them ('into the treasury'). The citation ends with a phrase that may reflect the opening words of Zech. 11.13 or a Pentateuchal formula found, among other places, in Exod. 9.12.[187]

Zechariah 11.4-17 is best understood as a symbolic prophetic action, in which the prophet follows the instruction of Yahweh to act as a shepherd for the 'flock doomed for slaughter'. In Zech. 11.12-13, the prophet requests a wage for his service as shepherd. In return, the sheep merchants weigh out a wage of thirty pieces of silver, not an insignificant amount in literal terms in other Old Testament contexts, but in this context an amount that signifies a trivial and thereby insulting amount. The wage is ironically described as 'this lordly price'. Following Yahweh's instructions, the prophet throws the silver to the potter, as a sign of contempt for the wage and rejection by Yahweh of those who offered it. This repudiation of the despicable sum of silver supports the MT's reading of יוֹצֵר ('potter') over the proposed emendation of אוֹצָר ('treasury'), based on the Peshitta and Targum. Even though the proposed meaning of 'founder' (that is, an official who melts down precious metals given to the temple) is attractive, this suggestion remains doubtful, since it depends too heavily on the inferior reading χωνευτήριον ('furnace')

15, 18, 23; 5.31; 9.13; 12.7; 27.9-10 among the formal citations unique to Matthew that are non-Septuagintal. Of the 21 words in Matthew's citation, only four words are also found in the LXX, according to John C. Hawkins, *Horae Synopticae: Contributions to the Study of the Synoptic Problem* (Oxford: Clarendon Press, 2nd edn, 1901; repr., Grand Rapids: Baker Book House, 1968), p. 154, who also indicates that of the formula quotations Mt. 27.9-10 shows the most divergence from the LXX. The sum of the multiple deviations from the MT and LXX in Mt. 27.9-10 has caused Gärtner, 'Habakkuk Commentary', p. 19, to conclude: 'The quotation must be considered as a sort of exposition, an allusion rather than a direct citation'.

187. The idiomatic expression καθὰ συνέταξεν κύριος appears in many places in the LXX, including Exod. 36.8 (39.1 MT), 12 (39.5 MT), 14 (39.7 MT), 28 (39.21 MT), 33 (39.26 MT); 37.20 (38.22 MT); 39.10 (39.32 MT); 40.19; Num. 8.3, 22; 9.5; 15.23; 20.9, 27; 27.11; 31.31, 41; the expression generally relates to some command given to Moses.

in the LXX, it does not adequately explain the irony of the noble price, and it does not suit the context of symbolic actions of Zech. 11.4-14.

The evidence for the use of Zech. 11.12-13 in the Dead Sea Scrolls and Old Testament Pseudepigrapha is entirely nonexistent. The biblical scrolls contain only parts of Zech. 11.1-2 in 4QXIIᵍ (= 4Q82) 104, 3-4. Two texts among the Dead Sea Scrolls (CD B 19.9 and 4QpIsᶜ [= 4Q163] 21, 7-8) contain the phrase 'the poor of the flock' from Zech. 11.11, but the phrase more likely relates to Mt. 26.31 and its use of Zech. 13.7. Two rabbinic writings of the Amoraic period (220–500 CE) consider conflicting interpretations of the thirty pieces of silver in Zech. 11.12-13 (*b. Ḥull.* 92a and *Gen. Rab.* 98.9 [on Gen. 49.11]). The monetary amount of thirty pieces of silver either refers to thirty commandments given to the Gentiles by the Messiah or to thirty righteous men who must always exist in the world. The second of these interpretations is similar to the written records of deeds in *Tg.* Zech. 11.12-13, although an alleged dependence cannot be corroborated.

Among the Early Church Fathers of the second century CE, Zech. 11.12-13 is apparently ignored except for Irenaeus, *Epid.* 81.7. The text used by Irenaeus is quite similar to Mt. 27.9-10, and Irenaeus even attributes the citation to Jeremiah. In the explanation that follows the citation, Irenaeus refers to the monetary amount as 'thirty *staters*' (στατῆρας for ἀργύρια), an alteration also appearing in several manuscripts at Mt. 26.15.

In the New Testament, only Mt. 27.9-10 cites Zech. 11.13. The citation is introduced with Matthew's characteristic formula, but the formula's wording corresponds with the wording of the only other formula quotation from Jeremiah. Both Mt. 2.17 and 27.9 begin with the adverb τότε rather than ἵνα or ὅπως to avoid ascribing the fulfilling event in question to a divine plan, as both 'envisage mortal opposition to the messiah on the part of those who, according to the Evangelist, should have received him'.[188] While the citation is primarily from Zech. 11.13, Matthew has attributed it to Jeremiah to cite the more notable prophet, to draw attention to allusions to Jeremiah in the passage, and to explain the death of Jesus with reference to Jeremiah as the prophet of rejection. Of the three texts from Jeremiah that may stand behind such allusions, Jer. 19.1-13 seems most likely, because it shares with Mt. 27.3-10, among other elements, the judgment against those guilty of shedding/betraying 'innocent blood'. The citation itself focuses on the thirty pieces of silver and their use for the purchase of the potter's field by the chief priests or, as denoted in the citation itself, (some) ἀπὸ υἱῶν ᾽Ισραήλ. In so doing, the chief priests implicate themselves in Jesus' death, even though this occurs according to the divine purpose, that is, according to the LORD's command.

---

188. Knowles, *Jeremiah in Matthew's Gospel*, p. 77.

Matthew alters the wording of Zech. 11.12-13 and expands the citation with the allusion to Jer. 19.1-13, but Matthew applies the citation to a situation with literal similarities to the one envisioned by Zechariah (that is, Israel's religious leaders have cheaply valued and repudiated their divinely chosen leader in the presence of the LORD). In contrast to the allegorical interpretations of the thirty pieces of silver (as referring to thirty messianic precepts or thirty righteous men) evidenced in the rabbinic literature, Matthew shows a respect for the original intention of Zechariah but also reworks the text according to his own 'original'[189] interpretive purpose. The citation in Mt. 27.9-10 underscores 'one of Matthew's more prominent emphases, the guilt of Judas (27.3-10) and the Jewish leaders (27.3-10, 19, 24-25)'.[190] Moreover, Matthew's creative combination of the words of Zechariah and the allusion to Jeremiah attest that even the betrayal of Jesus by Judas and the rejection of Jesus by Israel's religious leaders take place according to the divine purpose.[191]

Matthew 26.31

Both Matthew and Mark make explicit[192] the prophetic fulfillment of the desertion of the disciples by referring to Zech. 13.7. The Matthean citation is found in Mt. 26.31:

> Τότε λέγει αὐτοῖς ὁ Ἰησοῦς· πάντες ὑμεῖς σκανδαλισθήσεσθε ἐν ἐμοὶ ἐν τῇ νυκτὶ ταύτῃ, γέγραπται γάρ· πατάξω τὸν ποιμένα, καὶ διασκορπισθήσονται τὰ πρόβατα τῆς ποίμνης.

> Then Jesus said to them, 'You will all become deserters because of me this night; for it is written, "I will strike the shepherd, and the sheep of the flock will be scattered"'.

The text of Zech. 13.7 in the MT is as follows:

> חֶרֶב עוּרִי עַל־רֹעִי וְעַל־גֶּבֶר עֲמִיתִי נְאֻם יְהוָה צְבָאוֹת
> הַךְ אֶת־הָרֹעֶה וּתְפוּצֶיןָ הַצֹּאן וַהֲשִׁבֹתִי יָדִי עַל־הַצֹּעֲרִים׃

> 'Awake, O sword, against my shepherd, against the man who is my associate', says the LORD of hosts. Strike the shepherd, that the sheep may be scattered; I will turn my hand against the little ones.

189.	France, *Jesus and the Old Testament*, p. 207.

190.	Swartley, *Israel's Scripture Traditions*, p. 216.

191.	Brown, *Death of the Messiah*, p. 652.

192.	The citation is not introduced with the characteristic Matthean formula but with γέγραπται, an introductory formula found in Mt. 2.5; 4.4, 6, 7, 10; 11.10; 21.13; 26.24; 26.31. The reference to Zech. 13.7 in Mk 14.27 is discussed below, p. 80.

A comparison of the citation in Mt. 26.31 with Zech. 13.7 in the MT reveals that the citation is closer to the MT than to the standard LXX text.[193] Actually, the Matthean citation shows only two minor modifications from the MT, neither of which can readily be attributed to the influence of the LXX, namely, the opening verb form and the final noun phrase. The citation begins with the first singular future indicative πατάξω ('I will strike') for the MT's second singular *hiphil* imperative הַךְ ('Strike'); the Targum and Peshitta also have imperatives. The LXX, using the same word as Matthew, has the second plural imperative πατάξατε. This recasting of the imperative with the future indicative in Mt. 26.31 may be required grammatically, since the abbreviated citation does not mention the sword of Yahweh and is likely derived from the final clause in Zech. 13.7, וַהֲשִׁבֹתִי יָדִי עַל־הַצֹּעֲרִים ('I will turn my hand against the little ones'); this change indicates that the judgment against the shepherd and the scattering of the flock are ultimately initiated by Yahweh.[194] In addition to the plural verb πατάξατε, the LXX differs from the MT and Matthew in its rendering of the verb's object; the LXX has a plural object, τοὺς ποιμένας ('the shepherds'), while the MT (אֶת־הָרֹעֶה) and Matthew (τὸν ποιμένα) both have a singular object ('the shepherd').[195]

193.   Matthew includes only a portion of Zech. 13.7, omitting the opening and closing statements: 'Awake, O sword, against my shepherd, against the man who is my associate', says the LORD of hosts' (חֶרֶב עוּרִי עַל־רֹעִי וְעַל־גֶּבֶר עֲמִיתִי נְאֻם יְהוָה צְבָאוֹת) and 'I will turn my hand against the little ones' (וַהֲשִׁבֹתִי יָדִי עַל־הַצֹּעֲרִים).

194.   Gundry, *Use of the Old Testament*, p. 27; France, *Jesus and the Old Testament*, pp. 107-108; Moo, *Old Testament in the Passion Narratives*, p. 184; Archer and Chirichigno, *Old Testament Quotations in the New Testament*, pp. 163-65; and Davies and Allison, *Matthew*, III, p. 484.

195.   Some MSS for the LXX have both a sg. verb and object (e.g. A, Q, Sᶜ, and Lucian), and Cod. Alexandrinus adds the words τῆς ποίμνης, resulting in a reading with strong affinities to Matthew's citation: πάταξον τὸν ποιμένα, καὶ διασκορπισθήσονται τὰ πρόβατα τῆς ποίμνης. Alexander Sperber, 'New Testament and Septuagint', *JBL* 59 (1940), pp. 193-293 (281), suggests an interdependence between these LXX readings and the text of Matthew; however, Stendahl, *School of St Matthew*, p. 81, doubts that these other readings for the LXX were corrected from Matthew, since the variations (minus τῆς ποίμνης in Alexandrinus) clearly render the sg. forms of the MT better.

Tg. Zech. 13.7 reads: 'slay the *king* and the *princes* shall be scattered'. The text substitutes 'king' for 'shepherd', a frequent metaphor for 'ruler' or 'king' in ancient literature, according to Paul A. Porter, *Metaphors and Monsters: A Literary-Critical Study of Daniel 7 and 8* (ConBOT, 20; Lund: C.W.K. Gleerup, 1983; repr., Toronto: Paul A. Porter, 1985), pp. 61-120. The transposition occurs elsewhere in *Tg. Zech.* 10.2-3; 11.3. Likewise, the substitution of 'prince' for the MT 'flock' in *Tg. Zech.* 13.7 follows the substitution earlier in the verse of 'prince' for the MT 'man', which Cathcart and Gordon, *Targum of the Minor Prophets*, p. 222, attribute to 'the influence of the shepherd = king equivalence immediately preceding' ('O sword, *be revealed* against *the king* and against the *prince his* companion *who is his equal, who is like him*'). See also *Tg. Zech.* 10.2: 'For *the worshippers of idols* speak *deceit in their deceitful prophesying*; they afford *no*

In the second clause of the citation, the future passive verb διασκορπισ-θήσονται[196] ('they will be scattered') renders well the MT's *qal* imperfect וּתְפוּצֶין ('and they may be scattered'). In the LXX, διασκορπίζω is regularly used to translate פּוּץ;[197] however, the LXX reads ἐκσπάσατε (meaning to 'draw out' or 'remove'), a word which is not translated for פּוּץ in any other text in the LXX.[198] The nominative noun τὰ πρόβατα ('sheep'), found in Matthew and the LXX, translates the MT's הַצֹּאן; both the MT and Matthew make 'sheep' the subject of the verb, but Matthew adds the genitive phrase τῆς ποίμνης ('of the flock'), perhaps to emphasize such a scattering of Jesus' followers that one flock no longer exists.[199]

Zechariah 13.7

The poem in Zech. 13.7-9 resumes the shepherd motif from Zech. 9.16; 10.2-3; and 11.3-17.[200] Furthermore, the similarities between Zech. 13.7-9 and 11.3-17 have suggested to some that 13.7-9 should be transposed to follow 11.17; this would allow for 13.7-9 to complete the description of the worthless shepherd in 11.15-17 (that is, the worthless shepherd is finally smitten).[201] However, several factors favor the canonical position of 13.7-9: the different poetic meter, genre, and use of the shepherd motif in 11.4-17 and 13.7-9, the different imagery associated with the sword in 11.17 and 13.7, and the proleptic connection of 13.7-9 with 14.1-21.[202] In its canonical context,

---

comfort *at all*; therefore they have *been scattered* like *the scattering of* a flock, *they went into exile* because there is no *king*', where the scattering of the flock is identified with the exile.

196. The variant reading διασκορπισθήσεται ($\mathfrak{P}$[37.45] D K W G D Q *f*[1] 565 579 1424) evidently attempts to correct the grammatical construction so that the neut. pl. collective has a sg. verb. For examples of the *constructio ad sensum*, see Wallace, *Greek Grammar Beyond the Basics*, pp. 399-400.

197. For example Num. 10.35; Deut. 30.3; 2 Esd. 11.8 (Neh. 1.8 MT); Job 37.11; Ps. 67.2 (68.2 MT); Jer. 9.15; 10.21; 23.1, 2; Ezek. 11.16; 12.15; 20.34, 41; 22.15; 28.25; 29.13; 46.18.

198. The LXX witnesses, A, S[c], Q, and Lucian, correct the reading from ἐκσπάσατε (B S* V W) to various forms of διασκορπίζω. Cf. ἐκσπάω in Zech. 3.2, 'Is this man a brand plucked from the fire?', and in Amos 3.12, where it means to 'rescue'.

199. Brown, *Death of the Messiah*, p. 130.

200. Forms of רעה appear in Zech. 10.2, 3; 11.3, 4, 5, 7, 8, 9, 15, 16, 17; 13.7.

201. Hanson, *Dawn of Apocalyptic*, pp. 338-39, sees 13.7-9 as a poetic fragment, originally connected with 11.4-17 and later relocated to a place preceding 14.1, and the NEB, in agreement with such a transposition, has printed 13.7-9 following 11.17.

202. Stephen L. Cook, 'The Metamorphosis of a Shepherd: The Tradition History of Zechariah 11.17 + 13.7-9', *CBQ* 55 (1993), pp. 453-66 (455-56); Petersen, *Zechariah 9–14*, p. 124; and Meyers and Meyers, *Zechariah 9–14*, p. 384; others who argue for the canonical position of Zech. 13.7-9 include Paul Lamarche, *Zacharie IX–XIV: Structure littéraire et messianisme* (Ebib; Paris: J. Gabalda, 1961), pp. 108-109; Sæbø, *Sacharja 9–14*, pp. 276-77; and R.L. Smith, *Micah–Malachi*, p. 218.

Zech. 13.7-9 refers to a good shepherd whose probable death leaves the flock leaderless to undergo 'severe testing and loss, which result in deeper assurance of their identity as the Lord's people'.[203]

Zechariah 13.7 begins with Yahweh summoning the sword against the shepherd.[204] 'Sword' (חֶרֶב), which occurs in the initial position for emphasis, is used elsewhere as a metaphor for physical harm (Zech. 11.17), death (Amos 9.4), or judgment via war (Jer. 14.12-18; 21.7, 9; 24.10; Ezek. 14.17, 21). While the image of Yahweh's sword does reflect judgment upon the disobedient and the enemies of Israel in other texts, here the poetical summons envisages the sword as an instrument of divine judgment against 'my shepherd'.[205]

This designation 'my shepherd' (רֹעִי) indicates no ordinary leader and may evoke Isa. 44.28, where the Persian monarch Cyrus is called 'my shepherd', or less likely Ps. 23.1, where Yahweh is addressed with the same appellation. However, the one so identified here is best distinguished from the worthless shepherd of Zech. 11.15-17, since Yahweh calls him 'the man who is my associate'.[206] In addition, the striking of the shepherd results in the scattering of the sheep, a concept missing from Zech. 11.4-17 but prominent in two other texts with similarities to Zech. 13.7-9, namely, Jer. 23.1-6 and Ezek. 34.1-31. Both Jer. 23.5 and Ezek. 34.23-24 present the shepherd placed over the sheep by Yahweh in monarchical and messianic terms, suggesting that here a royal ruler is also indicated by 'shepherd' (as in earlier texts, such as 1 Kgs 22.17, which use 'shepherd' as a figure for 'king').[207]

---

203. Baldwin, *Haggai, Zechariah, Malachi*, p. 197. Sæbø, *Sacharja 9–14*, p. 279, describes an implicit narrative within the poem as a sequence of judgment, purification, and restitution.

204. The *qal* of עוּר ('awake') is often found in apostrophe or addressed to Yahweh; see Pss. 7.6 (7.7 MT); 44.24 (44.23 MT); 57.8 (57.9 MT); 59.5 (59.4 MT); 108.2 (108.3 MT); Isa. 51.9; 52.1; Zech. 2.13 (2.17 MT). The word is also found in Zech. 4.1; 9.13.

205. Other texts also include an address to or description of the sword of Yahweh (Deut. 32.41; Isa. 31.8; 34.6; 43.6; 66.16; Jer. 12.12; 47.6; Ezek. 21.16.); cf. the song of the sword in Ezek. 21.8-17, 28-32, which describes the destruction of the people and the leaders of Israel. According to Meyers and Meyers, *Zechariah 9–14*, p. 385, the preposition עַל ('against') 'has a negative sense when used with verbs indicating some sort of attack'; the preposition occurs 3x in Zech. 13.7.

206. The word עֲמִית occurs elsewhere only in Lev. 5.21; 18.20; 19.11, 15, 17; 24.19; 25.14, 15; 27.17 (cf. 1QS VI, 26), where it generally refers to a person's neighbors, fellow citizens, or own people. In Zech. 13.7, then, it may, according to Sweeney, *Twelve Prophets*, p. 696, draw upon the idea that Yahweh's chosen leader is also designated as Yahweh's son (e.g. 2 Sam. 7.14; Pss. 2.7; 89.26-27). What is more, Geza Vermes, *Scripture and Tradition in Judaism: Haggadic Studies* (StPB, 4; Leiden: E.J. Brill, 2nd edn, 1983), pp. 58-60, argues that גֶּבֶר ('man') may function symbolically as a messianic title in some texts (e.g. LXX Num. 24.17; 2 Sam. 23.1; Zech. 13.7; *T. Jud.* 24.1; *T. Naph.* 4.5).

207. Meyers and Meyers, *Zechariah 9–14*, p. 386, see 'my shepherd' as representing 'the Davidic line, whose rule comes to a violent end in the sixth century'. Cf. *Tg. Zech.*

Following the prophetic announcement formula ('says the LORD of hosts'),[208] Yahweh enjoins the sword to strike the shepherd, probably calling for the shepherd's execution.[209] The wording may draw upon Jer. 21.7, where a similar idiom depicts the violent death of King Zedekiah and the people of Jerusalem: Nebuchadnezzar 'shall strike them down with the edge of the sword'. Because Yahweh commands the sword, the shepherd's violent end may also parallel the experience of the Suffering Servant, who is struck down by God in Isa. 53.4 and crushed according to the will of Yahweh in Isa. 53.10.[210] However, the innocence of the shepherd (compared to the Servant) remains less certain, since the preceding context (Zech. 13.1-6) indicts both the royal and prophetic leadership in postexilic Judah.

While the imperatives, 'awake' and 'strike', are directed against the shepherd, Zech. 13.7 now draws attention to the result of his death: the sheep are scattered.[211] 'Sheep' (צֹאן) here is a metaphor for the people, and 'scattered' (פּוּץ), a metaphor for their dispersion.[212] This scattering of the sheep elicits

---

13.7: 'O sword, *be revealed* against *the king* and against the *prince his* companion *who is his equal, who is like him,* says the Lord of hosts; slay the *king* and the *princes* shall be scattered and I will bring back *a mighty stroke* upon the *underlings*'. Here the Targum clearly identifies the shepherd as the king and accordingly substitutes 'prince' for 'man'. K&D, X, p. 397 takes 'shepherd' as a reference to the Messiah, and McComiskey, *Zechariah*, p. 1223, identifies the shepherd with the pierced one of Zech. 12.10, whose piercing and death, like the Suffering Servant of Isa. 53, lead to redemption.

208.   This formula נְאֻם יְהוָה צְבָאוֹת appears in Zech. 3.9, 10; 5.4; 8.11; 13.2, 7 (cf. 1.3, 16; 8.6 with the verb אָמַר), and it accords well with the postexilic conceptualization of the restoration of the temple and the return of the divine presence to it, according to Tryggve N.D. Mettinger, *The Dethronement of Sabaoth: Studies in the Shem and Kabod Theologies* (trans. Frederick H. Cryer; ConBOT, 18; Uppsala: C.W.K. Gleerup, 1982), pp. 80-115.

209.   The word נָכָה can refer to a non-fatal blow (Exod. 21.18; Neh. 13.25; Isa. 10.24; 58.4; Jer. 37.15; Hos. 6.1; Zech. 13.6) or to a fatal blow (Gen. 37.21; Exod. 21.12; Josh. 10.26; 2 Sam. 1.15; Ps. 78.51; Isa. 37.36; Jer. 40.15; cf. esp. Deut. 20.13; Josh. 11.11-12, 14; Jer. 21.7, which also use the word in relation to 'sword'), and often Yahweh is its subject (Gen. 8.21; Exod. 3.20; 12.12; Deut. 28.22, 27-28; 2 Sam. 6.7; 2 Kgs 6.18; Isa. 5.25; 53.4; Jer. 21.6; Ezek. 7.9; Zech. 9.4; 12.4). GKC §144a lists Zech. 13.7 among those texts where 'masculine forms are used in referring to feminines', that is, 'strike' is masc., but 'sword' is fem.

210.   Lamarche, *Zacharie IX–XIV*, pp. 137-38, adds three other possible connections with Deutero-Isaiah, Isa. 51.9; 52.1; 53.6; however, he concludes (p. 138): 'Les rapprochements entre Zach 13,7-9 et le Deutéro-Isaïe sont donc possibles, mais loin d'être certains'.

211.   The clause הַךְ אֶת־הָרֹעֶה וּתְפוּצֶיןָ הַצֹּאן conforms to the criteria in *IBHS*, p. 577 for a juss. following an impv., that is, an impf. following an impv. has a juss. force and expresses result. It is thus correctly translated 'Strike the shepherd *that* the sheep may be scattered'. In that the pl. verb has a sg. subject, וּתְפוּצֶיןָ הַצֹּאן is a *constructio ad sensum*.

212.   According to *HALOT*, p. 993, the metaphor of sheep for people may appear in contexts denoting either divine protection (Pss. 74.1; 79.13; 95.7; Jer. 23.1-3; Ezek. 34.31;

the recurring biblical phrase: 'like sheep without a shepherd';[213] furthermore, it reflects the ovine imagery found in Jer. 10.21; 23.1-2, and Ezek. 34.5-6, 12. Its significance in this text focuses on the judgment of Yahweh against the shepherd and the people, for Yahweh does not merely act to bring about the death of the shepherd but to scatter the flock.[214] Such judgment is also indicated in the concluding expression in Zech. 13.7: 'I will turn my hand against the little ones'.[215] However, the little ones survive and are subsequently refined into the people of Yahweh (Zech. 13.8-9).

Zechariah 13.7 in Jewish and Christian Interpretation
Dead Sea Scrolls. The evidence for the use of Zech. 13.7 in the Dead Sea Scrolls is minimal; however, the *Damascus Document* (CD B XIX, 7-9) clearly quotes Zech. 13.7:[216]

> When there comes the word which is written by the hand of Zechariah: Wake up, sword, against my shepherd, against the male who is my companion—oracle of God—wound the shepherd and scatter the flock and I shall return my hand upon the little ones. Those who are faithful to him are the poor ones of the flock.

Mic. 7.14) or divine judgment (Ps. 44.11, 22; Zech. 11.4). The word פוץ is frequently used for the dispersal of a people away from their homeland (Gen. 10.18; 11.4, 8, 9; Isa. 24.1; 18.17; 40.15; Ezek. 29.12, 13; 30.23, 26) and especially the dispersal of Israel among the nations (Deut. 4.27; 28.64; 30.3; Neh. 1.8; Isa. 11.12; Jer. 9.16; 13.24; 30.11; Ezek. 11.16, 17; 12.15; 20.23, 34, 41; 22.15; 28.25; 36.19; Zech. 3.10).

213. Num. 27.17; 1 Kgs 22.17; 2 Chron. 18.16; Ezek. 34.5; Zech. 10.2; cf. Mt. 9.36.

214. Petersen, *Zechariah 9–14*, pp. 130-31; K&D, X, p. 397.

215. Although some take the expression as an image of protection (e.g. K&D, X, p. 398), the negative connotations of the verse's verbs (awake, strike, and turn) and the use of the construction elsewhere (e.g. Ps. 81.14; Isa. 1.25; Amos 1.8) confirm such a reference to Yahweh's judgment, according to Meyers and Meyers, *Zechariah 9–14*, p. 388. The term 'the little ones' (הַצֹּעֲרִים) appears twice in the expanded expression 'the little ones of the flock' in Jer. 49.20 and 50.45, and it may refer to the same group labeled as 'the flock doomed to slaughter' in Zech. 11.4, 7.

216. The biblical scrolls found in the Judean Desert contain no fragments from Zech. 13.1-9; the frgs. closest to Zech. 13 are from Zech. 12.7-12 in 4QXIIe (= 4Q80) 18, 1-8 and from Zech. 14.18 in 4QXIIa (= 4Q82) 1, 1-2. The Hebrew text of the citation in CD B XIX, 7-9 differs only in the prophetic announcement formula; CD B XIX, 8 has נאם אל ('oracle of God'), while Zech. 13.7 has נְאֻם יְהוָה צְבָאוֹת ('says the LORD of hosts'). The Cairo *Damascus Document* (CD) is unique among the Dead Sea Scrolls, since its two main MSS were found in a Cairo synagogue, not a Qumran cave. These medieval copies were first published by Solomon Schechter, *Fragments of a Zadokite Work* (DJS, 1; Cambridge: Cambridge University Press, 1910); additionally, ten MSS or frgs. have since been discovered at Qumran (4Q266–73, 5Q12, 6Q15). The work divides into two parts: admonitions (reviewing Israelite history to encourage faithfulness) and laws (elaborating on biblical laws and community organization). Generally it is accepted that the work was written about 100 BCE and that the work was foundationally important to the Qumran community, even though it differs at times from the regulations found in 1QS.

Only MS B contains the citation from Zech. 13.7, while in a parallel place MS A contains a citation of Isa. 7.17, and the relationship between the two MSS is unclear.[217] Since MS B omits a considerable section from MS A (VII, 10b-21a) before the citation, its interpretation in the present context remains difficult. Generally, the citation functions as a warning against those who reject the precepts and ordinances of God and a promise to those who are faithful: when the messiah comes, God will punish the wicked, but the 'poor ones of the flock' will escape this judgment.[218] Specifically, the citation may refer to a persecution during which the leading member of the community, that is, the Teacher of Righteousness, dies.[219] This persecution the community continues to experience. The phrase following the citation עניי הצאן ('the poor ones of the flock'), which CD B XIX, 9 shares with Zech. 11.11, confirms this application: apparently the sectarians relate the citation of Zech. 13.7 (and the allusion to Zech. 11.11) to their own past and present persecution 'between the suffering of the Teacher of Righteousness and the coming of the Messiah'.[220]

Old Testament Pseudepigrapha. Unfortunately the Old Testament Pseudepigrapha make no perceptible use of Zech. 13 or the imagery of shepherd or sheep.[221] 'Shepherd', while appearing less than ten times in the documents, refers most often to Joseph as 'the shepherd's son' in *Jos. Asen.* 4.10; 6.2; 13.13. 'Sheep' generally refers to an actual animal, as in *T. Jud.* 12.1; *T. Job* 9.2; 15.4; 16.3; 32.2; *1 En.* 89.42-49; and *Apoc. Sedr.* 8.3. Although *Sib. Or.*

---

217. For a summary of the par. material in CD A VII, 7–XIII, 21 and CD B XIX, 1–XX, 34, see Joseph M. Baumgarten and Daniel R. Schwartz, 'Damascus Document (CD)', in James H. Charlesworth (ed.), *The Dead Sea Scrolls: Hebrew, Aramaic, and Greek Texts with English Translations*. II. *Damascus Document, War Scrolls, and Related Documents* (PTSDSSP; Louisville, KY: Westminster/John Knox Press, 1995), p. 25. On the discrepancy between the two recs. of CD (A and B), see Jerome Murphy-O'Connor, 'The Original Text of CD 7.9–8.2 = 19.5-14', *HTR* 64 (1971), pp. 379-86; and Philip R. Davies, *The Damascus Covenant: An Interpretation of the 'Damascus Document'* (JSOTSup, 25; Sheffield: JSOT, 1982), pp. 145-48.

218. Fitzmyer, 'Use of Explicit Old Testament Quotations', p. 47.

219. Chaim Rabin, *The Zadokite Documents* (Oxford: Clarendon Press, 2nd edn, 1958), p. 31, suggests that the passage may refer here to the Teacher of Righteousness; however, Jan de Waard, *Comparative Study of the Old Testament Text in the Dead Sea Scrolls*, pp. 40-41, sees insufficient evidence for such an identification. Bruce, 'Book of Zechariah', p. 343, interprets the citation as a threat against a wicked ruler, while Davies, *Damascus Covenant*, p. 171, understands the passage as a general warning for the community 'to think of their plight in terms of Judah and Ephraim' and to resist any attraction to or 'compromise with the "princes of Judah"', who are destined to the same fate as Ephraim.

220. France, *Jesus and the Old Testament*, p. 177; see 1QH II, 34; V, 13, 14, 21; XVIII, 14 for the use of עני and ענו in reference to the community,

221. France, *Jesus and the Old Testament*, pp. 183-84.

3.541-44; 5.101-103 and *4 Ezra* 16.73 may compare generally with Zech. 13.8-9, the texts lack any interpretative value with reference to Zech. 13.7.

Rabbinic Literature. Zechariah 13.7 is not clearly cited in the Mishnah or Talmud and is completely ignored in the other rabbinic writings of the Tannaic and Amoraic period with one exception. One of 15 minor tractates gathered at the end of the Babylonian Talmud, '*Abot de Rabbi Nathan*,[222] does contain a legendary account of the martyrdoms of R. Ishmael and R. Simeon ben Gamaliel. As a tribute to R. Simeon at his death, R. Ishmael cites part of Zech. 13.7 in '*Abot R. Nat.* A §38: 'Concerning you was it stated, *Awake, O sword, against My shepherd, and against the man that is near unto Me*'. This eulogistic use of Zech. 13.7, however, is isolated and quite distant from its original context.[223]

Early Church Fathers. Several writings among the Early Church Fathers of the second century CE use Zech. 13.7.[224] The *Epistle of Barnabas*, written between 70–135 CE, elaborates upon the three basic doctrines of hope, righteousness, and love (*Barn.* 1.5-6). In a section on the reason for the death of Jesus Christ (*Barn.* 5.1–8.7), *Barn.* 5.12 cites Zech. 13.7 in reference to his suffering in the flesh as a completion of the sins of those who killed the prophets: 'It was for this reason, therefore, that he submitted. For God says that the wounds of his flesh came from them: "When they strike down their own shepherd, then the sheep of the flock will perish".' The citation itself reveals two noteworthy alterations. One, the first clause contains a third person plural verb and reflexive pronoun (ὅταν πατάξωσιν τὸν ποιμένα ἑαυτῶν), likely emphasizing the Jewish responsibility for Jesus' death.[225] Two, the citation adds the words τῆς ποίμνης to form the phrase τὰ πρόβατα τῆς ποίμνης, suggesting a possible literary dependence on Mt. 26.31.[226]

222. According to C.A. Evans, *Noncanonical Writings*, p. 127, '*Abot de Rabbi Nathan* was written in the late third century CE but may be Tannaic, since R. Ishmael ben Elisha dates from second Tannaic generation (120–40 CE) and R. Simeon ben Gamaliel from third Tannaic generation (140–165 CE).

223. France, *Jesus and the Old Testament*, p. 192.

224. Shepherd of Hermes, *Similitude* 9.31.6 (= 108.6) reads: 'And, if the shepherds themselves are found scattered, what will they say to the owner of the flock? That they were scattered by the sheep?' Massaux, *Influence of the Gospel of St Matthew*, II, p. 130, comments that, while this text is sometimes seen as par. to Mt. 26.31 (and Mk 14.27), the text is quite different, in that *Sim.* mentions the scattering of shepherds, and Matthew, the scattering of the flocks; the comparison has arisen merely from the word 'scattering', even though *Sim.* has διαπεπτωκότες and Matthew has διασκορπισθήσονται.

225. France, *Jesus and the Old Testament*, p. 213; such is also indicated in the phrase ἐξ αὐτῶν that ends *Barn.* 5.11.

226. Massaux, *Influence of the Gospel of St Matthew*, I, p. 62.

In a long section on the fulfillment of Old Testament scriptures in the life of Jesus Christ, Justin Martyr cites both Zech. 9.9 (*Dial.* 53.2-4)[227] and Zech. 13.7 (*Dial.* 53.6). Justin understands the crucifixion of Christ and the dispersion of the disciples as a fulfillment of Zech. 13.7: 'The following is said, too, by Zechariah: "O Sword, rise up against My Shepherd, and against the man of My people, saith the Lord of hosts. Smite the Shepherd, and His flock shall be scattered".' The citation renders well the MT, though it shares certain wording with some alternate readings to the LXX. For example, Symmachus also has καὶ ἐπὶ ἄνδρα τοῦ λαοῦ μου, and codex Alexandrinus has the singular τὸν ποιμένα, rather than the plural τοὺς ποιμένας found in the standard LXX text. Furthermore, Justin uses the singular imperative (πάτα-ξον) as does the MT, instead of the first singular future indicative (πατάξω) found in Mt. 26.31. These changes may suggest that Justin, while paraphrasing Matthew, has looked up the text of his testimony source in a biblical manuscript of the twelve prophets.[228]

Similar to Justin, *Dial.* 53.6 is Irenaeus, *Epid.* 76: 'And Zachariah says thus: Sword, awake, against my shepherd, and against the man (that is) my companion; Smite the shepherd, and the sheep of the flock shall be scattered. And this came to pass when He was taken by the Jews: for all the disciples forsook Him, fearing lest they should die with Him.' Like Justin, Irenaeus uses the imperative 'strike' rather than the indicative 'I will strike', and both quote the verse from the beginning. Irenaeus also understands the fulfillment of Zech. 13.7 in the dispersion of the disciples' at the arrest and crucifixion of Jesus.[229]

Zechariah 13.7 in the New Testament
The New Testament cites Zech. 13.7 in Mt. 26.31 and Mk 14.27. Luke 22.31-34 and Jn 13.36-38 only predict Peter's denial but do not cite Zech. 13.7. John 16.32 does mention the scattering (σκορπίζω) of the disciples, but without any verbal links to Zech. 13.7.[230]

227. For comments on Justin's citation of Zech. 9.9 in *Dial.* 53.2-4, see the discussion on p. 38, above.

228. Oskar Skarsaune, *The Proof from Prophecy: A Study in Justin Martyr's Proof-Text Tradition: Text-Type, Provenance, Theological Profile* (NovTSup, 56; Leiden: E.J. Brill, 1987), p. 121.

229. While Zech. 13.7 is generally applied to the suffering of Jesus, one exception is Tertullian (c. 160–c. 215 CE), who uses the text as a threat against false shepherds, that is, Christian leaders who abandoned the church in the midst of persecution, in *Fug.* 11.2: 'Thus Zechariah threatens: "Arise, O sword, against the shepherds, and pluck ye out the sheep; and I will turn my hand against the shepherds"'.

230. France, *Jesus and the Old Testament*, p. 208, suggests that any allusions in Jn 16.32 to Zech. 13.7 is 'more likely derived from Jesus' actual quotation of Zechariah 13.7 at this time, as recorded in Mk 14.27, than from an independent use of the text'. Or, in the

Matthew 26.31. The citation from Zech. 13.7 is not introduced with the characteristic Matthean formula but with γέγραπται, an introductory formula found in Mt. 2.5; 4.4, 6, 7, 10; 11.10; 21.13; 26.24; 26.31. In Matthew, γέγραπται is not used with citations from the evangelist but rather from characters within the narrative (e.g. the chief priests, the devil, and, most often, Jesus). According to Earle Ellis, the formula γέγραπται often connotes a correct interpretation (e.g. Mt. 4.7), even if the interpretation itself may be incorrect (e.g. Mt. 4.6).[231] In this context, the formula and citation appear on the lips of Jesus,[232] as he predicts the desertion of all the disciples.[233] The prediction itself is less ambiguous than its parallel in Mk 14.27, since Mt. 26.31 contains the emphatic pronoun ὑμεῖς and two dative phrases, one causal (ἐν ἐμοί) and the other temporal (ἐν τῇ νυκτὶ ταύτῃ). With these additions, Mt. 26.31 identifies 'You will all become deserters' with 'Drink from it, all of you' in Mt. 26.27, parallels the prophecy concerning Peter in Mt. 26.34, where Jesus says that Peter will deny him three times 'this very night', and provides a christological reason ('because of me'), as in Mt. 11.6; 13.56, for the desertion of all the disciples.[234]

The citation itself begins with the first singular future indicative πατάξω ('I will strike') for the MT's second singular imperative הַךְ ('Strike'). This change may be required grammatically, since the citation includes only a section from the middle of Zech. 13.7 and does not mention the sword of Yahweh. Thus, the personified sword of Zech. 13.7 gives way to the one who commands it, because both the Old Testament and New Testament texts

words of Keener, *Matthew*, p. 635, even though Jn 16.32 lacks the citation, it 'probably testifies to a common tradition of this shepherd logion'. In the LXX, σκορπίζω does translate פוץ three times (2 Kgdms 22.15 [2 Sam. 22.15 MT]; Pss. 17.14 [18.14 MT]; 143.6 [144.6 MT]); in the New Testament, it is found only in Mt. 12.30; Lk. 11.23; Jn 10.12; 16.32; 2 Cor. 9.9.

231. E. Earle Ellis, 'Interpretation of the Bible Within the Bible Itself', in William R. Farmer (ed.), *The International Bible Commentary: A Catholic and Ecumenical Commentary for the Twenty-First Century* (Collegeville, MN: Liturgical Press, 1998), pp. 53-63 (54).

232. N.T. Wright, *Jesus and the Victory of God*, p. 599, sees this citation 'as an indication of Jesus' own mindset'; so too Bruce, 'Book of Zechariah', p. 343. Bruner, *Matthew*, II, p. 972, expresses it more pointedly: Jesus 'apparently believed that *he* was the Zecharian Shepherd'.

233. In Matthew, σκανδαλίζω may mean to 'cause to sin' (Mt. 5.29-30; 18.6, 8-9), 'take offense' (Mt. 13.57; 15.12; 17.27), or 'fall away or desert' (Mt. 11.6; 13.21; 24.10; 26.31). Four of these texts focus the 'scandal' upon Jesus with a causal dat. phrase: ἐν ἐμοι in Mt. 11.6; 26.31; ἐν αὐτῷ in Mt. 13.57; and ἐν σοί in Mt. 26.33.

234. Bruner, *Matthew*, II, p. 971; Brown, *Death of the Messiah*, p. 127; and Gundry, *Matthew*, p. 529. In the words of Davies and Allison, *Matthew*, III, p. 484, 'the prophecy expands the betrayal beyond Judas: all the disciples are implicated'.

intimate that the action against the shepherd and the scattering of the flock are ultimately initiated by Yahweh.[235] Presumably 'strike' in this context refers to the death of Jesus,[236] for Peter expresses his willingness to 'die' with Jesus in Mt. 26.35 (κἂν δέῃ με σὺν σοὶ ἀποθανεῖν). Moreover, if the word 'strike' denotes Jesus' death, the citation also identifies Jesus as the 'shepherd'.[237]

The second part of the citation describes the dispersion of the disciples with the image of scattered sheep. If, in the citation, Jesus is identified as the shepherd, then the disciples are 'the sheep of the flock'.[238] In Matthew, the word πρόβατον generally appears in a context of mission (Mt. 9.36; 10.6, 16; 15.24) or judgment/salvation (Mt. 18.12; 25.32-33), and the word often describes the people of God (e.g. 'the lost sheep of the house of Israel' in Mt. 10.6; 15.24) in contrast to those who are not (e.g. false teachers as 'wolves' in Mt. 7.16; 10.16 or the unrighteous as 'goats' in Mt. 25.32-33). The words τὰ πρόβατα are modified by the genitive phrase τῆς ποίμνης; the addition may allude to Ezekiel 34 and its description of the regathering of the scattered sheep (Ezek. 34.12-13), which somewhat resembles Jesus' promise to go ahead (προάγω) of the disciples to Galilee after he is raised up (Mt. 26.32).[239] The word 'scattered' (διασκορπίζω) relates to the earlier word

235. Davies and Allison, *Matthew*, III, p. 486; Gundry *Matthew*, p. 530; and Carson, *Matthew*, p. 541; cf. Yahweh as subj. of 'I will strike' in Exod. 3.20; 12.12; Lev. 26.24; Jer. 21.6; Ezek. 21.7; Zech. 12.4.

236. Cf. Acts 7.24; 12.23, where πατάσσω signifies a fatal blow.

237. John Paul Heil, 'Ezekiel 34 and the Narrative Strategy of the Shepherd and Sheep Metaphor in Matthew', *CBQ* 55 (1993), pp. 698-708 (706), comments: 'The first and only use of the word "shepherd" (ποιμήν) for Jesus and of "flock" (ποίμνη) for the disciples makes the prediction of their separation all the more traumatic'. Another occurrence of ποιμήν in Matthew corroborates this identification of Jesus as ποιμήν: Mt. 25.32 uses the word in a simile that describes the Son of Man.

238. While rendering the MT better than the standard text of the LXX, the citation in Matthew adds the words τῆς ποίμνης. On the possible relation of the text of Matthew to LXX reading in Cod. Alexandrinus, see n. 195, above. While it is sometimes suspected that Cod. Alexandrinus has conformed to Matthew's text, it seems more likely that the cod. preserves a reading known by Matthew, according to Gundry, *Matthew*, p. 530, and Davies and Allison, *Matthew*, III, p. 485.

239. Gundry, *Use of the Old Testament*, p. 27, lists four possibilities for Matthew's addition of τῆς ποίμνης: it appears in contrast to shepherd in the preceding line; it denotes the unity of the flock before it is scattered; it exemplifies a targumic expansion; or it alludes to Ezek. 34.31. Heil, 'Shepherd and Sheep in Matthew', p. 706, favors the allusion to Ezek. 34.31 based on the common vocabulary of shepherd, sheep, and flock (although the LXX uses ποίμνιον rather than ποίμνη, which appears in the New Testament only in Mt. 26.31; Lk. 2.8; Jn 10.16; 1 Cor. 9.7.) and the common theme of the preceding and regathering of the sheep in both Ezek. 34.12-13 and Mt. 26.32. Keener, *Matthew*, p. 636, also sees a possible connection between Mt. 26, Zech. 13, and Ezek. 34. According to Joachim Jeremias, 'ποιμήν', in *TDNT*, VI, pp. 485-502 (493), 'go before' (προάγω) in

'become deserters' (σκανδαλίζω). Whereas σκανδαλίζω can refer to apostasy, as in Mt. 11.6; 13.21; 24.10, and possibly 5.29-30, this text explains the word in terms of the scattering (διασκορπίζω) of the disciples, that is, their flight at the arrest of Jesus in Mt. 26.56.[240] Still, σκανδαλίζω cannot be completely disassociated from the loss of faith in view of Peter's absolute avowal to Jesus in Mt. 26.35 (οὐ μή σε ἀπαρνήσομαι),[241] a declaration evidently made by all the disciples (ὁμοίως καὶ πάντες οἱ μαθηταὶ εἶπαν).

Mark 14.27. The citation of Zech. 13.7 in Mk 14.27, the only explicit citation in the Markan Passion Narrative, appears in the same context as it does in Mt. 26.31. After eating the Passover supper and leaving for the Mount of Olives, Jesus predicts his death, the disciples' dispersion, and Peter's denial. Mark uses the same introductory formula γέγραπται, although the conjunction ὅτι, rather than γάρ, links the citation to the prediction.[242] The prediction is shorter in Mark, as it does not contain the emphatic pronoun ὑμεῖς and two dative phrases, ἐν ἐμοὶ and ἐν τῇ νυκτὶ ταύτῃ. The citation itself differs slightly from Matthew's in the second line, which places the subject before the verb (τὰ πρόβατα διασκορπισθήσονται) and does not expand the subject with the genitive phrase, τῆς ποίμνης. As the context of the citation is similar to that in Matthew, so too is its literary purpose: it anticipates the subsequent accounts of the flight of the disciples (Mk 14.43-50) and the denial of Peter (Mk 14.66-72). In its context, the citation of Zech. 13.7 in Mk 14.27 supports Jesus' prediction that all the disciples would desert him,[243] for Peter seizes this part of the prediction in 'his bold affirmation of absolute loyalty' in Mk 14.29, 31.[244]

Mt. 26.32 is a shepherd term (cf. Jn 10.4) that continues the shepherd metaphor from the preceding verse. Jesus' promise to go before the disciples to Galilee anticipates the restoration of the disciples after their desertion of Jesus. For Galilee with positive connotations, see Mt. 4.12, 15, 23, 25; 28.7, 10, 16.

240. Brown, *Death of the Messiah*, p. 127, says the verse defines 'the scandal in terms of being scattered, i.e., fleeing when Jesus is arrested, and so the use of "scandalized" suggests that in the Christian mind the flight of the disciples was on a par with denying Jesus'.

241. In this text, Wolfgang Schenk, 'ἀρνέομαι', in *EDNT*, I, pp. 154-55, regards ἀπαρνέομαι as a synonym for σκανδαλίζω, and, in BDAG, p. 97, ἀπαρνέομαι is defined as 'to refuse to recognize/acknowledge' (see Mt. 16.24; 26.75); related is ἀρνέομαι, meaning 'to disclaim association with a pers. or event, *deny, repudiate, disown*', according to BDAG, p. 132 (see Mt. 10.33; 26.70, 72; cf. Wis. 12.27; 16.16; *4 Macc.* 8.7; 10.15; Philo, *Spec. Laws* 2.255).

242. Mark does not use γάρ with the introductory formula γέγραπται; rather, Mark usually uses the comparative conjunctions καθώς or ὡς (see Mk 1.2; 7.6; 9.13; 14.21).

243. Robert H. Gundry, *Mark: A Commentary on His Apology for the Cross* (Grand Rapids: Eerdmans, 1993), p. 844.

244. William L. Lane, *The Gospel according to Mark* (NICNT; Grand Rapids: Eerdmans, 1974), p. 511.

Summary
The citation of Zech. 13.7 in Mt. 26.31 is closer to the MT than the standard LXX text. Indeed, the Matthean citation shows only two minor modifications from the MT, and neither of these can readily be attributed to the influence of the LXX. One, the citation begins with a first person singular future indicative verb instead of the MT's imperative. This rephrasing of the imperative as a future indicative may have arisen because the citation does not mention the sword of Yahweh and is likely derived from the final clause in Zech. 13.7 ('I will turn my hand against the little ones'). Two, the citation adds the phrase 'of the flock' to 'sheep', which is the subject of the verb 'scattered'. The first alteration emphasizes that the judgment against the shepherd and the scattering of the sheep is ultimately initiated by Yahweh; the second alteration may emphasize such a scattering of Jesus' followers that one flock no longer exists. Otherwise, the citation comes closer to the MT than does the LXX, since both the MT and Mt. 26.31 have a singular object ('shepherd') for the verb 'strike', and 'scattered' in Mt. 26.31 renders better the MT than does the LXX's 'draw out'.

The poem in Zech. 13.7-9 resumes the shepherd motif from Zechariah 9–11. Even though certain similarities between Zech. 13.7-9 and 11.3-17 may suggest that 13.7-9 should follow 11.17, the two texts contain different poetic meters, genres, and imagery, favoring the canonical position of 13.7-9. Zechariah 13.7 begins with Yahweh summoning the sword, as an instrument of divine judgment, against the shepherd. The designation 'my shepherd' may evoke Cyrus in Isa. 44.28 or, less likely, Yahweh in Ps. 23.1, but here it describes a royal ruler, as it does in Jer. 23.1-6 and Ezek. 34.1-31. The LORD of hosts enjoins the sword to strike the shepherd with a similar idiom to the one that depicts the death of King Zedekiah in Jer. 21.7. The shepherd's violent end may parallel the experience of the Suffering Servant in Isa. 53.4, 10, but the innocence of the shepherd may not be undoubtedly surmised from the context of Zech. 13.7. The text now draws attention to the result of the shepherd's death: the sheep are scattered. This scattering of the sheep elicits the recurring biblical phrase: 'like sheep without a shepherd'. Moreover, it reflects upon the ovine imagery found in Jer. 1.21; 23.1-2, and Ezek. 34.5-6, 12. The judgment of Yahweh brings death to the shepherd but also scatters the sheep; yet the 'little ones' who undergo severe suffering are refined into the people of Yahweh (Zech. 13.8-9).

The evidence for the use of Zech. 13.7 in early Jewish interpretation is limited to two citations. The *Damascus Document* (CD B XIX, 7-9) clearly quotes Zech. 13.7, but its interpretation is complicated by the ambiguous relationship between MS B and MS A, which does not contain the citation. Probably the sectarians understood the text to refer to the death of their leader, the Teacher of Righteousness, and to their own persecution resulting

from his death.[245] They continue to experience this persecution, while await-
ing deliverance at the coming of the Messiah. The minor tractate *'Abot de
Rabbi Nathan* cites Zech. 13.7 as a tribute to R. Simeon at his death (*'Abot R.
Nat.* A §38). This eulogistic use of Zech. 13.7, however, is isolated and
distant from its original context.

Several writings among the Early Church Fathers use Zech. 13.7. *Barnabas*
5.12 cites Zech. 13.7 in reference to the suffering of Jesus Christ in the flesh
as a completion of the sins of those who killed the prophets. The citation
emphasizes the Jewish responsibility for Jesus' death ('When they strike
down their own shepherd') and may display some literary dependence on Mt.
26.31 in the phrase 'the sheep of the flock'. Justin (*Dial.* 53.6) and Irenaeus
(*Epid.* 76) understand the crucifixion of Christ and the dispersion of the
disciples as fulfilling Zech. 13.7. Both Justin and Irenaeus seem to quote the
verse from a source other than Matthew's Gospel, since both quote the verse
from the beginning and use the imperative 'Strike' rather than the indicative
'I will strike'.

The New Testament cites Zech. 13.7 in Mt. 26.31 and Mk 14.27; in both
texts the citation appears in the same context. After eating the Passover supper and leaving for the Mount of Olives, Jesus predicts his death, the disciples' dispersion, and Peter's denial. Both gospels introduce the citation with
γέγραπται, an introductory formula that often connotes a correct interpretation. In both gospels, the formula and citation appear on the lips of Jesus,
rather than from the evangelists. However, the prediction is less ambiguous
in Matthew, since Mt. 26.31 adds the pronoun 'you', the causal phrase
'because of me', and the temporal phrase 'this night'. These elements link the
text with 'Drink from it, all of you' in Mt. 26.17 and the prophecy concerning
Peter's denial in Mt. 26.34, and the causal phrase offers a christological
reason for the desertion of the disciples at Jesus' arrest in Mt. 26.56.[246]

The citation itself begins with the future indicative 'I will strike' for the
MT's imperative 'Strike'. The change may have arisen for grammatical
reasons, since the citation only includes the middle portion of Zech. 13.7 and
does not mention the sword of Yahweh. While the personified sword gives
way to the one who commands it, 'the unidentification of the striker' avoids
the suggestion that the enemies of Yahweh blamelessly obey the command to
strike the shepherd; rather, the Old Testament citation corroborates the fate of
Jesus and the actions of the disciples.[247] When Peter expresses his willingness

---

245. In the words of France, *Jesus and the Old Testament*, p. 198: 'The fate of the
leader is followed by the suffering of the group'.

246. Although the difference is slight, *Barn.* 5.12, Justin (*Dial.* 53.6), and Irenaeus
(*Epid.* 76) understand the crucifixion of Christ and the dispersion of the disciples as
fulfilling Zech. 13.7, rather than the disciples' flight from Gethsemane.

247. Gundry, *Mark*, p. 845.

to die with Jesus in Mt. 26.35, the word 'strike' refers to the death of Jesus, and thus 'shepherd', to Jesus himself. The citation continues the metaphor in its description of the dispersion of the disciples as the scattering of the sheep of the flock.[248] The word 'scattered' is basically synonymous with 'become deserters' and possibly Peter's promise that he will never 'desert' Jesus, a promise also made by all the disciples. In Matthew, 'sheep' often describes the people of God, and, in this context, it denotes the disciples. The addition of the phrase 'of the flock' may allude to Ezekiel 34 and its description of the regathering of the scattered sheep (Ezek. 34.12-13), which has some resemblance with Jesus' promise to go ahead (προάγω) of the disciples to Galilee after he is raised up (Mt. 26.32).

In Mt. 26.31-35, the citation of Zech. 13.7 explains Jesus' prediction about the desertion of the disciples. As the tragic death of the shepherd has a devastating effect on the sheep in Zech. 13.7, so does the arrest of Jesus occasion the flight of his disciples. In this way, 'the metaphorical level corresponds with the historical reality'.[249] Thus, the citation of Zech. 13.7 functions theologically to establish that 'the disciples' defection, though tragic and irresponsible, does not fall outside God's sovereign plan'.[250] However, beyond this prediction of the disciples' deserting Jesus at his arrest and crucifixion stands the promise of their restoration to him in Mt. 26.32: 'But after I am raised up, I will go ahead of you to Galilee'. Even though Zech. 13.8-9 is not cited explicitly, it may be that Mt. 26.31 presupposes this full context of Zech. 13.7, in which a remnant is purified through testing and becomes the renewed people of Yahweh.[251]

---

248. Matthew's use of Zech. 13.7 has some similarities with the use of the Old Testament text in CD B XIX, 7-9, where it probably refers to the present persecution of the sectarians resulting from the death of their leader and it also promises that the 'poor ones of the flock' will escape God's punishment of the wicked at the coming of the Messiah. Keener, *Matthew*, p. 635, notes, however, that the citations differ in that CD B XIX, 7-9 interprets the text eschatologically and Mt. 26.31 may intend the shepherd imagery messianically.

249. Frankemölle, *Matthäus*, p. 453.

250. Carson, 'Matthew', p. 540.

251. David H. Johnson, 'Shepherd, Sheep', in *DJG*, p. 752; Davies and Allison, *Matthew*, III, p. 486; Carson, *Matthew*, p. 541.

2

THE ALLUSIONS TO ZECHARIAH IN
MATTHEW'S GOSPEL

This chapter considers the probable presence and intention of both textual and conceptual allusions to Zechariah in the Gospel of Matthew. The compilation of allusions from the NA27, the UBS4, Dittmar, and Davies and Allison includes 18 texts, which are divided into two sections. Five of these are found in Matthew before the Passion Narrative (Mt. 5.33; 9.4, 36; 11.21-22; 19.26). Thirteen of them are found in Matthew's Passion Narrative and the material directly preceding it (Mt. 21.1, 12; 23.23, 35; 24.30, 31, 36; 25.31; 26.15, 28, 56, 64; 27.51-53). As is appropriate for each text, the chapter uses the seven methodological criteria for discerning the presence of Old Testament allusions in the New Testament to guide the specific analysis of these 18 allusions.[1] In the case of composite references, the discussion seeks to determine whether the allusion to Zechariah is primary, and it attempts to clarify the unique contribution of the reference to Zechariah.

Allusions before the Passion Narrative

Five alleged allusions to Zechariah are found in Matthew before the Passion Narrative: Mt. 5.33; 9.4, 36; 11.21-22; 19.26.

Matthew 5.33
The wording 'you shall not swear falsely' in Mt. 5.33 may allude to Zech. 8.17. In Zech. 8.16-17, Yahweh calls upon the people to practice judicial honesty while the temple is rebuilt. The unit contains a general introduction, two positive commands, two prohibitions, and a concluding basis for these instructions. The second of the prohibitions, 'love no false oath', reiterates a basic precept found in the Decalogue (Exod. 20.16; Deut. 5.20) and relates to the problem of bringing false charges against an innocent person (Exod. 23.6-7;

---

1. Hays, *Echoes of Scripture*, pp. 29-31; see pp. 15-18 above for a description of this research methodology.

Deut. 19.15-21).² The MT of Zech. 8.17 reads וּשְׁבֻעַת שֶׁקֶר אַל־תֶּאֱהָבוּ, which the LXX translates as καὶ ὅρκον ψευδῆ μὴ ἀγαπᾶτε; however, Mt. 5.33 reads οὐκ ἐπιορκήσεις. The word ἐπιορκέω appears only twice in the LXX (1 Esd. 1.46 [1.48 NRSV] and Wis. 14.28),³ and the LXX does not use the word to translate combinations of שבע or שבעה and שקר.⁴ Matthew 5.33 does not have any specific verbal similarities with the MT or LXX text of Zech. 8.17, which is why other texts, such as Lev. 19.12 and Exod. 20.7, are generally identified as standing behind the prohibition in Mt. 5.33.⁵ Thus, any allusion to Zech. 8.17 in Mt. 5.33 is doubtful.

Matthew 9.4
The wording 'Why do you think evil in your hearts?' in Mt. 9.4 may allude to Zech. 8.17, which is described in the preceding paragraph. The first of the two prohibitions in the verse, 'do not devise evil in your hearts against one another', repeats a similar prohibition found in Zech. 7.10, 'do not devise evil

2. Sweeney, *Twelve Prophets*, p. 653. On the various Old Testament vocabulary for 'oath' and 'vow', see Jon Nelson Bailey, 'Vowing Away the Fifth Commandment: Matthew 15.3-6//Mark 7.9-13', *RestQ* 42 (2000), pp. 193-209.

3. BDAG, p. 376, defines ἐπιορκέω as 'to swear that someth. is true when one knows it is false, *swear falsely, perjure oneself*', as in *Did.* 2.3, or 'to fail to do what one has promised under oath, *break one's oath*', as with the noun ἐπίορκος in Wis. 14.25; 1 Tim. 1.10. The positive command in Mt. 5.33, 'carry out the vow you have made to the Lord', may suggest the latter meaning for ἐπιορκέω; however, the meaning 'swear falsely' better suits the context of the antithesis in Mt. 5.34-37, according to Robert A. Guelich, *The Sermon on the Mount: A Foundation for Understanding* (Waco, TX: Word Books, 1982), p. 212.

4. For example, Lev. 6.3, 5 (5.22, 24 MT); 19.12; Jer. 7.9; Zech. 5.4; 8.17; Mal. 3.5. Actually, the coinciding prohibition is found only in Ps.-Phoc. 16: 'And do not commit perjury (μὴ ἐπιορκήσῃς), either ignorantly or willingly'. Pseudo-Phocylides was written in the first century BCE or CE to demonstrate the similarities between Jewish ethics and the ethics of the sixth-century BCE Greek poet Phocylides. The prohibition against swearing falsely or committing perjury is, according to Hans Dieter Betz, *The Sermon on the Mount: A Commentary on the Sermon on the Mount, including the Sermon on the Plain* (ed. Adela Yarbro Collins; Hermeneia; Minneapolis: Fortress Press, 1995), p. 263, regarded by Hellenistic Judaism as part of the Torah, even if it is not found in the written MT (cf. Zech. 5.4; 1 Esd. 4.46; Wis. 14.25; Philo, *Decal.* 88; *Spec. Laws* 1.235; 2.26-27; 4.40; Josephus, *Ant.* 5.169-70; 8.20; *J.W.* 1.260; 2.135). For this reason, Stendahl, *School of St Matthew*, pp. 137-38, suggests that Matthew draws from an early Jewish or Christian catechism (cf. *Barn.* 2.8; Irenaeus, *Haer.* 4.17.3; 4.36.2), rather than a specific text from the MT or LXX.

5. Samuel Tobias Lachs, *A Rabbinic Commentary on the New Testament: The Gospels of Matthew, Mark, and Luke* (Hoboken, NJ: Ktav, 1987), p. 101; Gundry, *Use of the Old Testament*, p. 108; Carson, *Matthew*, p. 153; France, *Matthew*, p. 124. The positive command, 'carry out the vows you have made to the Lord', is generally connected with Ps. 50.14.

in your hearts against one another'.[6] These prohibitions may draw on similar language from Gen. 50.20; Pss. 35.4; 41.8; Jer. 48.2; Ezek. 38.10; and Nah. 1.11, and, while the prohibitions address all levels of Israelite community, Zech. 7.10 focuses on behavior against socially and economically deprived groups within that community, namely, widows, orphans, aliens, and the poor.[7] The MT of Zech. 8.17 reads וְאִישׁ אֶת־רָעַת רֵעֵהוּ אַל־תַּחְשְׁבוּ בִּלְבַבְכֶם, and Zech. 7.10 has the identical prohibition, וְרָעַת אִישׁ...אַל־תַּחְשְׁבוּ בִּלְבַבְכֶם. In the LXX, Zech. 8.17 uses the second person prohibition, μὴ λογίζεσθε, while Zech. 7.10 uses the third person prohibition, μὴ μνησικακείτω. Matthew 9.4, however, uses the indicative verb ἐνθυμεῖσθε.[8] What is more, Mt. 9.4 is a question, with which Jesus confronts the evil thoughts of the scribes against himself. The distinct differences in wording and context may suggest that a closer parallel is Wis. 3.14: 'Blessed also is the eunuch…who had not devised wicked things against the Lord' (εὐνοῦχος ὁ…μηδὲ ἐνθυμηθεὶς κατὰ τοῦ κυρίου πονηρά). If so, rather than accuse the scribes of judicial dishonesty, Mt. 9.4 likely applies to Jesus the common Jewish belief that only God knows everything about human hearts.[9] Therefore, because of verbal and contextual dissimilarity, any allusion to Zech. 7.10 or 8.17 in Mt. 9.4 is dubious.

Matthew 9.36
The wording 'like sheep without a shepherd' in Mt. 9.36 may allude to Zech. 10.2. Zechariah 10.1-2 consists of three elements: the exhortation to ask Yahweh for rain, the reason that the people are to request rain from Yahweh, and the result of the people having turned to deities and diviners for guidance and comfort. The people suffer since they have rejected Yahweh and sought other prophetic leadership; therefore, as 'sheep', they have no legitimate leader or 'shepherd'.[10]

---

6. The difference between Zech. 8.17 and 7.10 is slight, relating basically to the object of the prohibition; Zech. 8.17 has רֵעֵהוּ, 'against your neighbor', and Zech. 7.10 has אָחִיו, 'against another person'. The texts differ also in their placement of the word 'evil'.

7. Sweeney, *Twelve Prophets*, p. 644; David L. Petersen, *Haggai and Zechariah 1–9: A Commentary* (OTL; Philadelphia: Westminster Press, 1984), p. 291.

8. According to BDAG, p. 336, ἐνθυμέομαι means 'to process information by thinking about it carefully, *reflect (on), consider, think*'; the word is used in the New Testament only in Mt. 1.20; 9.4. The parallel passages in Mk 2.8 and Lk. 5.22 use the verb διαλογίζομαι, which is used by Matthew in Mt. 16.7, 8; 21.25 to denote detailed discussion.

9. Keener, *Matthew*, p. 290; e.g. 1 Sam. 16.7; 1 Kgs 8.39; Pss. 44.21; 139.1-2, 23; Jer. 12.3; 17.10; *Jub.* 15.30; *1 En.* 84.3; *Pss. Sol.* 9.3; 14.8; *Let. Arist.* 132-33; *T. Zeb.* 5.2; *m. 'Abot* 2.1; Lk. 16.15; Acts 15.8; Rom. 8.17; 1 Thess. 2.4; cf. Mt. 12.12, 25; 16.8; 22.18; Rev. 2.23. 'Evil' often applies to the religious leaders in Mt. 12.33-35, 38-45; 16.1-4; 22.18.

10. In the words of Petersen, *Zechariah 9–14*, p. 72, 'the people set out *like* a flock, which symbolizes their search for the deity in a time of distress', and, as a result, 'the

The MT of Zech. 10.2 reads עַל־כֵּן נָסְעוּ כְמוֹ־צֹאן יַעֲנוּ כִּי־אֵין רֹעֶה, which the LXX renders διὰ τοῦτο ἐξήρθησαν ὡς πρόβατα καὶ ἐκακώθησαν διότι οὐκ ἦν ἴασις.[11] Matthew 9.36 reads ὡσεὶ πρόβατα μὴ ἔχοντα ποιμένα. This wording, however, more nearly approximates such texts as Num. 27.17, 1 Kgs 22.17, and 2 Chron. 18.16, where the people of Yahweh are presented as lacking divinely appointed leaders. Of these, Num. 27.17, in which Moses appoints Joshua to lead Israel, presents the closest verbal parallel with its use of the adverb ὡσεί; it reads in the LXX: ὡσεὶ πρόβατα οἷς οὐκ ἔστιν ποιμήν.[12] Another text with verbal and conceptual similarities is Ezek. 34.5, which reads in the LXX: καὶ διεσπάρη τὰ πρόβατά μου διὰ τὸ μὴ εἶναι ποιμένας. In contrast to Ezek. 34.4, which castigates the shepherds of Israel for not healing the sick nor binding up the injured, Mt. 9.35 presents Jesus as 'curing every disease and every sickness' as he travels from one village to another. Moreover, Matthew repeatedly employs the shepherd motif, drawing especially upon Ezekiel 34 but also Mic. 5.2 and Zech. 13.7.[13] Yet, since Matthew does not cite Zech. 13.7 until Mt. 26.31 nor Zechariah 10 at any other point in the gospel, Mt. 9.36 probably does not allude to Zech. 10.2 over either Num. 27.17 or Ezek. 34.5, both of which illustrate the rich background of this Old Testament metaphor that can connote a lack of political leadership or a lack of spiritual guidance and can refer to the Davidic Messiah Yahweh will send.[14]

Matthew 11.21-22
With the mention of Tyre and Sidon, Mt. 11.21-22 is speciously linked with Zech. 9.2-4, which portrays the two cities as wise, fortified, wealthy, but unable to withstand the judgment of Yahweh. These Phoenician cities on the coast of the Mediterranean Sea north of Mt Carmel are regularly paired, several of the Old Testament prophets attacking them for their rejection of

people have let themselves suffer by accepting inappropriate leadership'. In view of the first part of Zech. 10.2, which deals with false prophecy, Meyers and Meyers, *Zechariah 9–14*, p. 194, suggest that the 'shepherd' may refer to a true prophet, in whose absence the people must endure their present affliction.

11. With the word ἴασις, meaning 'healing', as defined in Takamitsu Muraoka, *A Greek–English Lexicon of the Septuagint (Twelve Prophets)* (Leuven: Peeters, 1993), p. 113, the LXX differs significantly from the MT's רֹעֶה; however, Aquila, Symmachus, and Theodotion correctly render רֹעֶה as ποιμήν.

12. The word ὡσεί also appears in Mt. 3.16; 14.21; it is used only 21x in the New Testament. The other comparable texts in the LXX read as follows: 3 Kgdms 22.17, ὡς ποίμνιον ᾧ οὐκ ἔστιν ποιμήν; and 2 Chron. 18.16, ὡς πρόβατα οἷς οὐκ ἔστιν ποιμήν; cf. also Jdt 11.19, ὡς πρόβατα οἷς οὐκ ἔστιν ποιμήν.

13. Mt. 2.6; 9.36; 10.6, 16; 15.24; 18.12-14; 25.32; 26.31; Heil, 'Ezekiel 34', pp. 698-708; Keener, *Matthew*, p. 309.

14. Gundry, *Use of the Old Testament*, p. 32; France, *Matthew*, p. 175; Carson, *Matthew*, p. 235.

Yahweh.[15] The texts of Zech. 9.2-4 (צֹר וְצִידוֹן) and Mt. 11.21-22 (Τύρος καὶ Σιδών) share only the names of the two cities; therefore, Mt. 11.21-22 does not allude specifically to Zech. 9.2-4. Rather, Matthew refers to the 'comparable lightness' of the judgment upon Tyre and Sidon compared to the Galilean towns, which do not respond repentantly to the miracles of Jesus: their failure is worse than the arrogant paganism of Tyre and Sidon.[16]

Matthew 19.26

The wording 'for mortals it is impossible, but for God all things are possible' in Mt. 19.26 may allude to Zech. 8.6, which is the fourth of ten short oracles about Jerusalem in Zechariah 8. The oracle in Zech. 8.6 addresses the problem of allowing human expectations to distrust Yahweh's promise to restore Jerusalem (Zech. 8.1-5); the oracle presents a rhetorical question from the LORD of hosts: 'even though it seems impossible to the remnant of this people in these days, should it also seem impossible to me?'[17] In the MT, Zech. 8.6 reads: כִּי יִפָּלֵא בְּעֵינֵי שְׁאֵרִית הָעָם הַזֶּה בַּיָּמִים הָהֵם גַּם־בְּעֵינַי יִפָּלֵא,[18] and it is translated in the LXX as: εἰ ἀδυνατήσει ἐνώπιον τῶν καταλοίπων τοῦ λαοῦ τούτου ἐν ταῖς ἡμέραις ἐκείναις μὴ καὶ ἐνώπιον ἐμοῦ ἀδυνατήσει. The verb פָּלֵא connotes impossibility from a human standpoint but also wonder at the power of Yahweh;[19] it is translated by ἀδυνατέω in this text and in Gen. 18.14 and Deut. 17.8 (cf. ἀδύνατος, which translates פָּלֵא in Prov. 30.18). Similarly, Mt. 19.26 uses the adjective form of ἀδυνατεω: παρὰ ἀνθρώποις τοῦτο ἀδύνατόν ἐστιν, παρὰ δὲ θεῷ πάντα δυνατά. Such wording has a closer parallel in Gen. 18.14, μὴ ἀδυνατεῖ παρὰ τῷ θεῷ ῥῆμα. While πάντα differs from ῥῆμα, the unusual use of παρά as a dative of association may suggest a literary dependence upon the LXX of Gen. 18.14.[20] However, the context of Mt. 19.26 does not agree with the Yahweh's

---

15.　Isa. 23.1-18; Jer. 25.22; 27.3; 47.4; Ezek. 26.1–28.26; 27.8; 32.30; Joel 3.4; Amos 1.9-10. On these cities, see Josette Elayi, 'The Phoenician Cities in the Persian Period', *JANESCU* 12 (1980), pp. 13-28.

16.　Gundry, *Matthew*, p. 214; so also France, *Matthew*, p. 198.

17.　Petersen, *Haggai and Zechariah 1–8*, p. 301; Baldwin, *Haggai, Zechariah, Malachi*, p. 150; W.A.M. Beuken, *Haggai–Sacharja 1–8* (SSN, 10; Assen: Van Gorcum, 1967), p. 177, calls the form of the oracle a *Streitfrage* or 'disputation question', as in Gen. 18.14 and Jer. 32.27.

18.　The last part of this sentence is best read as an interrogative, even though no particle is present, according to GKC §150a, which states: 'A question need not necessarily be introduced by a special interrogative pronoun or adverb. Frequently the natural emphasis upon the words is of itself sufficient to indicate an interrogative sentence as such.'

19.　*HALOT*, p. 927; Sweeney, *Twelve Prophets*, p. 468; cf. the use of פָּלֵא with the prepositional phrase 'in the eyes of' in 2 Sam. 13.2; Ps. 118.23.

20.　Gundry, *Matthew*, p. 391; cf. Mt. 8.10; 22.25. Also, noting this verbal resemblance with Gen. 18.14 are Stendahl, *School of St Matthew*, p. 173; France, *Matthew*, p. 287; and Davies and Allison, *Matthew*, I, p. 37.

promise of a son to Abraham and Sarah (Gen. 18.9-15), nor does the context of Mt. 19.26 correspond with Yahweh's promise to restore Jerusalem (Zech. 8.1-5). What Zech. 8.6 shares uniquely with Mt. 19.26 is the contrasting expression of the limitation of human abilities and the unlimited abilities of Yahweh, but, without a clearer connection, one probably cannot assert that Mt. 19.26 unambiguously alludes to Zech. 8.6. Rather, Mt. 19.26 reflects in general the view that the remarkable actions of Yahweh exceed human expectations.[21]

Allusions in the Passion Narrative

Thirteen allusions are found in the Passion Narrative and the material directly preceding it: Mt. 21.1, 12; 23.23, 35; 24.30, 31, 36; 25.31; 26.15, 28, 56, 64; 27.51-53.

Matthew 21.1, 12
The wording 'Mount of Olives' in Mt. 21.1 may allude to Zech. 14.4. The prophecy of Zech. 14.1-5 concerns the coming Day of Yahweh, a time when Jerusalem will be destroyed by the nations who attack the city. But Yahweh will intervene, fighting against those nations that threaten the city, and will stand on the Mount of Olives, causing it to split into two parts, and thereby creating a valley through which the remaining inhabitants of Jerusalem will escape. The text takes up not only the theme of Yahweh's defense of Jerusalem against enemy nations, but also, using imagery similar to the Exodus tradition of the 'splitting' (בָּקַע) of the Red Sea, it presents Yahweh as one who transforms the cosmos.[22] The only other Old Testament reference to the Mount of Olives is 2 Sam. 15.30, where it is called מַעֲלֵה הַזֵּיתִים or 'the ascent of the Olives'.[23] Here David, his household, and his officials leave

---

21. Gen. 18.14; Jer. 32.17, 27; Job 42.2; Zech. 8.6; cf. Lk. 1.37; Mk 9.23; 10.27; 14.36; Lk. 18.27; cf. Philo, *Virt.* 26: πάντα γὰρ θεῷ δυνατά.

22. Exod. 14.16, 21; Neh. 9.11; Ps. 78.13; Isa. 63.12; Sweeney, *Twelve Prophets*, p. 699, also notes the possible similarity with the conquest tradition of the crossing of the Jordan (Josh. 3) and the exilic tradition of the exiles' return via the road created through the wilderness (Isa. 35.8-10; 40.3-4; 43.14-21).

23. The Mount of Olives is a ridge running parallel to the Kidron Valley, East of Jerusalem; the ridge rises more than one hundred feet higher than Jerusalem. Although they do not mention it by name, 1 Kgs 11.7; 2 Kgs 23.13; and Ezek. 11.13 probably refer to the Mount of Olives (cf. 2 Esd. 13.6). On the Mount of Olives in the Old Testament, see John Briggs Curtis, 'An Investigation of the Mount of Olives in the Judaeo-Christian Tradition', *HUCA* 28 (1957), pp. 137-80 (139-41). Josephus mentions the Mount of Olives by name in *J.W.* 2.262; 5.70, 135, 504; 6.157; *Ant.* 7.202; 20.169, and possibly as Mount Scopus in *J.W.* 2.528, 542; 5.67, 106. The New Testament refers to the Mount of Olives in Jn 8.1; Mt. 21.1 = Mk 11.1 = Lk. 19.29; Lk. 19.37; Mt. 24.3 = Mk 13.3; Lk. 21.37; 22.39; Mt. 26.30 = Mk 14.26.

Jerusalem to escape from Absalom; David ascends the Mount of Olives, while weeping over Absalom's rebellion. The wording in Mt. 21.1 corresponds with both the MT of Zech. 14.4, which reads הַר הַזֵּתִים, and the LXX, τὸ ὄρος τῶν ἐλαιῶν. In the present context, Mt. 21.5 explicitly refers to Zech. 9.9, confirming the availability and the recurrence of the Old Testament source.

More difficult, however, is assessing the allusion with relation to thematic coherence and historical plausibility. Matthew 21.1-11 differs from Zech. 14.1-5 in that Jesus does not fight against the nations and Jesus enters Jerusalem, rather than its inhabitants exit (cf. Jn 12.13). That Jesus rides a donkey into Jerusalem (Mt. 21.2-10) possibly evokes 2 Sam. 15.30; King David leaves Jerusalem during Absalom's rebellion, presumably riding on a donkey (2 Sam. 16.1-2). If so, Jesus' use of a donkey may suggest 'the peaceful yet triumphant return of King David back over the Mount of Olives', an identification confirmed by the accolades of the crowds in Mt. 21.9: 'Hosanna to the Son of David!'[24] Thus, the reference to the Mount of Olives in Mt. 21.1 probably serves less of an eschatological purpose (vis-à-vis Zech. 14.5), than a messianic one, in which case 'Matthew's geographical reference says, "here he is!"'.[25]

The wording in Mt. 21.12, 'all who were selling and buying in the temple', may allude to Zech. 14.21, which concludes the narration of Yahweh's defeat of the nations who fight against Jerusalem. These nations now join in the universal acknowledgment of Yahweh's kingship, expressed in their worship of Yahweh and their participation in the festival of booths (Zech. 14.16).[26] In the midst of this new social order, a redefined holiness displaces the old distinctions between sacred and profane, as even the Canaanites, who in the past have presented an archetypal threat to the religious and political integrity of Israel, now lose their identity with their integration into the people of Yahweh.[27] Unfortunately, the NRSV translates the last sentence of Zech. 14.21 as 'and there shall no longer be traders in the house of the LORD of hosts on that

24. France, *Matthew*, p. 297. Cf. *Tg.* Zech. 14.4, which reads: 'And at that *time he shall reveal himself in his might* upon the mount of Olives which is before Jerusalem on the east', that is, Yahweh, who is named in 14.3, will be revealed on the Mount of Olives.

25. Bruner, *Matthew*, p. 748.

26. In the words of Stuhlmueller, *Rebuilding with Hope*, p. 161: 'Zechariah is extending the canopy of the sacred over foreigners. There is this proviso: everyone must worship Yahweh and join in Israel's traditions of the Exodus out of Egypt and the settlement of the land of Canaan, at least symbolically, by celebrating the Feast of Booths. The Jerusalem temple is beginning to reach out and consecrate the rest of the world.' Cf. *Sib. Or.* 3.772-74: 'From every land they will bring incense and gifts to the house of the great God. There will be no other house among men, even for future generations to know.'

27. Michael H. Floyd, *Minor Prophets, Part 2* (The Forms of the Old Testament Literature, 22; Grand Rapids: Eerdmans, 2000), pp. 555-56; Meyers and Meyers, *Zechariah 9–14*, pp. 490-91; see Exod. 34.11-16; Lev. 18.2-5, 24-30; 20.22-26; Deut. 7.1-6; Ezra 9.1.

day', when the better translation of the MT's כְּנַעֲנִי would be 'Canaanite', as with the LXX's Χαναναῖος.[28] Neither of the words in Mt. 21.12, πωλοῦντας or ἀγοράζοντας, suggest that an alleged allusion to Zech. 14.21 has an audible volume. More importantly, Mt. 21.13 presents Jesus' action as the explicit fulfillment of Isa. 56.7 and Jer. 7.11, which substantiate Jesus' concern for use of the temple for prayer and his protest about exorbitant rates of exchange and excessive prices for sacrifices.[29] Therefore, Mt. 21.12 probably does not intentionally allude to Zech. 14.21.[30]

Matthew 23.23, 35
The wording 'justice and mercy and faith' in Mt. 23.23 may allude to Zech. 7.9. Introduced by a prophetic word formula, Zech. 7.9-14 presents an exhortation to practice social justice while the temple is rebuilt and a narration of what happened when Judah stubbornly refused to obey these same commands spoken previously by the prophets of Yahweh.[31] The unit Zech. 7.9-10, which is similar to Zech. 8.16-17, contains a messenger formula followed by two positive commands and two prohibitions. These two commands are worded in the MT as מִשְׁפַּט אֱמֶת שְׁפֹטוּ וְחֶסֶד וְרַחֲמִים עֲשׂוּ, while the LXX renders them, κρίμα δίκαιον κρίνατε καὶ ἔλεος καὶ οἰκτιρμὸν ποιεῖτε. Matthew 23.23 ostensibly shares three words with the MT—κρίσις, ἔλεος, and πίστις —which correspond with מִשְׁפַּט, חֶסֶד, and אֱמֶת.[32] Of these three, 'justice' and 'mercy' are frequently paired,[33] but the three words evidently appear together

---

28. See p. 51 n. 132, above, for a discussion of the word's occurrence in Zech. 11.11. Meyers and Meyers, *Zechariah 9–14*, p. 489, are likely correct in their assertion that the New Testament references to buying and selling in the temple—e.g., Mt. 21.12-13; Mk 11.15-18; Lk. 19.45-46; Jn 2.13-16—have been erroneously used to support the idea that כְּנַעֲנִי should be translated 'traders' in Zech. 14.21; they do not see these gospel texts as deriving from Zechariah.

29. For a comparison of the explicit citation with the two Old Testament texts, see Gundry, *Use of the Old Testament*, p. 19.

30. If Mt. 21.12 does allude to Zech. 14.21, it does so, according to Davies and Allison, *Matthew*, III, pp. 138-39, only in a general sense with several texts that anticipate the sanctification of the temple; for example, Hos. 9.15; Mal. 3.1-3; cf. *Pss. Sol.* 17.30: 'And he will purge Jerusalem (and make it) holy as it was even from the beginning'. In favor of the allusion to Zech. 14.21, see Cecil Roth, 'The Cleansing of the Temple and Zechariah 14.21', *New Testament* 4 (1960), pp. 142-81; Bruce Chilton, *The Temple of Jesus: His Sacrificial Program within a Cultural History of Sacrifice* (University Park, PA: Pennsylvania State University Press, 1992), p. 136; C.A. Evans, 'Jesus and Zechariah's Messianic Hope', p. 383.

31. Floyd, *Minor Prophets*, pp. 425-26.

32. This correspondence is closer to the MT, since the LXX uses δίκαιος rather than πίστις to render אֱמֶת. These three words appear elsewhere, though separately, in Mt. 5.22; 8.10; 9.13; 23.33.

33. Deut. 7.12; Pss. 33.5; 101.1; 119.149; Jer. 9.24; Hos. 2.19; 12.6; Mic. 6.8.

in the MT only in Ps. 89.14; Isa. 16.5; and Zech. 7.9. Matthew 23.23 does not allude to Ps. 89.14, since it includes the three words in its praise of Yahweh, nor to Isa. 16.5, since it uses them in reference to the Davidic promise. An intentional allusion to Zech. 7.9 in Mt. 23.23 also remains doubtful, since Matthew does not explicitly cite material from Zechariah 1–8. Moreover, any verbal correspondence between the two texts is complicated by the cognate accusative structure in the MT, which coalesces two qualities into a single one, that is, אֱמֶת modifies מִשְׁפָּט in the first command, 'render true judgments'. Generally, Mt. 23.23 has been connected with Mic. 6.8, even though the text contains only מִשְׁפָּט and חֶסֶד, because the two texts share the thematic similarities of torah commands and cultic offerings.[34] The absence of this latter thematic element from Zech. 7.9 suggests that Mt. 23.23 probably does not relate to it intentionally or specifically.[35]

The naming of 'Zechariah son of Barachiah' (Ζαχαρίου υἱοῦ Βαραχίου) in Mt. 23.35 allegedly alludes to the postexilic prophet.[36] Zechariah, whose name means 'Yahweh has remembered', is identified in Zech. 1.1, 7 as 'Zechariah son of Berechiah son of Iddo'. Ezra 5.1 and 6.14, however, omit any reference to Berechiah, referring to him as 'Zechariah son of Iddo', one who, along with Haggai, calls for the rebuilding of the temple. According to Neh. 12.4, Iddo is among those priests who accompanied Zerubbabel and Jeshua on their return to Jerusalem from Babylon, and Neh. 12.16 names Zechariah as the head of the priestly house of Iddo. Thus, the identification of Zech. 1.1 raises questions about the relationship of Zechariah and Iddo, whether Iddo is Zechariah's father or grandfather. In addition, any relationship between Mt. 23.35 and Zech. 1.1 is complicated by the lack of any biblical evidence for the death of the prophet Zechariah as a martyr.[37] As a result, many suggestions about the identity of the Zechariah in Mt. 23.35 have been offered; nonetheless, the only biblical martyr named Zechariah is the son of

---

34. Davies and Allison, *Matthew*, III, p. 294; France, *Matthew*, p. 328; however, Bruner, *Matthew*, p. 832, has certainly overstated the case: Matthew's triad 'is very close to being an exact paraphrase of Micah 6.8'.

35. However, Mt. 23.23 may reflect, according to David E. Garland, *The Intention of Matthew 23* (NovTSup, 52; Leiden: E.J. Brill, 1979), p. 139 n. 63, the same general understanding of the will of Yahweh presented throughout the Old Testament prophets; for example, Isa. 1.17; Jer. 5.28; Hos. 6.6; Amos 5.21-24; Mic. 6.8; and Zech. 7.9; cf. Irenaeus, *Haer.* 4.17.3; 4.36.2.

36. As one might expect, the wording of Mt. 23.35, Ζαχαρίου υἱοῦ Βαραχίου, translates well the MT זְכַרְיָה בֶּן־בֶּרֶכְיָה, with wording almost identical to the LXX, Ζαχαρίαν τὸν τοῦ Βαραχίου. The parallel in Lk. 11.51 contains only the name 'Zechariah'.

37. On the tradition that Zechariah became ill and died in his old age and that he was buried beside Haggai, see Charles Culter Torrey, *The Lives of the Prophets* (JBL Monograph Series, 1; Philadelphia: Society of Biblical Literature and Exegesis, 1946).

Jehoiada, a priest whose death is recorded in 2 Chron. 24.20-22.[38] Contextual features confirm that Mt. 23.35 has in view this Zechariah, for the son of Jehoiada is murdered 'between the sanctuary and the altar' (cf. 'in the court of the house of the LORD' in 2 Chron. 24.21), and his bloody murder, as does Abel's (Gen. 4.10), cries out for vengeance (cf. the mention of Zechariah's blood in 2 Chron. 24.25) and later becomes the subject of popular legend (*b. Giṭ.* 57b; *b. Sanh.* 96b; *Eccl. Rab.* 3.16 §1).[39] Furthermore, given the rabbinic tendency to merge two distinct persons, Matthew has likely conflated the prophet Zechariah with the son of Jehoiada, as is done in *Tg.* Lam. 2.20: 'Is it right to kill priest and prophet in the Temple of YHWH, as you killed Zechariah son of Iddo, the High Priest and faithful prophet, in the Temple of YHWH on the Day of Atonement, because he reproached you, that you refrain from evil before YHWH?'[40] In so doing, Matthew correlates the betrayal of Jesus' 'innocent blood' (Mt. 27.4, which is in the context of the citation of Zech. 11.12-13) with the shedding of the righteous blood of all the Old Testament

38. The name Zechariah appears more than 40x in the Old Testament, referring to almost 30 different individuals; this makes it 'one of the most popular of all biblical names', so say Meyers and Meyers, *Zechariah 1–8*, p. 91. Options for the identity of Zechariah in Mt. 23.35 include the minor prophet (Zech. 1.1), the son of Jehoiada (2 Chron. 24.20-22), the son of Jeberechiah (Isa. 8.2; cf. *b. Mak.* 24b), the father of John the Baptist (Lk. 1.5; cf. *Prot. Jas.* 23.1–24.4; see Roger W. Cowley, 'The "Blood of Zechariah" [Mt 23.35] in Ethiopian Exegetical Tradition', in Elizabeth A. Livingstone [ed.], *Studia Patristica XVIII* [4 vols.; Kalamazoo, MI: Cistercian Publications, 1985], I, pp. 293-302), the son of Baris (other MSS have Baruch or Bariscaeus), who is murdered by two Zealots (Josephus, *J.W.* 4.334-44), or a Zechariah, who remains otherwise unknown. For further discussion, see Gundry, *Use of the Old Testament*, pp. 86-88; Carson, *Matthew*, pp. 485-86; Garland, *Intention of Matthew 23*, pp. 182-83. The omission of υἱοῦ Βαραχίου in MS ℵ may suggest that 'son of Barachiah' is a later gloss, but its omission from ℵ is more easily explained than its insertion into all other MSS. Jerome, *Comm. Matt.* 23.35, mentions a reading, 'son of Joiada', from the *Gospel of the Hebrews*.

39. Davies and Allison, *Matthew*, III, pp. 318-19.

40. The English translation of *Tg.* Lamentations is from Étan Levine, *The Aramaic Version of Lamentations* (New York: Sepher-Hermon, 1976). So Eberhard Nestle, 'Über Zacharias in Matth 23', *ZNW* 6 (1905), pp. 198-200; Theodor Zahn, *Introduction to the New Testament* (trans. Melancthon Williams Jacobus *et al.*; 3 vols.; Edinburgh: T. & T. Clark, 1909; repr., Minneapolis: Klock & Klock, 1977), II, p. 590; John Chapman, 'Zacharias, Slain between the Temple and the Altar', *JTS* 13 (1912), pp. 398-410; Sheldon H. Blank, 'The Death of Zechariah in Rabbinic Literature', *HUCA* 12–13 (1937–38), pp. 327-46; Martin McNamara, *The New Testament and the Palestinian Targum to the Pentateuch* (AnBib, 27; Rome: Pontifical Biblical Institute, 1966), pp. 162-63; Gundry, *Matthew*, pp. 471-72; France, *Matthew*, pp. 330-32; Lachs, *Rabbinic Commentary*, p. 372; Keener, *Matthew*, p. 556; Davies and Allison, *Matthew*, III, pp. 318-19. For rabbinic examples of the quoting of various persons under one name to praise righteous people (or to disparage the wicked), see Z.H. Chajes, *The Student's Guide through the Talmud* (trans. Jacob Shachter; London: East and West Library, 1952), pp. 172-75.

martyrs, beginning with Abel and culminating with Zechariah the son of Jehoiada; their deaths anticipate that Jesus, although innocent, also suffers a violent death.[41] While Matthew does not here allude to a specific 'text' from Zechariah, it does seem that his conflation may suggest a general allusion to the prophetic book, based on several criteria, including volume, thematic coherence, and satisfaction, and one which anticipates Jesus' own violent death.

Matthew 24.30, 31, 36

Two phrases in Mt. 24.30 may allude to several elements in Zech. 12.10-14. Following the promise of Yahweh in Zech. 12.9 to defend Jerusalem against the nations, Zech. 12.10-14 contains two distinct descriptions: the favorable response of Yahweh toward Jerusalem and the mourning of all families over some unknown person.[42] Specifically, Yahweh pours out upon the people 'a spirit of compassion and supplication', so that, when they 'look on the one whom they have pierced', all families, along with 'the land', mourn, as if they were mourning for an only child.[43] In Mt. 24.30 (although absent from Mk 13.26 and Lk. 21.27), the phrase 'all the tribes of the earth will mourn' may relate to 'they shall mourn for him' in Zech. 12.10, 'land' in Zech. 12.12, and 'all the families' in Zech. 12.14. Here Matthew shares several words with the LXX: the verb form κόψονται, the phrase πᾶσαι αἱ φυλαὶ (minus the ptc. ὑπολελειμμέναι), and the word γῆ. Also, the phrase 'they will see "the Son of Man"' may relate to 'when they look on the one whom they have pierced'

---

41.   Gundry, *Matthew*, p. 471; Ham, 'Last Supper', pp. 67-68. Since Chronicles ends the HB, the deaths of Abel and the son of Jehoiada constitute the first and last 'literary' martyrdoms. Chronologically, the death of Uriah son of Shemaiah occurs last (Jer. 26.20-23). Nonetheless, the death of Zechariah son of Jehoiada cannot be used as evidence for an early closing of the Old Testament canon, according to H.G.L. Peels, 'The Blood "from Abel to Zechariah" (Matthew 23.35; Luke 11.50f) and the Canon of the Old Testament', *ZAW* 113 (2001), pp. 583-601.

42.   Petersen, *Zechariah 9–14*, pp. 120-21. On the possibility that the mourning may portray Jerusalem's concern for enemy casualties instead of the death of a particular individual, see Floyd, *Minor Prophets*, pp. 524-28.

43.   Although the NRSV translates the phrase 'on the one whom they have pierced', both the MT and LXX read 'on me', אֵלַי and πρός με, a preferable reading on text-critical grounds, according to Matthias Delcor, 'Un problème de critique textuelle et d'exégèse: Zach 12.10 et aspicient ad me quem confixerunt', *RB* 58 (1951), pp. 189-99 (192). The text does not identify the one who is pierced, but various figures have been suggested, including someone associated with King Josiah (see 2 Kgs 22.29-30), Zerubbabel following his possible displacement by Joshua (Zech. 6), the Suffering Servant (Isa. 53.5), the shepherd of Zech. 13.7, and even Yahweh (as indicated by the first per. construction beginning in Zech. 12.9 and by the first sg. prep. suf. in Zech. 12.10). This mourning like that for an only child or firstborn may draw upon the language of Gen. 22.2, 12, 16 (cf. Jer. 6.26; Amos 8.10) or perhaps the language of Exod. 4.22; 12.29; 13.15.

in Zech. 12.10; however, in this instance, Matthew (ὄψονται τὸν υἱὸν τοῦ ἀνθρώπου) and the LXX (ἐπιβλέψονται πρός με ἀνθ' ὧν κατωρχήσαντο) use different, though synonymous, verbs and contain different objects for these verbs.[44] The convergence of the language from Zech. 12.10-14 and its density in the context of Mt. 24.30 strongly suggest that Matthew has borrowed such Old Testament phraseology to emphasize the visibility of the Son of Man's coming and more so the reaction of universal mourning.[45] Furthermore, others in the history of interpretation have 'heard' the same allusion, applying Zech. 12.10 to the 'piercing' at the crucifixion of Jesus and to the 'mourning' at the Parousia; for example, Justin, *Dial.* 32, reads: 'and if I had not explained that there would be two advents of His, one in which He was pierced by you; a second, when you shall know Him whom you have pierced, and your tribes shall mourn, each tribe by itself, the women apart, and the men apart'.[46] What remains less clear is the degree to which Mt. 24.30 may identify Jesus, as the Son of Man, with the one pierced in Zech. 12.10, similar to the citation of Zech. 12.10 in Jn 19.37.[47] As in Mk 13.26 and Lk. 21.27, Mt. 24.30 relates 'they will see' to 'the Son of Man coming on the clouds of heaven', an allusion to Dan. 7.13 (cf. Rev. 1.7); however, 'they will see' in

---

44. The LXX evidently does not use ὁράω to translate *hiphil* forms of נבט in the MT, which means 'to look, in a particular direction', according to *HALOT*, p. 661. In contrast, the New Testament uses ἐπιβλέπω only in Lk. 1.48; 9.38; Jas 2.3; it means, according to BDAG, p. 368, 'to look intently' or 'to pay close attention to, with implication of obsequiousness'; cf. Muraoka, *Greek–English Lexicon of the Septuagint*, p. 89. Nonetheless, Jn 19.36 and Rev. 1.7 use ὁράω instead of ἐπιβλέπω in their citations of Zech. 12.10, and in Mt. 24.30 the use of ὁράω allows for the word-play between κόψονται and ὄψονται.

45. Gundry, *Matthew*, pp. 488-89; John Dominic Crossan, *The Historical Jesus: The Life of a Mediterranean Jewish Peasant* (San Francisco: HarperSanFrancisco, 1991), pp. 377-78. France, *Jesus and the Old Testament*, pp. 106-107, understands here an allusion to the mourning of (the tribes of) Israel, specifically at the destruction of Jerusalem in 70 CE and at the realization of their rejection of Jesus Christ, who is now their judge; however, Matthew seems to generalize the word φυλή so that it applies to 'all nations of the earth', as translated in the NIV, according to Keener, *Matthew*, p. 586 (cf. Gen. 12.3; 28.14; Rev. 1.7; *1 Clem.* 10.3, where the expression has more universal connotations).

46. See also Jn 19.37; Rev. 1.7; *Barn.* 7.9 (some MSS read: 'Is this not the one whom we once crucified, insulting and piercing and spitting upon him?'); Justin, *1 Apol.* 52.11; *Dial.* 14; 64; 118; Irenaeus, *Haer.* 4.33.11; moreover, even the rabbinic tradition (*b. Suk.* 52a) comes to read Zech. 12.10 as a prophecy of the slaying of Messiah the son of Joseph.

47. Jn 19.37 explicitly cites Zech. 12.10, following the MT over the LXX's misreading of דָּקָרוּ as רָקְדוּ, evidenced in the LXX with κατωρχήσαντο, which means 'they danced in triumph over' or 'they treated despitefully'. Zech. 12.10 shares several contextual similarities with Jn 19.37, including pouring out the spirit, looking, piercing, and the inhabitants of Jerusalem. Moreover, the image of a fountain for cleansing from sin in Zech. 13.1 is thematically congruent with the 'spring of water gushing up to eternal life' in Jn 4.14, 'rivers of living water' in Jn 7.38, and the flow of blood and water in Jn 19.34.

Mt. 24.30 may still relate with Zech. 12.10 to a lesser extent, since the preceding statement in Mt. 24.30, 'all the tribes of the earth will mourn', alludes to Zech. 12.10.[48] In addition, if the death of 'the one whom they have pierced' in Zech. 12.10 can be identified with the 'shepherd' who dies by the sword in Zech. 13.7, then Mt. 24.30, in distinction from its synoptic parallels, may connect thematically with the citation of Zech. 13.7 in Mt. 26.31.[49] If so, while Mt. 26.31 explicitly presents Jesus as the shepherd who is struck with the sword, Mt. 24.30 implicitly portrays Jesus as the one who is pierced.

The wording 'the four winds, from one end of heaven to the other' in Mt. 24.31 may allude to Zech. 2.6 (2.10 LXX/MT). Zechariah 2.6-13 (2.10-17 LXX/MT) comprises a series of commands each with motivations based on 'prophetic claims about Yahweh' and composed of 'oracular speech of Yahweh'.[50] As the first command in this sequence, Zech. 2.6 constitutes Yahweh's call for the exiles to flee from Babylon, since Yahweh has scattered abroad the exiles 'like the four winds of heaven'.[51] Because Yahweh has scattered Judah among the nations, Yahweh is now capable of reversing the exile and bringing the exiles back to Jerusalem.[52] While the exiles return from 'the land of the north', their diaspora is described as global (cf. Deut. 30.4; Ps. 106.47; Isa. 11.12; *Pss. Sol.* 9.1-2); that is, the exiles are scattered 'like the four winds of heaven', an expression which appears no less than five times in the MT (Jer. 49.36; Dan. 8.8; 11.4; Zech. 2.6; 6.5) and signifies universal or cosmic comprehensiveness.[53] Matthew 24.31 contains the same words as the LXX, ἐκ τῶν τεσσάρων ἀνέμων, but adds the descriptive phrase, ἀπ' ἄκρων οὐρανῶν ἕως [τῶν] ἄκρων αὐτῶν. This wording is similar to the LXX's expansion of the MT (מִקְצֵה הַשָּׁמַיִם) in Deut. 30.4: ἀπ' ἄκρου τοῦ οὐρανοῦ

---

48.   The same association appears in Jesus' response to the high priest in Mt. 26.64 and Mk 14.62. In his discussion of the Markan text, Darrell L. Bock, *Blasphemy and Exaltation in Judaism and the Final Examination of Jesus: A Philological-Historical Study of the Key Jewish Themes Impacting Mark 14.61-64* (WUNT, 2.106; Tübingen: Mohr Siebeck, 1998), pp. 206-207, argues that Jesus' expectation that he will be vindicated and his claim that he will act as a judging figure appeal not to Zech. 12.10 but to a martyrdom tradition evident in such texts as Wis. 5.2; *Apoc. El.* 5.28; and *1 En.* 62.5.

49.   McComiskey, *Zechariah*, p. 1214; France, *Jesus and the Old Testament*, p. 106; Davies and Allison, *Matthew*, III, p. 360, although such an identification should be made with some caution, as advocated by Sweeney, *Twelve Prophets*, pp. 688-89.

50.   Floyd, *Minor Prophets*, p. 369.

51.   'The land of the north' is equated to Babylon in the next verse; 'north' is the direction from which invaders enter Palestine (Jer. 1.14-19; 6.22; 10.22; Zech. 6.6, 8) and the direction from which the exiles return (Jer. 3.18; 16.15; 23.8; 31.8).

52.   In the words of Sweeney, *Twelve Prophets*, p. 587, 'YHWH as sovereign of the cosmos called for Judah's exile and now calls for the exiles to return home'.

53.   In Old Testament, the phrase 'the four winds of heaven' signifies 'the four sides of the world, or the four points of the compass', according to *HALOT*, p. 1198; cf. Mk 13.27; Rev. 7.1; Josephus, *J.W.* 6.301; *Ant.* 8.80; *Did.* 10.5.

ἕως ἄκρου τοῦ οὐρανοῦ, except that Mt. 24.31 assimilates all four case endings to the genitive plural as in the earlier phrase, τῶν τεσσάρων ἀνέμων.[54] Both Deut. 30.4 and Zech. 2.6 refer to the regathering of the exiles, and Mt. 24.31 calls those to be gathered the 'elect'.[55] Therefore, on the basis of such criteria as volume, thematic coherence, and history of interpretation (see Justin, *1 Apol.* 52; cf. *Did.* 10.5), it would appear that Mt. 24.31 contains a plausible allusion to Zech. 2.6.

The wording 'about that day and hour no one knows...but only the Father' in Mt. 24.36 allegedly alludes to Zech. 14.7. Zechariah 14.1-21 offers a narrative description of the coming day of Yahweh in four episodes (14.1-5, 6-7, 8-12, 13-21); the second and third of these envision new temporal and topographical distinctions of the new creation effected 'on that day'. In particular, Zech. 14.7 describes a reversal of the first act of creation that produces the division of day and night (Gen. 1.3-5); thus, this diurnal pattern ceases in 'that day', but its absence results, not in darkness, but in perpetual light.[56] Such a 'continuous day' is beyond human comprehension and 'known to the LORD' only.[57] The text of Mt. 24.36 shares with the LXX only the words τῆς ἡμέρας ἐκείνης, although the LXX renders the words as the subject of the assertion, ἡ ἡμέρα ἐκείνη γνωστὴ τῷ κυρίῳ. The MT, however, is more concise (הוּא יָדַע לַיהוָה) and does not repeat 'that day' in reference to the earlier יוֹם־אֶחָד (although יוֹם הַהוּא occurs 7x in Zech. 14). Furthermore, the word οἶδεν in Mt. 24.36 differs from the LXX form γνωστὴ (although the LXX often uses forms of οἶδα to translate the verb יָדַע in the MT), and Matthew's appellation πατὴρ does not appear in either the MT or the LXX. These verbal similarities suggest that the volume of any allusion here is moderate at best. With its reference to 'that day', Mt. 24.36 shares a significant contextual similarity with Zech. 14.7, since 'that day' in Zech. 14.7 is properly understood as the Old Testament's 'day of the LORD' (cf. Zech. 14.1), a day which Matthew identifies as the Parousia (Mt. 7.22; 24.3, 27, 37, 39). However, the two texts differ in that Zech. 14.7 emphasizes the unique quality of 'that day' and Yahweh's knowledge of it while Mt. 24.36 stresses the chronological arrival of 'that day' and the lack of knowledge of its timing by anyone, except the

54. Gundry, *Use of the Old Testament*, p. 55; France, *Matthew*, p. 345.

55. Cf. Mt. 8.11-12; 22.14; 24.22, 24, where the designation clearly describes those beyond the boundaries of Israel. Thus, Mt. 24.31 corresponds thematically with Zech. 2.11 (MT 2.15), in which the nations join themselves to Yahweh; in the words of Floyd, *Minor Prophets*, p. 369: 'The sign of Yahweh's renewed presence in Jerusalem, which authenticates the prophets' interpretation of the restoration as an act of cosmic significance, is the new possibility of the Gentiles' inclusion among the people of Yahweh'.

56. Meyers and Meyers, *Zechariah 9–14*, pp. 433-34; Sweeney, *Twelve Prophets*, p. 700; cf. Isa. 24.23; 60.19-20; Rev. 21.25; 22.5.

57. For יוֹם־אֶחָד, *HALOT*, p. 30, suggests a 'never-ending day', but the NASB and the NIV translate the phrase as 'unique day'.

Father.[58] According to the criteria of volume, recurrence, and thematic coherence, an allusion to Zech. 14.7 in Mt. 24.36 remains a possibility, although less likely than the earlier allusions in the immediate context Mt. 24.30-31.[59]

Matthew 25.31
The wording 'when the Son of Man comes in his glory, and all the angels with him' in Mt. 25.31 may allude to Zech. 14.5. The first of four episodes concerning the coming Day of Yahweh in Zech. 14.1-21, 14.1-5 describes a time when Jerusalem will be destroyed by the nations who attack the city. But Yahweh will intervene, fighting against those nations that threaten the city, and provide a way of escape for the remaining inhabitants of Jerusalem. At the end of the narrative unit in Zech. 14.5, the prophet declares: 'then the LORD my God will come, and all the holy ones with him'. 'Holy ones' here denotes angelic beings;[60] therefore, if Matthew does allude to this text, Mt. 25.31 'interpretively (and correctly) renders קְדֹשִׁים by οἱ ἄγγελοι'.[61] In fact,

58. Divine omniscience relating to the end-time is illustrated in both Jewish and Christian literature; see Zech. 14.7; *Pss. Sol.* 17.21; *2 Bar.* 21.8; 48.8; 54.1; 1QM I, 8-10; Acts 1.7; Mk 13.32; 1 Thess. 5.1; Irenaeus, *Haer.* 2.28.6. While the phrase οὐδὲ ὁ υἱός is missing from some MSS (e.g. א¹ L W f¹ 33 vg sy co), its omission is best explained by doctrinal difficulties; its inclusion and authenticity is likely, since, as Albrecht Oepke, 'παρουσία', in *TDNT*, V, pp. 858-71 (867), has remarked, 'Who would have dared invent such a saying?'

59. Gundry, *Matthew*, p. 492, suggests that the saying seems to rely on the LXX text of Dan. 12.13, but the possibility of an allusion to Dan. 12.13 in Mt. 24.36 is quite doubtful, especially in view of the criteria of volume, thematic coherence, and satisfaction.

60. The designation 'holy ones' may intimate that 'the holiness of the heavenly realm will surely and at last become pervasive on earth in the eschatological age', according to Meyers and Meyers, *Zechariah 9–14*, pp. 429-30. While קְדֹשִׁים, generally translated as οἱ ἅγιοι in the LXX, can refer to 'people' (Lev. 21.7-8; Num. 16.5, 7; 2 Chron. 35.3; Ps. 34.9; Dan. 7.18; 8.22, 24), קְדֹשִׁים usually refers to heavenly beings in the Old Testament (Deut. 33.2-3; Job 5.1; 15.15; Ps. 89.5, 7; Prov. 30.3; Dan. 4.13, 17, 23; 8.13; cf. οἱ ἅγιοι in Exod. 15.11 LXX; Tob. 12.15 LXX; Sir. 42.17 LXX; *Pss. Sol.* 17.43). In the New Testament, οἱ ἅγιοι may also denote angelic beings (1 Thess 3.13, and possibly 2 Thess. 1.10), but more often the New Testament uses the designation for believers (Mt. 27.52; Acts 9.13, 32, 41; 26.10; Rom. 1.7; 8.27; 12.13; 15.25, etc.). Thus, the older distinction, which understands celestial beings as 'holy' because of their closeness to the 'Holy One' (cf. 1QM XII, 1; *1 En.* 14.23), has evidently been transferred in the New Testament to the 'saints' in view of a new relationship with Yahweh, according to Stephen Woodward, 'The Provenance of the Term "Saints": A *Religionsgeschichtliche* Study', *JETS* 24 (1981), pp. 107-16 (110-11); cf. Dan. 7.27; 1QS XI, 7-8; 1QM X, 10-11. Later rabbinic works identify the 'holy ones' of Zech. 14.5 as the prophets mentioned in 2 Kgs 2.3 (*Ruth Rab.* 2 [on Ruth 1.1]; *Song Rab.* 4.11 §1; *Eccl. Rab.* 1.11§1). In Matthew, ἅγιος generally denotes the Holy Spirit (Mt. 1.18, 20; 3.11; 12.32; 28.19) but may also describe Jerusalem as the holy city (Mt. 4.5; 27.53), a holy place in the temple (Mt. 24.15), or something holy (Mt. 7.6).

61. Gundry, *Use of the Old Testament*, p. 142.

Mt. 25.31 duplicates the entire clause from the LXX: καὶ πάντες οἱ ἄγγελοι
μετ' αὐτοῦ.[62] While the Old Testament and the Old Testament Pseudepigrapha do not suggest that the Messiah will come with angels at the end of
the age, the New Testament transfers the expectation without hesitation from
Yahweh to Jesus (see Mt. 16.27-28; 24.30-31).[63] Such is also attested in *Did.*
16.7 in its own citation of Zech. 14.5 in relation to the Parousia of Jesus: 'as
it has been said, "The Lord will come, and all his saints with him"'.[64] Therefore, on the basis of such criteria as volume, recurrence, history of interpretation, and satisfaction (cf. 'king' in Zech. 14.9 and Mt. 25.34), Mt. 25.31
probably does allude to Zech. 14.5 in its depiction of Jesus as the Son of Man
coming at the Parousia, 'and all the angels with him'.[65]

Matthew 26.15, 28, 56, 64
The wording 'They paid him thirty pieces of silver' in Mt. 26.15 surely
alludes to Zech. 11.12. Zechariah 11.4-17 contains a symbolic prophetic
action, in which the prophet follows Yahweh's instruction to act as a shepherd for the 'flock doomed for slaughter'. In Zech. 11.12-13,[66] the prophet
requests a wage for his service as shepherd. In return, the sheep merchants
weigh out a wage of thirty pieces of silver, not an insignificant amount in literal terms, but in this context an amount that signifies a trivial and thereby
insulting amount.[67] The text of Mt. 26.15, οἱ δὲ ἔστησαν αὐτῷ τριάκοντα
ἀργύρια, shows a similarity to the LXX of Zech. 11.12, καὶ ἔστησαν τὸν
μισθόν μου τριάκοντα ἀργυροῦς,[68] which translates well the MT, וַיִּשְׁקְלוּ
אֶת־שְׂכָרִי שְׁלֹשִׁים כָּסֶף. Indeed, the use of the word ἔστησαν indicates that
the allusion in Mt. 26.15 complies more closely with the MT (יִּשְׁקְלוּ) and
the LXX of Zech. 11.12 than does the citation of the same passage in Mt.
27.9, which uses instead the verb ἔλαβον.[69] Thus, the recurrent citation of

62. Some MSS (A W *f*[13] 𝔐 sy[p.h] bo[pt]) omit the article οἱ in Mt. 25.31.
63. France, *Jesus and the Old Testament*, p. 184; Carson, *Matthew*, p. 521; cf. Mt.
16.27-28; 24.31; 1 Thess. 3.13; 2 Thess. 1.7; Jude 14; *Did.* 16.7; Justin, *1 Apol.* 51.9.
64. Even closer than Mt. 25.31 to the LXX rending of Zech. 14.5 is *Did.* 16.7: ἥξει ὁ
κύριος, καὶ πάντες οἱ ἅγιοι μετ' αὐτοῦ.
65. France, *Matthew*, p. 356; Davies and Allison, *Matthew*, III, p. 420.
66. On the meaning of Zech. 11.12-13, see pp. 51-57, above.
67. On the connotation of the thirty pieces of silver, see pp. 52-53, above.
68. On Matthew's use of the neut. pl. ἀργύρια and the LXX's use of the masc. pl.
ἀργυροῦς, see p. 48 n. 118, above. Mk 14.11 and Lk. 22.5 mention only that a promise of
monetary payment (ἀργύριον) is agreed upon; they do not specify an amount, as does Mt.
26.15, and therefore they do not allude to Zech. 11.12.
69. In this context, BDAG, p. 482, indicates that ἵστημι means to 'determine monetary amount', since Matthew's 'readers would know that coinage of their time was not
"weighed out" and would understand ἱ. in the sense of striking a bargain'. The use of
ἵστημι for שָׁקַל, meaning to 'to weigh out (money)', appears with some frequency in the

Zech. 11.12 in Mt. 27.9-10 offers unambiguous support for the availability of
Zech. 11.12 to Matthew. The allusion is quite loud, since Mt. 26.15 specifies
both the sum (i.e. 'thirty pieces of silver') and the manner in which the money
is paid (i.e. 'weighed out') and anticipates the narrative of Judas's suicide in
Mt. 27.3-10.[70] Thematically, the allusion implicates Judas and the Jewish
leaders for their rejection of Jesus as the divinely appointed 'shepherd', a
reading whose intended effect is clearly heard in Irenaeus, *Epid.* 81.7.

The wording 'this is my blood of the covenant' in Mt. 26.28 may allude to
Zech. 9.11. Zechariah 9.11-17 describes Yahweh's restoration of the people,
following the king's procession into Jerusalem (Zech. 9.9) and the proclamation concerning the end of military conflict and the beginning of peace
among the nations (Zech. 9.10). Zechariah 9.11 explains the reason for Yahweh's favorable actions toward Judah: Yahweh liberates the Babylonian
exiles because of the covenant made by the blood of sacrifice, specifically the
covenant ceremony of Exod. 24.8.[71] The phrase 'the blood of the covenant'
appears in only these two Old Testament texts: Exod. 24.8 and Zech. 9.11.
The text of Mt. 26.28, τὸ αἷμά μου τῆς διαθήκης, is identical to the LXX of
Exod. 24.8, except that Exod. 24.8 does not contain the first-person pronoun.
The text of Mt. 26.28 is also similar to the LXX of Zech. 9.11, although Zech.
9.11 lacks both articles and the pronoun and renders 'blood' as the dative
object of the preposition, translating well the MT's בְּדַם־בְּרִיתֵךְ as ἐν αἵματι
διαθήκης. Based on these verbal similarities, the allusion in Mt. 26.28 to
Zech. 9.11 may be slightly less loud than one to Exod. 24.8.[72] Still, an allusion

LXX (see 2 Kgdms 14.26; 18.12; 2 Esd. 8.25, 26, 29, 33; Job 6.2; 28.15; 31.6; Isa. 46.6;
Zech. 11.12).

70. Stendahl, *School of St Matthew*, p. 121, writes: 'The words in 26.15 and the
passage 27.3-10 are dominated by Matthew's interpretation of Zech. 11.12-13'. According
to Davies and Allison, *Matthew*, III, p. 453, Mt. 26.15 and 27.3-10 may also connect
thematically with Mt. 10.9, where Jesus commands his disciples to take no silver on their
mission, and with Mt. 28.12-15, where the soldiers accept silver to lie about the disappear-
ance of Jesus' body, suggesting that the desire for monetary gain reveals one to be a
disingenuous follower of Jesus.

71. Petersen, *Zechariah 9–14*, p. 60; Meyers and Meyers, *Zechariah 9–14*, p. 139.
Such an identification is intimated by the expansion based on the Exodus theme in *Tg.*
Zech. 9.11: 'You also, *for whom* a covenant *was made* by blood, *I have delivered you*
from bondage to the Egyptians, I have supplied your needs in a wilderness desolate as an
empty pit in which there is no water'. The connection is made clearly in *Lev. Rab.* 6.5 (on
Lev. 5.1): 'God said to them: *As for thee also, because of the blood of thy covenant* (Zech.
IX, 11), i.e. because you remembered that blood of [the covenant at] Sinai'; and *Lev. Rab.*
19.6 (on Lev. 15.25): 'as it is said, *As for thee also, because of the blood of thy covenant*
I send forth thy prisoners out of the pit (Zech. IX, 11) [which means], You have
remembered the blood of Sinai'.

72. As Carson, *Matthew*, p. 537, says, 'the textual affinities are clearly in favor of
Exodus 24.8'. So also I. Howard Marshall, *Last Supper and Lord's Supper* (Exeter:

to Zech. 9.11 should not be overlooked, since the context of Zech. 9.11 is redemptive and eschatological, whereas Exod. 24.8 is merely descriptive of the covenant ceremony.[73] Matthew 21.5 has already cited Zech. 9.9, confirming the availability of Zech. 9.11. Moreover, the citation of Zech. 13.7 in Mt. 26.31 evokes the bloody death of Jesus the shepherd, by whose death the covenant is established in the context of messianic victory;[74] these themes also appear together again in Heb. 13.20. Thus, the allusion to Zech. 9.11 is corroborated by several of the seven criteria, including availability, volume, coherence, history of interpretation, and satisfaction.

Matthew 26.56 contains an introductory formula similar to the one that introduces the first of the ten formula quotations. Both Mt. 1.22 and Mt. 26.56 begin with the same five words, τοῦτο δὲ ὅλον γέγονεν ἵνα, but the two formulas differ in at least two ways. The remaining words in Mt. 1.22, except for the prepositions, are singular (πληρωθῇ τὸ ῥηθὲν ὑπὸ κυρίου διὰ τοῦ προφήτου), while all the other words in Mt. 26.56 are plural (πληρωθῶσιν αἱ γραφαὶ τῶν προφητῶν). Also, Mt. 1.23 explicitly cites Isa. 7.14, but Mt. 26.56 does not cite any Old Testament text. Because the following clause in Mt. 26.56, 'then all the disciples deserted him and fled', clearly relates to the earlier prediction of the disciples' dispersion in Mt. 26.31 and its citation of Zech. 13.7,[75] Mt. 26.56 may also allude to Zech. 13.7. However, the plural phrase αἱ γραφαὶ τῶν προφητῶν (cf. Mt. 26.54) probably indicates that no single scripture is in view, as with Mt. 2.23, the only other fulfillment formula with the plural form προφητῶν and itself a citation without a clear Old Testament source.[76] Furthermore, it seems doubtful that τοῦτο δὲ ὅλον γέγονεν refers simply to the dispersion of the disciples, although their desertion is certainly included among 'all this'.[77] Thus, any allusion to Zech. 13.7

Paternoster Press, 1980), p. 43, and Peter Stuhlmacher, *Jesus of Nazareth—Christ of Faith* (trans. Siegfried S. Schatzmann; Peabody: Hendrickson, 1993), p. 72. On the allusions to Exod. 24.8, Isa. 53.11-12, and Jer. 31.31-34 in Mt. 26.28, see Ham, 'Last Supper', pp. 60-66.

73. Anna Maria Schwemer, 'Jesus Christus als Prophet, König und Priester: Das *munus triplex* und die frühe Christologie', in Martin Hengel and Anna Maria Schwemer (eds.), *Der messianische Anspruch Jesu und die Anfänge der Christologie: vier Studien* (WUNT, 138; Tübingen: Mohr Siebeck, 2001), p. 227; Lindars, *New Testament Apologetic*, pp. 132-34; C.F. Evans, 'I Will Go before You', p. 6. Nonetheless, Mt. 26.28 applies Exod. 24.8 typologically, evidenced in the word 'my', and Exod. 24.8 exerts some influence upon the wording of Mt. 26.28. Cf. Heb. 9.20; 10.29; *1 Clem.* 7.4.

74. N.T. Wright, *Jesus and the Victory of God*, pp. 560-61; C.A. Evans, 'Jesus and Zechariah's Messianic Hope', p. 386.

75. On the citation of Zech. 13.7 in Mt. 26.31, see pp. 69-83, above.

76. Ulrich Luz, *Das Evangelium nach Matthäus* (EKKNT, 1; 3 vols.; Zürich: Benziger, 1985–2000), IV, p. 169.

77. Davies and Allison, *Matthew*, III, p. 516; Carson, *Matthew*, p. 548. Cf. Mt. 22.40. The parallel passage in Mk 14.49 does not contain the clause τοῦτο δὲ ὅλον γέγονεν.

in Mt. 26.56 cannot be confirmed on the basis of volume; however, the criteria of recurrence and thematic coherence establish that Zech. 13.7 can be identified as one of several Old Testament texts fulfilled in events of the Passion Narrative.

The wording 'you will see the Son of Man seated at the right hand of Power and coming on the clouds of heaven' in Mt. 26.64 allegedly alludes to Zech. 12.10, a text discussed under Mt. 24.30 above.[78] Here, however, the only verbal similarity between Zech. 12.10 and Mt. 26.64 is 'they look on' and 'you will see', ἐπιβλέψονται in the LXX and ὄψεσθε in Mt. 26.64.[79] Furthermore, the context of Mt. 26.64 does not contain the same density of language from Zech. 12.10-14 as does Mt. 24.30, specifically the statement 'all the tribes of the earth will mourn', which emphasizes the reaction of universal mourning at the Son of Man's coming. While the history of interpretation has heard allusions to Zech. 12.10 in Mt. 24.30, it generally applies the wording 'they look on the one whom they have pierced' in Zech. 12.10 to the crucifixion of Jesus, rather than the eschatological context envisioned here.[80] In Mt. 26.64, as in Mk 14.62, Jesus' response to the high priest, expressing his expectation concerning his vindication and his role as eschatological judge, probably draws upon a martyrdom tradition and more likely alludes to Ps. 110.1 and Dan. 7.13 than to Zech. 12.10.[81] Therefore, if Mt. 26.64 alludes to Zech. 12.10, it can only do so on account of the recurrence of one expression it shares with Mt. 24.30. When the criteria are applied to the wording and context of Mt. 26.64 itself, any allusion to Zech. 12.10 is effectively inaudible.[82]

Matthew 27.51-53

Some of the wording in Mt. 27.51-53 may allude to Zech. 14.4-5, a text discussed under Mt. 21.1 and 25.31 above.[83] Zechariah 14.4-5 concludes the first of four episodes concerning the coming Day of Yahweh in Zech. 14.1-21. Yahweh will fight against those nations that threaten Jerusalem and will stand on the Mount of Olives, causing it to 'split in two', and thereby creating a valley through which the remaining inhabitants of Jerusalem will escape. The people will flee from Jerusalem, as they 'fled from the earthquake in the days

78. See pp. 95-97, above.

79. On the meaning and use of these verbs in the LXX, see n. 44, above.

80. See Jn 19.37; Rev. 1.7; Justin, *1 Apol.* 52.11; *Dial.* 14; 32; 64; 118; Irenaeus, *Haer.* 4.33.11.

81. Bock, *Blasphemy and Exaltation*, pp. 206-207; Davies and Allison, *Matthew*, III, p. 529; cf. Wis. 5.2; *Apoc. El.* 5.28; *1 En.* 62.5; *Midr. Ps.* 2.9 (on Ps. 2.7).

82. Gundry, *Use of the Old Testament*, p. 60, calls ὄψεσθε 'a faint reflection of Zech. 12.10', but he recognizes the primary allusions to Ps. 110.1 and Dan. 7.13, asserting that Zech. 12.10 is more fully alluded to in Mt. 24.30.

83. See pp. 89-90 and 98-99, above.

of King Uzziah of Judah',[84] and Yahweh will come 'with all the holy ones'. Using some of the traditional biblical descriptions of an apocalyptic eschatology, Mt. 27.51-53 lists several of the astounding phenomena occurring after Jesus' death.[85] At least three of them may relate to Zech. 14.4-5: the earthquake, the 'splitting', and the (re)appearance of the 'holy ones'.[86] Matthew 27.51 mentions the earthquake, which accompanies the tearing of the temple veil, as a sign of divine judgment at the death of Jesus in the simple statement, ἡ γῆ ἐσείσθη, and Mt. 27.54 refers to it again in the phrase, ἰδόντες τὸν σεισμὸν. The LXX of Zech. 14.5 uses the noun σεισμός to translate רַעַשׁ; however, phrases similar to the one in Mt. 27.51, which contain the noun γῆ and the aorist passive ἐσείσθη, appear at other places in the LXX,[87] suggesting that Mt. 27.51 may not draw upon the language of any specific Old Testament text.[88] Moreover, Zech. 14.4 does not record or predict an

---

84.   Amos 1.1 also mentions an earthquake during the reign of Uzziah, and apparently Amos 1.1 and Zech. 14.5 refer to the same earthquake; it is otherwise unknown. Josephus, *Ant.* 9.225, purportedly connects the earthquake in Zech. 14.5 and Amos 1.1 with 2 Chron. 26.16-21, where Uzziah becomes afflicted with a leprous disease since he inappropriately enters the temple to make an offering on the altar of incense. That the book of Amos uses this natural phenomenon to date Amos's prophecy is unusual, according to Meyers and Meyers, *Zechariah 9–14*, p. 427, but it signals the significant and lasting impact of the seismic event, which the prophet likely views as reinforcing his own prophetic message. In general, the biblical text presents the occurrence of an earthquake as a demonstration of divine presence or power (Exod. 19.18; Pss. 68.8; 77.18; 114.7; Isa. 64.2-3), and more often divine judgment (Judg. 5.4; Isa. 5.25; 13.13; 24.18-20; 29.6; Jer. 4.23-24; 10.10; Ezek. 26.18; 38.19-20; Joel 2.10-11; 3.16; Mic. 1.4; Nah. 1.5-6; cf. *T. Levi* 4.1; *1 En.* 1.6-8).

85.   Brown, *Death of the Messiah*, p. 1118. A description similar to Mt. 27.51-53, in which individual couplets implicate the Jews and describe earthly and heavenly phenomena, appears in Melito of Sardis, *On Pascha and Fragments* (trans. Stuart George Hall; OECT; Oxford: Clarendon Press, 1979), p. 98: 'For when the people did not tremble, the earth quaked; when the people were not terrified, the heavens were terrified; when the people did not tear their clothes, the angel tore his; when the people did not lament, *the Lord thundered out of heaven and the Highest gave voice*'. The image of the heavens terrified probably refers to darkness, and torn angel's clothes, to the torn veil. The text is from Melito of Sardis, *On Pascha and Fragments*.

86.   Dale C. Allison, Jr, *The End of the Ages Has Come: An Early Interpretation of the Passion and Resurrection of Jesus* (Philadelphia: Fortress Press, 1985), pp. 40-46, suggests that the combination of these three elements may suggest an allusion to Zech. 14.4-5.

87.   The LXX also translates רַעַשׁ with σεισμός in Job 41.20; Isa. 29.6; Jer. 10.22; 29.3 (47.3 MT); Ezek. 3.12, 13; 37.7; 38.19; Amos 1.1; Nah. 3.2; Zech. 14.5; cf. συσσεισμός in 3 Kgdms 19.11-12 (1 Kgs 19.11-12 MT). Other texts with a phrase similar to ἡ γῆ ἐσείσθη include Judg. 5.4; 2 Kgdms 22.8; Ps. 67.9 (68.9 MT); Jer. 8.16; 28.29 (51.29 MT); 1 Macc. 1.28.

88.   Nevertheless, Gundry, *Matthew*, p. 576, and Donald Senior, 'The Death of Jesus and the Resurrection of the Holy Ones (MT 27.51-53)', *CBQ* 38 (1976), pp. 312-29 (321), propose Ezek. 37.7 as the particular background to the earthquake in Mt. 27.51, even

earthquake but commands a particular action during a future crisis that is comparable to one during a past catastrophe, that is, 'the earthquake in the days of King Uzziah of Judah'. Along with the earthquake, Mt. 27.51 mentions the splitting of rocks, καὶ αἱ πέτραι ἐσχίσθησαν. Zechariah 14.4, where the LXX uses σχίζω to translate בָּקַע, portends the splitting of the Mount of Olives as a way of escape for the inhabitants of Jerusalem, an escape like the exodus through the wind-split sea in Exod. 14.21.[89] The image of splitting rocks is less common in the Old Testament than that of the earthquake, but it has Old Testament roots nonetheless.[90] It seems difficult, however, to align an allusion in Mt. 27.51 with a specific Old Testament text, since the splitting of rocks, like the earthquake, is 'a traditional element in the description of Yahweh's activity at the final time';[91] here the splitting of the rocks connects the earthquake with the resurrection of the saints, a symbolic sign in Mt. 27.52-53 emphasizing the significance of Jesus' death. In general, Mt. 27.52-53 affirms the association of the resurrection of the dead with the Day of Yahweh and the messianic age found in later Jewish writings[92] but already in two Old Testament texts, Ezek. 37.12-13 and Dan. 12.2. While Dan. 12.2 shares a similar syntactical structure with Mt. 27.52,[93]

though σεισμός in Ezek. 37.7 probably does not denote an 'earthquake', according to Walther Zimmerli, *Ezekiel 2: A Commentary on the Book of the Prophet Ezekiel Chapters 25–48* (trans. James D. Martin; ed. Paul D. Hanson and Leonard Jay Greenspoon; Hermeneia (Philadelphia: Fortress Press, 1983), p. 261, and *HALOT*, p. 1272, which suggests the meaning 'rustling' for רַעַשׁ in Ezek. 37.7.

89.   Floyd, *Minor Prophets*, p. 545.

90.   The word σχίζω, when translating בָּקַע, is often used for splitting wood (Gen. 22.3; 1 Kgdms 6.14 [1 Sam. 6.14 MT]; Eccl. 10.9), but it refers to the parting of the wind by a bird's wings in Eccl. 10.9. In Isa. 48.21 (cf. Ps. 114.7-8), the word alludes to the flow of water from the rock (see Exod. 17.1-7). 1 Kgs 19.11 and Nah. 1.5-6 use the imagery of splitting rocks in an eschatological context that includes an earthquake, but with slightly different vocabulary.

91.   Donald Senior, *The Passion Narrative according to Matthew: A Redactional Study* (BETL, 39; Leuven: Leuven University Press, 1975), p. 314. Gundry, *Matthew*, p. 576, suggests that the rocks are derived 'from Matthew's own interest in πέτρα...and especially from his anticipating the rock of Jesus' tomb in v. 60'.

92.   For example, 2 Macc. 7.9; 12.43-44; *1 En.* 91.10; *T. Benj.* 10.7-11; *Pss. Sol.* 3.10-12; *4 Ezra* 7.26-44; for other texts, see Str-B 4.1166-98. One MS of the targum (Cod. Reuchlinianus) interprets Zech. 14.4 as referring to the resurrection by adding these words to the beginning of *Tg.* Zech. 14.4: 'At that time the LORD will take in his hand the great trumpet and will blow ten blasts upon it to revive the dead'. Curtis, 'Mount of Olives', p. 171, connects the crevasse in Zech. 14.4 with the resurrection of Ezek. 37, because of a popular view that the Mount of Olives, as a place sacred to the god of the dead, contains an entrance to the realm of the dead.

93.   Cf. Dan. 12.2, καὶ πολλοὶ τῶν καθευδόντων ἐν γῆς χώματι ἐξεγερθήσονται with Mt. 27.52, καὶ πολλὰ σώματα τῶν κεκοιμημένων ἁγίων ἠγέρθησαν. Matthew

Ezek. 37.12-13 shares with Mt. 27.52-53 precise conceptual parallels relating to the resurrection motif, including the opening of graves and the return of the risen saints to Jerusalem/Israel. Either of these texts, in particular Ezek. 37.12-13, provides a more probable Old Testament source for Matthew;[94] moreover, Mt. 27.52 and Zech. 14.5 have in common only forms of ἅγιος, a word correctly interpreted as ἄγγελοι in Mt. 25.31. Collectively, then, these three apocalyptic signs, the earthquake, the splitting of rocks, and the resurrection of the saints, present a theological understanding of Jesus' death introducing the coming day of Yahweh with its negative and positive effects,[95] but in all likelihood they do not allude to Zech. 14.4-5.

Summary

The NA27, the UBS4, Dittmar, and Davies and Allison list 18 potential allusions to Zechariah in the Gospel of Matthew. Of these, ten cannot be confirmed as intentional allusions, based on the seven methodological criteria for discerning the presence of Old Testament allusions in the New Testament; these texts include all five found in Matthew before the Passion Narrative, Mt. 5.33; 9.4, 36; 11.21-22; 19.26, and five found in Matthew's Passion Narrative and the material directly preceding it, Mt. 21.1, 12; 23.23; 26.64; 27.51-53. Of the eight remaining, the criteria clearly corroborate six allusions, Mt. 23.35; 24.30, 31; 25.31; 26.15; 26.28, and probably substantiate two more, Mt. 24.36; 26.56.

These eight allusions occur between Mt. 21.5 and 27.9-10, the first and last citations being from Zechariah. One of them, Mt. 26.15, relates directly to the citation of Zech. 11.12-13 in Mt. 27.9-10, using some of the same language found therein. Another, Mt. 26.56, refers to the citation of Zech. 13.7 in Mt. 26.31, even if the introductory formula used in this text does not cite any specific Old Testament text and certainly envisions additional Old Testament texts as 'fulfilled' in the events of the Passion Narrative. Still another, Mt. 23.35, does not relate to a specific text in Zechariah but alludes generally to the prophet Zechariah, since Matthew conflates this Zechariah with Zechariah the son of Jehoiada (2 Chron. 24.20-22) in anticipation of Jesus' own violent death. Also, the allusion to Zech. 9.11 in Mt. 26.28 evokes the bloody death of Jesus the shepherd, by whose death the covenant is established in the context of messianic victory.

---

more characteristically uses οἱ προφῆται or οἱ δίκαιοι than οἱ ἅγιοι for exemplary characters from Israel's past (Mt. 5.12; 9.13; 10.41; 13.17; 23.29, 30, 31, 34, 35, 37).

94. Senior, *Passion Narrative according to Matthew*, p. 320; Gundry, *Matthew*, p. 576; France, *Matthew*, pp. 400-401. On Mt. 25.31, see pp. 98-99, above.

95. Brown, *Death of the Messiah*, p. 1137.

Three of the allusions occur within a limited context of the Olivet Discourse; these allusions in Mt. 24.30-36 reflect an eschatological use of material from Zechariah, rather than merely the messianic use presented in the three explicit citations. Specifically, Mt. 24.30 alludes to Zech. 12.10-14, describing the reaction of universal mourning at the Son of Man's coming and, to a lesser degree, implicitly identifying Jesus with the one pierced in Zech. 12.10. Matthew 24.31 alludes to Zech. 2.6, a unique use of material from Zechariah 1–8 in Matthew, in order to signify the universal regathering of the elect. Matthew 24.36 alludes to Zech. 14.7, emphasizing the chronological arrival of the day of the LORD, which Matthew identifies as the Parousia, and the lack of knowledge of its timing by anyone, except the Father. Yet another eschatological use is the allusion to Zech. 14.5 in Mt. 25.31, where the expectation of the coming of Yahweh 'and all the holy ones with him' is transferred without hesitation to a depiction of Jesus as the Son of Man coming at the Parousia.

3

THE THEOLOGICAL USE OF ZECHARIAH
IN MATTHEW'S GOSPEL

The previous two chapters have examined in detail three citations from Zechariah and have identified eight allusions to Zechariah (see Table 1 below).

Table 1. *Citations from and Allusions to Zechariah in Matthew's Gospel*

Matthew	Zechariah	Citation or Allusion
21.5	9.9	'Look, your king is coming to you...'
23.35	1.1	The blood of Zechariah son of Barachiah
24.30	12.10-14	The universal mourning of all nations of the earth
24.31	2.6	The universal gathering of the elect
24.36	14.7	The chronological arrival of the day of the Lord
25.31	14.5	The coming of the Son of Man with all the holy ones
26.15	11.12	The thirty pieces of silver
26.28	9.11	The blood of the covenant
26.31	13.7	'I will strike the shepherd...'
26.56	13.7	The desertion of Jesus by all the disciples
27.9-10	11.12-13	'And they took the thirty pieces of silver...'

These eight allusions occur between the first and last citations in Mt. 21.5 and 27.9-10, and, taken together, the three citations and the eight allusions indicate that the theology of Zechariah has influenced the theology of Matthew.[1] This chapter describes the thematic and theological function of Matthew's use of Zechariah. Through a literary and exegetical analysis of themes derived from and related to the material from Zechariah, the chapter describes how Matthew has used Zechariah in the portrayal of Jesus and his mission. In several instances, Jesus' actions and words correspond with important themes in Zechariah, namely, the presentation of the Davidic king and the rejection of the divinely appointed shepherd. Together these themes portray Zechariah's predominant messianic image, the shepherd-king, an image which is most

---

1. C.A. Evans, 'Jesus and Zechariah's Messianic Hope', p. 386; van Tilborg, 'Matthew 27.3-10', p. 161.

influential on the use of Zechariah in the Gospels in general[2] and in Matthew in particular. Of special interest for this study, then, is the Gospel of Matthew's presentation of Jesus as coming king and rejected shepherd.

Coming King

The Greek word for 'king', βασιλεύς, occurs 22 times in Matthew. It refers to kings in general (Mt. 10.18; 11.8; 17.25) and identifies several specific rulers, including David (Mt. 1.6), Herod the Great (Mt. 2.1, 3, 9), and Herod Antipas (Mt. 14.9). In these instances, βασιλεύς denotes 'one who rules as possessor of the highest office in a political realm', but by extension the word may also indicate 'one who possesses unusual or transcendent power'.[3] In this sense, 'king' is also applied to God or Jesus. Seven times in Matthew βασιλεύς names God, albeit indirectly. One of these occurs within the designation for Jerusalem, 'the city of the great King' (Mt. 5.35), a phrase that alludes to Ps. 48.2 (48.3 MT). Six of these are in the parable of the unmerciful servant (Mt. 18.23) and the parable of the wedding banquet (Mt. 22.2, 7, 11, 13) in which the king stands for God.[4] The remaining eight occurrences of βασιλεύς in Matthew denote Jesus as messianic king (Mt. 2.2; 21.5; 25.34, 40; 27.11, 29, 37, 42).

Sometime after the birth of Jesus, wise men or magi (μάγοι)[5] come to Jerusalem. In Mt. 2.2, the magi inquire of Herod the Great where they might find 'the child who has been born king of the Jews'. Herod becomes frightened at their request, and he asks the chief priests and scribes about the birthplace of the Messiah (χριστός). In Mt. 2.6, they identify Bethlehem as the Messiah's

2. Bruce, *New Testament Development of Old Testament Themes*, p. 347; cf. Lamarche, *Zacharie IX–XIV*, pp. 114-23.

3. BDAG, p. 169.

4. Craig L. Blomberg, *Matthew* (NAC, 22; Nashville: Broadman, 1992), pp. 282-83, 326; Robert W. Funk, Roy W. Hoover and the Jesus Seminar, *The Five Gospels: The Search for the Authentic Words of Jesus* (San Francisco: Harper & Row, 1993), pp. 218, 235. For a lengthy list of later rabbinic parables in which 'king' stands for God, see Keener, *Matthew*, p. 457 n. 34.

5. The readers of Matthew's Gospel would not have understood the magi as kings, according to Mark Allan Powell, 'The Magi as Kings: An Adventure in Reader-Response Criticism', *CBQ* 62 (2000), pp. 459-73. Gerhard Delling, 'μάγος', in *TDNT*, IV, pp. 356-59 (356-57), has identified four meanings of μάγος in the ancient Near East: a Persian priest, a person who possesses supernatural knowledge or ability (such as interpreting dreams), a magician, or a deceiver (e.g. Josephus, *Ant.* 20.142). According to Brown, *Birth of the Messiah*, p. 167, and Delling, 'μάγος', p. 358, μάγοι in Mt. 2.1, 7, 16 designates Persian priests, who were experts in astrology, interpreted dreams and other special signs, and engaged in various occult arts; cf. the use of the word μάγος in Dan. 1.20; 2.2, 27; 4.4 (4.7 LXX); 5.7, 15; Josephus, *Ant.* 10.216. On the expectation for a world-ruler who would come from Judea, see Suetonius, *Vesp.* 4; Tacitus, *Hist.* 5.13.

birthplace according to the prophecy in Mic. 5.2, a citation, as it appears in Matthew, which also draws upon the description of David as shepherd of Israel in 2 Sam. 5.2: 'And you, Bethlehem, in the land of Judah, are by no means least among the rulers of Judah; for from you shall come a ruler who is to shepherd my people Israel'.

Specifically, Matthew's citation uses the words 'ruler' (ἡγέομαι), and 'shepherd' (ποιμάνω)[6] from 2 Sam. 5.2 in the LXX. The first of these also appears in the citation in a form of its corresponding noun, ἡγεμών, a noun appearing ten times in Matthew, eight of which refer to Pilate as 'governor' (Mt. 27.2, 11, 11, 14, 15, 21, 27; 28.14). In these instances and in Mt. 10.18, the word represents the Greek equivalent of the Latin term *praefectus*, that is, 'a person who ruled over a minor Roman province'.[7] In Mt. 2.6, however, ἡγεμόσιν appears as 'a personification of the cities of Judah in the persons of the clan heads',[8] and it anticipates the corresponding verb ἡγούμενος in the next line that refers to Jesus.[9] Thus, Matthew's citation from Mic. 5.2, which draws on the wording of 2 Sam. 5.2, 'makes clearer the status of Jesus as son of David, born in the city of David, to rule like David over the people of God'.[10]

From an exegetical perspective, Mt. 2.1-6 clearly connects several titles for Jesus, namely, 'king' (βασιλεύς), 'messiah' (χριστός), 'ruler' (ἡγούμενος), and 'shepherd' (ποιμήν). Herod understands the terms 'king of the Jews' and 'Messiah' with political overtones, but Matthew has qualified these titles by referring to 2 Sam. 5.2, which describes the anointing of David as 'shepherd' and 'ruler' over Israel.[11] From a literary perspective, the passage presents

6. The image of Jesus as shepherd is discussed below, pp. 115-20.

7. L&N, I, p. 482; Everett Ferguson, *Backgrounds of Early Christianity* (Grand Rapids: Eerdmans, 2nd edn, 1993), p. 42; cf. Josephus, *Ant.* 18.55. Other provincial governors called ἡγεμών in the New Testament include Felix (Acts 23.22, 24, 26; 24.1, 10) and Festus (Acts 26.30). The title 'prefect of Judea' for Pontius Pilate is confirmed by the inscription described in Jerry Vardaman, 'A New Inscription which Mentions Pilate as "Prefect"', *JBL* 81 (1962), pp. 70-71. According to L&N, I, p. 479, ἡγεμών may also designate 'one who rules, with the implication of preeminent position'; cf. Josephus, *Ant.* 19.217, where the word is used to mean 'emperor'.

8. Gundry, *Use of the Old Testament*, p. 92.

9. In the LXX, forms of ἡγέομαι refer to tribal chiefs (Deut. 5.23; 2 Chron. 5.2), kings, for example, David (1 Sam. 25.30), Solomon (2 Chron. 9.26), and Jehu (1 Kgs 16.2), or military leaders (Jdt 5.3). In 1 Sam. 15.17, ἡγούμενος is equated with βασιλεὺς. On the uses of ἡγέομαι for leaders of various types and levels, see Spicq, 'ἡγούμενος', in *TLNT*, II, pp. 166-70.

10. France, *Matthew*, p. 84. The title 'king' is earlier associated with David in Mt. 1.6.

11. According to Jack Dean Kingsbury, *Matthew: Structure, Christology, Kingdom* (Philadelphia: Fortress Press, 2nd edn, 1988), pp. 97-98, Matthew characteristically qualifies the title 'Messiah' with the term 'Son of God'; cf. Mt. 16.16; 26.63. On the Old Testament background of the title 'Son of God' and its relationship to 'King' and 'Messiah',

some significant contrasts. While the Gentile magi look for the child born king of the Jews to worship him, King Herod seeks to destroy Jesus;[12] Herod, then, is the first of several Jewish leaders to reject Jesus in Matthew (see Mt. 26.65; 27.1, 25). While Herod is king over Judea, Jesus is recognized by the magi as King of the Jews, and, after the magi worship Jesus, Herod is never called 'king' again in Matthew (Mt. 2.12-22).[13] While later in Matthew's narrative Pilate is ruler over Palestine, Jesus is here recognized by Matthew as the Davidic ruler who shepherds the people of Israel.

The way in which the magi refer to Jesus anticipates the reoccurrence of the phrases, 'the king of the Jews' and 'the king of Israel', in the accounts of Jesus' interrogation, mockery, and crucifixion. In Mt. 27.11, Pilate asks Jesus if he is 'the King of the Jews'. These words indicate Pilate's understanding that the accusation by the Jewish leaders against Jesus' claim to be the Messiah (cf. Mt. 27.17, 22) carries political overtones.[14] Jesus' response, σὺ λέγεις, has the sense 'the words are yours', as rendered in the NEB, suggesting that the Gentile Pilate has unwittingly acknowledged the kingship of Jesus, even as the Gentile magi have done earlier in Mt. 2.1-12.[15] After Pilate's interrogation of Jesus, Pilate's soldiers dress Jesus in a scarlet robe, put on his head a crown of twisted thorns, and place in his right hand a reed.[16] In Mt. 27.29, the soldiers kneel before Jesus, saying, 'Hail, King of the Jews'.[17] Thus, the soldiers feign adoration and thereby allege Jesus' kingship

see Harmut Gese, *Essays on Biblical Theology* (trans. Keith Crum; Minneapolis: Augsburg Press, 1981), pp. 142-51.

12. In Mt. 2.1-18, two programmatic statements are signaled by the ironic use of 'king of the Jews': the Jews reject Jesus' kingship, while non-Jews accept him, and Jesus is labeled 'king of the Jews' in contexts of dishonor and execution, according to Bruce Malina and Jerome H. Neyrey, *Calling Jesus Names: The Social Value of Labels in Matthew* (Sonoma, CA: Polebridge, 1988), p. 115.

13. Brian M. Nolan, *The Royal Son of God: The Christology of Matthew 1–2 in the Setting of the Gospel* (OBO, 23; Fribourg Suisse: Éditions Universitaires, 1982–92), p. 39.

14. Darrell L. Bock, *Jesus according to Scripture: Restoring the Portrait from the Gospels* (Downers Grove, IL: Intervarsity Press, 2002), p. 596.

15. Blomberg, *Matthew*, p. 410.

16. Only Matthew mentions that the soldiers 'put a reed in his right hand', an action which Swartley, *Israel's Scripture Traditions*, p. 218, understands as 'a parody of the royal scepter (Gen. 49.10)'. The word κάλαμος appears 5x in Matthew. It refers to either a tall grass (e.g. Mt. 11.7; 12.20; cf. 3 Kgdms 14.15; Job 40.21; Isa. 35.7; 42.3; *3 Macc.* 2.22) or a stalk (e.g. Mt. 27.29-30; 27.48; cf. 4 Kgdms 18.21; Josephus, *Ant.* 10.7). In the LXX, the word often refers to a 'measuring reed', for example, Ezek. 40.3, 5, 6, 7, 8; 41.8; 42.12, 16, 17, 18; 42.20; cf. Rev. 11.1.

17. Even though the variant reading ὁ βασιλεὺς is supported by MSS ℵ, A, L, W, *f*[13], 33, and 𝔐, the voc. sg. form, βασιλεῦ, supported by MSS B, D, Δ, Θ, 0250, 0281, *f*[1], and *al*, should be favored on intrinsic probabilities. Leopold Sabourin, *The Gospel according*

through their mockery.[18] In Mt. 27.37, the charge written against Jesus, 'This is Jesus, the King of the Jews', recalls Pilate's question to Jesus in Mt. 27.11 and the soldier's ridicule in Mt. 27.29.[19] The wording of the charge, which 'makes no sense apart from the presence of royal messianic sayings and actions',[20] characterizes Jesus as a political figure and undoubtedly offends the Jews who demand that Pilate crucify Jesus (cf. Jn 19.21), but the wording also ironically expresses to the readers of Matthew the truth of Jesus' kingship. While Jesus is crucified, three groups deride him: the passersby, the Jewish leaders, and the two bandits. While both the passersby and the Jewish leaders sarcastically challenge Jesus to save himself, the Jewish leaders, including the chief priests, scribes, and elders,[21] mock[22] Jesus, calling him 'King of Israel' and 'God's son'. For the fourth time in the chapter (Mt. 27.11, 29, 37, 42), Jesus is called 'king', but this time, 'King of Israel' rather than 'King of the Jews', since the mockery is spoken by Jews and not Gentiles (cf. Zeph. 3.15; Jn 12.13). The contempt expressed in their taunt for God to deliver Jesus as 'God's son' alludes to Ps. 22.8 and Wis. 2.20 and reflects

to St Matthew (Bandra, Bombay: St Paul, 1982), p. 907, compares the entire episode to a 'coronation parody, involving investiture, crowning, homage, and acclamation'.

18. In the words of Malina and Neyrey, *Calling Jesus Names*, p. 118: 'when non-Jews acclaim Jesus as king in the Passion Narrative, albeit ironically and sarcastically, this label is intended by the evangelist to be taken literally and seriously'.

19. Both Mk 15.26 and Lk. 23.38 refer to the written notice as an 'inscription', ἐπιγραφή, but Mark expands the phrase to ἡ ἐπιγραφὴ τῆς αἰτίας, 'the inscription of the charge'. Jn 19.19 refers to it by its Latin name, since the Greek τίτλος comes from the Latin *titulus*. Typically a condemned person would carry such a placard on the way to the place of death; however, here the written charge is placed on the cross. Suetonius, *Cal.* 32, mentions the practice of a condemned person carrying a placard as he illustrates the cruelty of Caligula: 'at a public dinner in the City he sent to his executioners a slave who had stolen a strip of silver from a couch; they were to lop off the man's hands, tie them around his neck so that they hung on his breast, and take him for a tour of the tables, displaying a placard [*titulo*] in explanation of his punishment'. The citation is from Gaius Suetonius Tranquillus, *The Twelve Caesars* (trans. Robert Graves; Baltimore: Penguin Books, 1957), p. 165. See also Suetonius, *Dom.* 10, where Domitian places a placard [*titulo*] around the neck of a Thracian supporter. Eusebius, *Hist. eccl.* 5.1.44, relates an account of one Attalus who was martyred under Marcus Aurelius; in the amphitheater a placard (πίνακος) was carried before him which read, 'This is Attalus, the Christian'. On the authenticity of the wording of the inscription, see Ernst Bammel, 'The *Titulus*', in Ernst Bammel and C.F.D. Moule (eds.), *Jesus and the Politics of His Day* (New York: Cambridge University Press, 1984), pp. 353-64 (363).

20. C.A. Evans, 'Jesus and Zechariah', p. 387.

21. This full listing of Jewish leaders 'serves to underline the total rejection of Jesus by official Judaism', according to France, *Matthew*, p. 397; cf. Mt. 26.57.

22. According to L&N, I, p. 435, ἐμπαίζω means 'to make fun of someone by pretending that he is not what he is or by imitating him in a distorted manner'. It occurs 5x in Matthew (2.16; 20.19; 27.29, 31, 41).

Matthew's emphasis on Jesus' identity as Son of God.[23] Thus, the four times in Mt. 27 that Jesus is called 'King of the Jews/Israel' in the context of dishonor and execution ironically assert Jesus' true identity.[24]

While the title 'king' appears in the negative context of dishonor in Matthew 27, in Mt. 21.1-12 the term appears in the positive context of humility. The portrayal of Jesus as king at his entry into Jerusalem is qualified by Matthew's citation of Zech. 9.9.[25] While Jesus enters Jerusalem to public acclaim (Mt. 21.8-11), he does so as a king, 'humble, and mounted on a donkey' (Mt. 21.5).[26] This 'demeaned status'[27] is further emphasized in Matthew's omission of 'triumphant and victorious' from Zech. 9.9. In this way, Matthew has unequivocally repudiated any undue nationalistic expectations surrounding Jesus' entry into Jerusalem, particularly any expectations that Jesus as the Davidic Messiah would forcefully free Judea by the military conquest of the political enemies of the Jews.[28] Rather, Matthew's citation directs the reader to the context of Zechariah 9, in which Yahweh, rather than the king, conquers Israel's enemies.[29] In Zech. 9.9, the king, who is fully qualified to assume the Davidic throne and has received deliverance without military means, enters Jerusalem for the purpose of bringing peace and salvation to all nations (Zech. 9.10). The king rides into Jerusalem on a donkey, portraying the king's legitimate reign (cf. Gen. 49.10-11); so too Jesus rides into Jerusalem on a donkey as the legitimate heir of David, a theme reinforced by the cheers of the crowd in Mt. 21.9: 'Hosanna to the son of David'.[30] Therefore,

23. Davies and Allison, *Matthew*, III, p. 620. Kingsbury, *Matthew*, pp. 77-78; *idem*, 'The Composition and Christology of Mt. 28.6-20', *JBL* 93 (1974), pp. 580-84, contends that 'Son of God' ranks foremost among the christological titles in Matthew.

24. Malina and Neyrey, *Calling Jesus Names*, p. 117.

25. On the citation of Zech. 9.9 in Mt. 21.5, see pp. 20-47, above.

26. On the use of πραΰς in Matthew, see p. 41, above. Deirdre J. Good, *Jesus the Meek King* (Harrisburg, PA: Trinity Press International, 1999), pp. 61-93, argues, on the basis of Mt. 21.5, *Gosp. Thom.* 90, and *Sib. Or.* 8.324-38, that Mt. 11.29-30, in addition to Mt. 21.5, portrays Jesus as a humble king.

27. Malina and Neyrey, *Calling Jesus Names*, p. 117.

28. Swartley, *Israel's Scripture Traditions*, p. 225.

29. Duguid, 'Messianic Themes in Zechariah 9–14', p. 168, correctly comments: 'The warlike language is still present in Zechariah 9, but it has been transferred from the royal figure to the Lord himself'. Mason, 'Relation of Zech. 9–14 to Proto-Zechariah', p. 237, says that the coming king in Zech. 9.9 is 'a figure far more akin to the Suffering Servant than the Warrior King'.

30. A rabbinic tradition found in one of the Middle Age Midrashim (*Eccl. Rab.* 1.9 §1) draws a parallel between Exod. 4.20, where Moses takes his family and puts them on a donkey, and Zech. 9.9. Thus, according to Dale C. Allison, Jr, *The New Moses: A Matthean Typology* (Minneapolis: Fortress Press, 1993), p. 249, one could also 'interpret the fulfillment of Zechariah's oracle as establishing Jesus' status as Mosaic Messiah'.

Mt. 21.5 makes positive use of the title 'king' to counter any political mis-understandings and to label Jesus as a humble king in the line of David.[31]

Two other occurrences of βασιλεύς which denote Jesus as king appear in the story of the sheep and goats in Mt. 25.31-46. The story initially mentions the coming of 'the Son of Man', but then the story compares his actions to a shepherd who separates sheep from goats and later refers to him twice as 'the king' (Mt. 25.34, 40). In the manner that Matthew records the story, these terms, 'Son of Man' and 'king', refer to Jesus, since the first person pronouns (Mt. 25.34, 35, 36, 40, 41, 42, 43, 45) and second person pronouns (Mt. 25.37, 38, 39, 44) clearly identify the story's speaker with the Son of Man and the king. Indeed, the king in the story does not represent God the Father, since the king calls God, 'my Father' (Mt. 25.34).[32] In this way, the story discloses how Matthew may envisage that Jesus the humble king relates to God the Father as a client king, one who confers the blessings of the kingdom upon his subjects;[33] that is, the king directs to his right[34] the heirs who inherit the kingdom, which is itself, in the language of Matthew, 'the kingdom of heaven'.[35] Even so, Jesus assumes the role of eschatological judge, a role normally reserved for God alone but one now transferred to Jesus.[36] Such a transfer is also evident in the allusion of Mt. 25.31 to Zech. 14.5, which describes the coming of Yahweh with all the holy ones to intervene against the enemies of Jerusalem and provide an escape for the inhabitants of the city.[37] Here the one who comes with all the angels is Jesus, the apocalyptic Son of Man, who judges 'all nations at the end of time in the same way as a king presides over his court'.[38]

---

31. Kingsbury, *Matthew*, pp. 98-99.

32. David C. Sim, *Apocalyptic Eschatology in the Gospel of Matthew* (SNTSMS, 88; Cambridge: Cambridge University Press, 1996), p. 125. According to Gundry, *Matthew*, p. 512, Matthew distinctively ascribes the kingdom to the Son of Man on the basis that Jesus is God and the Son of Man; therefore, Jesus 'is the king in the kingdom of heaven just as much as the Father is—1.23; 13.41; 16.28; 20.21'.

33. Good, *Jesus the Meek King*, p. 91; cf. Col. 1.13: 'the kingdom of his beloved Son'.

34. On the metaphorical use of right and left in Jewish and Christian literature, see J.M. Court, 'Right and Left: The Implications for Matthew 25.31-46', *NTS* 31 (1985), pp. 223-33.

35. Mt. 3.2; 4.17; 5.3, 10, 19, 20; 7.21; 8.11; 10.7; 11.11, 12; 13.11, 24, 31, 33, 44, 45, 47, 52; 16.19; 18.1, 3, 4, 23; 19.12, 14, 23; 20.1; 22.2; 23.13; 25.1.

36. Even though final judgment is normally reserved for God alone, some Jewish texts expect that others may also fill the role of final judge (see Dan. 7.13-14; 11QMelch [= 11Q13] II, 13; 1 *En.* 9.4; 47.3; 60.2; 62.2-3; *T. Ab.* 13.1-14A; 11.1-10B).

37. On the allusion to Zech. 14.5 in Mt. 25.31, see pp. 98-99, above.

38. Kingsbury, *Matthew*, p. 99. In addition, Davies and Allison, *Matthew*, III, p. 424, suggests that the title 'king' in Mt. 25.34, 40 recalls Jesus' status as Son of David in Mt. 2.2; 21.5 and anticipates the irony of the those who call Jesus 'the King of the Jews' in Mt. 27.11, 29, 37, and 'the King of Israel' in Mt. 27.42.

The eight occurrences of βασιλεύς demonstrate that the kingship of Jesus is important for Matthew's Christology. The title appears first in the context of the magi's search for the child born king of the Jews (Mt. 2.2), but it does not occur again until Jesus enters Jerusalem as the humble king mounted upon a donkey (Mt. 21.5). Toward the end of the Olivet Discourse, Jesus tells the story of the sheep and goats, in which the Son of Man comes with all the angels to judge all nations as a king presides over his court (Mt. 25.34, 40). During the interrogation and crucifixion, Jesus is called 'king' four times (Mt. 27.11, 29, 37, 42), a mockery which ironically asserts the kingship of Jesus. In this way, Matthew's Gospel, perhaps more explicitly than the other Synoptic Gospels, develops the nature of Jesus' kingship,[39] but Matthew does so in a way which emphasizes the humility of the Davidic king, whose 'enthronement must await his return'.[40]

In this regard, three additional allusions to Zechariah may relate to Matthew's portrayal of Jesus as the humble king who awaits enthronement. Matthew 24.30 alludes to Zech. 12.10-14 and depicts the reaction of universal mourning at the Son of Man's coming; the nations mourn, since they realize that they have rejected Jesus Christ, who is now their judge.[41] Matthew 24.31 alludes to Zech. 2.11 (2.15 MT) and describes the universal regathering of the elect, a designation in Matthew that includes those beyond the boundaries of Israel (Mt. 8.11-12; 22.14; 24.22, 24).[42] In Zech. 2.11 (2.15 MT), Yahweh calls for the return of the exiles scattered among the nations; in Mt. 24.31, the Son of Man sends the angels to gather the elect from the four winds. Here the Son of Man assumes the role of Yahweh in gathering the nations, an action which parallels the Son of Man's assuming the role of Yahweh as eschatological judge in Mt. 25.34. Finally, Mt. 24.36 alludes to Zech. 14.7 and identifies the coming day of Yahweh as the Parousia, a day whose arrival is known only by Yahweh.[43] Thus, Matthew reminds the reader that the enthronement of the humble king in the line of David comes at a time unknown to the king himself.

---

39. Swartley, *Israel's Scripture Traditions*, p. 217.
40. Donald Verseput, *The Rejection of the Humble Messianic King: A Study of the Composition of Matthew 11–12* (EurUS, 23; Theology, 291; Frankfurt: Peter Lang, 1986), p. 305.
41. On the allusion to Zech. 12.10-14 in Mt. 24.30, see pp. 94-96, above. The allusion in Mt. 24.30 may also implicitly identify Jesus with the one pierced in Zech. 12.10, if the text is read in conjunction with Mt. 26.31, where Jesus the shepherd dies by the sword; however, Matthew does not appropriate the image of mourning for an only child in Zech. 12.10.
42. On the allusion to Zech. 2.11 (MT 2.15) in Mt. 24.31, see pp. 96-97, above.
43. On the allusion to Zech. 14.7 in Mt. 24.36, see pp. 97-98, above.

Rejected Shepherd

The Greek noun for 'shepherd', ποιμήν, occurs three times in Matthew, and the Greek verb, ποιμαίνω, meaning 'to shepherd', occurs once. While the Gospel of Luke uses ποιμήν for those who herd sheep (Lk. 2.8, 15, 20, 28), Matthew uses only the metaphorical connotation of the term for one who protects or leads people.[44] In general, the shepherd metaphor in the New Testament may refer to three categories of people: leaders of the Jewish people (Mt. 9.36), Jesus as the messianic shepherd (Mt. 26.31; Jn 10.11, 14, 16; Heb. 13.20; 1 Pet. 2.25; Rev. 7.17; cf. Ignatius, *Rom.* 9.1), and leaders of a Christian congregation (Eph. 4.11; cf. Ignatius, *Phld.* 2.1).[45] Of these, Matthew clearly uses the first and second categories, but not the third.[46] More specifically, Joachim Jeremias has identified three ways in which the Synoptic Gospels use the shepherd metaphor: to describe Jesus' mission to gather the scattered flock (Mt. 10.6; 15.24), to intimate Jesus' death (and return) to the disciples (Mt. 26.31-32), and to illustrate Jesus' role as eschatological judge (Mt. 25.32).[47] These three uses are evidenced by Matthew in the four texts which use ποιμήν and ποιμαίνω: Mt. 2.6; 9.36; 25.32; 26.31.

Matthew's first clear reference to the shepherd metaphor is in Mt. 2.6.[48] When the magi inquire of Herod where they might find 'the child who has

44. The frequency with which the shepherd and sheep metaphor appears in the Bible 'grows out of two phenomena—the importance of sheep to the nomadic and agricultural life of the Hebrews, and the qualities of sheep and shepherds that made them particularly apt sources of metaphor for spiritual realities', according to Leland Ryken, James C. Wilhoit and Tremper Longman, III (eds.), *Dictionary of Biblical Imagery* (Downers Grove, IL: Intervarsity Press, 1998), p. 782. In the Old Testament, writes I.M. Duguid, *Ezekiel and the Leaders of Israel* (VTSup, 56; Leiden: E.J. Brill, 1994), pp. 39-40, 'shepherd' invariably denotes either Yahweh or 'some kind of earthly ruler, though not necessarily a king'. More specifically, J.G. Thomson, 'The Shepherd-Ruler Concept in the Old Testament and its Application in the New Testament', *SJT* 8 (1955), pp. 406-12, has categorized the use of the word רעה, 'shepherd', in the Old Testament; it appears as a designation for Yahweh (Gen. 48.15; 49.24; Pss. 23.1; 80.1; Isa. 40.11), for national leaders in Israel (Num. 27.17; 2 Sam. 7.7), for nobility in Israel (Jer. 2.8; 23.1-2; 25.34-36), for Gentile military commanders (Isa. 44.28; Mic. 5.5-6; Nah. 3.18), and for the Messiah (Ezek. 34.23-24; 37.24-25).

45. Thomson, 'Shepherd-Ruler Concept', pp. 412-18.

46. When Jesus commissions his disciples to go 'to the lost sheep of the house of Israel' (Mt. 10.6; cf. 15.24; 18.12-14), the disciples are implicitly 'shepherds'; however, Jesus sends them out, with a different orientation of the imagery, not as 'shepherds', but 'like sheep into the midst of wolves' (Mt. 10.16; cf. Mt. 7.15). Cf. the mixed metaphor in Rev. 7.17, which portrays 'the Lamb' as 'shepherd'. Cf. also *1 En.* 89.45-46.

47. Jeremias, 'ποιμήν', pp. 492-93. Wilfred Tooley, 'The Shepherd and Sheep Image in the Teaching of Jesus', *New Testament* 7 (1964), pp. 15-25 (24), asserts that, of the three categories proposed by Jeremias, the mission of Jesus has the best authenticated texts.

48. See pp. 107-14, above, for discussion of the use of 'king' in Mt. 2.1-6.

been born king of the Jews' (Mt. 2.2), Herod consults all the chief priests and scribes about the birthplace of the Messiah. The response given by the chief priests and scribes locates the Messiah's birthplace in Bethlehem according to the prophecy in Mic. 5.2, but the citation, as it appears in Mt. 2.6, also draws upon the description of David as shepherd of Israel in 2 Sam. 5.2. In the context of Mic. 5.2, the ruler of Israel is described as one who will 'shepherd his flock' (Mic. 5.4). In 2 Sam. 5.2, David is described as 'king' and 'shepherd'; the term 'ruler' (נָגִיד) in 2 Sam. 5.2 clearly parallels the three occurrences of 'king' (מֶלֶךְ) in 2 Sam. 5.3. This change in imagery from 'king' to 'shepherd' is certainly not surprising, since kings in the ancient Near East are often portrayed as shepherds of the people.[49] Although 1 Kgs 22.17 extends the image of shepherd generally to other Israelite kings, David is the only Israelite king to whom the verb 'shepherd' explicitly refers (2 Sam. 5.2)[50] and is par excellence the shepherd of Israel (Ps. 78.70-72). An additional association between Jesus and David is evoked by the town of Bethlehem, since Bethlehem is the location of David's first appearance when he is anointed as king of Israel by Samuel (1 Sam. 16.1-11).[51] So too, in the narrative of Matthew, Jesus appears first when he is born in Bethlehem (Mt. 2.1). From the prophetic vision of Mic. 5.2 and the narrative description of 2 Sam. 5.2 arises the expectation of a future Davidic leader from Bethlehem who shepherds the people of Israel. Therefore, the composite citation of these two texts, Mic. 5.2 and 2 Sam. 5.2, in Mt. 2.1-6 implies that Jesus comes as God's messianic shepherd who shepherds God's people.[52]

Matthew's second use of the shepherd metaphor occurs in Mt. 9.35-38, a general introduction to the mission of the twelve in Matthew 10. The text is composed of a summary and a saying. The summary, Mt. 9.35-36, describes Jesus' journey through the cities and villages, his ministry of teaching, preaching, and healing, and his compassion for the crowds, 'because they were harassed and helpless, like sheep without a shepherd'. The saying, Mt. 9.37-38, envisions the readiness of people to respond to the good news of the

49. See Jeremias, 'ποιμήν', pp. 486-87; Baldwin, *Haggai, Zechariah, Malachi*, p. 171; and Bruce, *New Testament Development of Old Testament Themes*, p. 100, for examples from Assyria, Babylonia, Canaan, Egypt, and Sumeria.

50. The words of Jeremias, 'ποιμήν', p. 488, are surprising but true: there is 'no single instance in the Old Testament of "shepherd" ever being used in Israel as a title for the ruling king'.

51. Francis Martin, 'The Image of Shepherd in the Gospel of Saint Matthew', *ScEs* 27 (1975), pp. 261-301 (273).

52. Swartley, *Israel's Scripture Traditions*, p. 224. Heil, 'Ezekiel 34', p. 700, notes that in Mt. 1–2 the word λαός, 'people', intimates that, in contrast to the present leaders of Jerusalem, that is, 'all the chief priests and scribes of the *people*' (Mt. 2.4), Jesus is presented as the shepherd of God's '*people* Israel' (Mt. 2.6) who saves 'his *people* from their sins' (Mt. 1.21) (emphasis added).

kingdom and the need for the disciples, whom Jesus is sending out, to proclaim that good news. Of specific importance for the shepherd image in
Matthew is the expression 'like sheep without a shepherd' in Mt. 9.36. This
Old Testament metaphor, which more nearly approximates either Num.
27.17, 1 Kgs 22.17, or 2 Chron. 18.16 than Zech. 10.2,[53] connotes a lack of
political leadership or a lack of spiritual guidance. Moreover, both Ezekiel
and Jeremiah denounce wicked rulers as bad shepherds (Jer. 25.34-38; Ezek.
34.7-10) and look forward to a faithful shepherd, a future prince in the line of
David (Jer. 23.4-6; Ezek. 34.23-24). In this way, the metaphor is a stinging
rebuke against the Jewish leaders who have failed to shepherd God's people
Israel and an implication that Jesus is the Davidic messianic shepherd sent by
God. The expression 'like sheep without a shepherd' also shares verbal and
conceptual similarities with Ezek. 34.5. However, in contrast to Ezek. 34.4,
which castigates the shepherds of Israel for not healing the sick nor binding
up the injured,[54] Mt. 9.35 presents Jesus as 'curing every disease and every
sickness'. Jesus' healing of the demoniac (Mt. 9.32-33) confirms Jesus as the
shepherd of God's people in spite of the Pharisees' objection that Jesus casts
out demons by the ruler of the demons (Mt. 9.34). The healing of the
demoniac, then, exemplifies Jesus' fulfillment of the responsibility that the
Jewish leaders have neglected, that is, the responsibility of the messianic
shepherd to heal the people and to gather 'the lost sheep of the house of
Israel' (Mt. 10.6; 15.24; cf. Mt. 18.12-14).[55]

The third occurrence of the shepherd metaphor appears in the story of the
sheep and goats in Mt. 25.31-46.[56] The story begins with the coming and
enthronement of the Son of Man but then compares his action of separating people of all the nations to a shepherd separating sheep from goats

53. On the potential allusion to Zech. 10.2 in Mt. 9.36, see pp. 86-87, above.

54. The responsibility of Israel's shepherds to heal the sick and bind up the injured
may also be suggested in the LXX text of Zech. 10.2, which replaces 'shepherd' with
'healing': the people suffer 'because there is no healing', rather than 'for lack of a
shepherd'. The expectation, as noted by Evans, 'Jesus and Zechariah', p. 386, is consistent
with the eschatology of Zech. 9.16: 'On that day the LORD their God will save them for
they are the flock of his people'. Cf. CD XIII, 9-10: 'He shall have pity on them like a
father on his sons, and will heal all the strays like a shepherd his flock. He will undo all
the chains which bind them, so that there will be neither harassed nor oppressed in his
congregation'; and *Pss. Sol.* 17.40: 'Faithfully and righteously shepherding the Lord's
flock, he will not let any of them stumble in their pasture. He will lead them all in holiness
and there will be no arrogance among them, that any should be oppressed. This is the
beauty of the king of Israel which God knew, to raise him over the house of Israel to
discipline it.'

55. Martin, 'Image of the Shepherd', pp. 276-77; van Tilborg, 'Matthew 27.3-10',
p. 168.

56. Mt. 25.31-46 has already been discussed regarding its use of 'king' on p. 113.

(Mt. 25.32).[57] While the story begins with an allusion to Zech. 14.5,[58] the image of the shepherd who judges the sheep likely evokes the description of Yahweh's action in Ezek. 34.17: 'As for you, my flock, thus says the Lord GOD: I shall judge between sheep and sheep, between rams and goats' (cf. Ezek. 34.20-22).[59] In Mt. 25.31-46, Jesus, as the Son of Man, assumes this role of eschatological judge, a role normally reserved for God alone but now transferred to the Son of Man. Whether the text assumes Jesus' deity or merely his exalted role as the Davidic shepherd, Jesus 'clearly becomes the focus of the final judgment, spelling disaster to those who ignore him on this side of judgment', those who fail to receive the messengers of the gospel, that is, the disciples of Jesus.[60]

The fourth occurrence of the shepherd metaphor in Matthew appears in Mt. 26.31. After eating the Passover supper (Mt. 26.17-30), Jesus predicts his death, the disciples' dispersion, and Peter's denial (Mt. 26.31-35). The predictions of Jesus' death and the disciples' dispersion are corroborated by the citation of Zech. 13.7 in Mt. 26.31.[61] Just as the tragic death of the shepherd has a devastating effect on the sheep in Zech. 13.7, so does the arrest of Jesus cause the flight of his disciples. The citation, then, describes the dispersion of the disciples metaphorically in terms of the scattering of the sheep of the flock. The addition of the phrase 'of the flock' may allude to the regathering of the scattered sheep in Ezek. 34.12-13, which resembles somewhat Jesus' promise to go ahead of the disciples to Galilee after he is raised up (Mt. 26.32). Yet the phrase probably also presupposes the context of Zech. 13.7-9, in which a remnant is purified through testing and becomes the renewed people of Yahweh. Moreover, Peter's expression of his willingness to die with Jesus in Mt. 26.35 clarifies the significance of the words 'strike', which refers to the death of Jesus, and 'shepherd', which refers to Jesus himself. Since the narrative of Matthew has not explicitly designated Jesus as the shepherd until this prediction, the shock of the shepherd's imminent death is intensified.[62] Even though Ezekiel 34 has provided many of the concepts and images used in Matthew's shepherd metaphor, it cannot, in spite of Heil's

---

57. This expands upon previous uses of sheep in Matthew, for, in the words of Heil, 'Ezekiel 34', p. 705, 'now the sheep are not limited to the people of Israel (2.6; 9.36; 10.6; 15.24), to the disciples (10.16), or to believers (18.12-14) but to include the righteous among all peoples'. This expansion corresponds with the expectation that some from among the nations join with the Jews in worship of Yahweh in Zech. 2.11 (2.15 MT); 8.20-23; 14.16.

58. On the allusion to Zech. 14.5 in Mt. 25.31, see pp. 98-99, above.

59. Heil, 'Ezekiel 34', p. 705; Martin, 'Image of the Shepherd', p. 291.

60. Keener, *Matthew*, p. 603.

61. On the citation of Zech. 13.7 in Mt. 26.31, see pp. 69-83, above.

62. Heil, 'Ezekiel 34', p. 707.

assertion to the contrary,[63] account for this new development based upon
Zech. 13.7: before the scattered sheep are gathered, Jesus the shepherd, struck
by God, dies.

The four occurrences of ποιμήν and ποιμαίνω demonstrate that the shepherd metaphor has importance for Matthew's Christology. The description
appears first in the magi's search for the child born king of the Jews; when
Herod asks about the birthplace of the Messiah, the chief priests and scribes
point to the town of Bethlehem on the basis of Mic. 5.2 and 2 Sam. 5.2 (Mt.
2.6). In a summary of Jesus' ministry of teaching, preaching, and healing in
various cities and villages, the image, 'like sheep without a shepherd' (Mt.
9.36), indicts the Jewish leaders for their failure to shepherd God's people
and confirms Jesus as the Davidic messianic shepherd who heals the sick and
gathers 'the lost sheep of the house of Israel' (Mt. 10.6). Toward the end of
the Olivet Discourse, Jesus tells the story of the sheep and goats, in which the
Son of Man comes with all the angels to judge all nations as a shepherd separates sheep from goats (Mt. 25.32). Following the Passover supper, Jesus
predicts his death and the disciples' dispersion, predictions supported by the
citation of Zech. 13.7 (Mt. 26.31); the text compares the flight of the disciples
to the scattering of sheep and identifies Jesus as the shepherd who is struck
and dies. In this way, Matthew, perhaps more explicitly than any of the other
Gospels except for John 10, develops the metaphor of Jesus as shepherd; the
description emphasizes that Jesus, in contrast to the Jewish leaders, fulfills
the expectation of a future Davidic leader from Bethlehem. Jesus the shepherd heals the sick, gathers 'the lost sheep of the house of Israel', dies by the
sword of divine judgment, regathers the scattered people of Yahweh, and
ultimately judges all nations.

Three additional allusions to Zechariah and one additional citation from
Zechariah may relate to Matthew's portrayal of Jesus as the messianic shepherd who dies. The naming of 'Zechariah son of Barachiah' in Mt. 23.35
conflates the postexilic prophet Zechariah (Zech. 1.1, 7) with Zechariah son
of Jehoiada, who is murdered 'between the sanctuary and the altar' (cf.
2 Chron. 24.25).[64] In this way, Matthew correlates the betrayal of Jesus'
'innocent blood' (Mt. 27.4) with the shedding of the righteous blood of all
the Old Testament martyrs; their deaths imply that Jesus, although innocent,
also suffers a violent death. Matthew 26.28 alludes to Zech. 9.11[65] and, in the
context of the citation of Zech. 13.7 in Mt. 26.31, envisions the bloody death
of Jesus the shepherd, by whose death the covenant is established and after

63. Heil, 'Ezekiel 34', p. 708: 'The narrative strategy of Matthew's shepherd metaphor is guided and unified by Ezekiel 34, which supplies the reader with some of its terms
and with all of its concepts and images'.
64. On the allusion to Zech. 1.1, 7 in Mt. 23.35, see pp. 92-94, above.
65. On the allusion to Zech. 9.11 in Mt. 26.28, see pp. 100-101, above.

whose death the scattered disciples are gathered into the purified people of God.[66] Matthew 27.9-10 expands the citation from Zech. 11.12-13, a text already alluded to in Mt. 26.51, with an allusion to Jer. 19.1-13.[67] Of these two Old Testament texts, Matthew uses Zech. 11.12-13 to explain the significance of the sum of thirty pieces of silver Judas receives for betraying Jesus and their use for the purchase of the potter's field by the chief priests. Moreover, Zech. 11.12-13 provides significant background for the image of shepherd in Matthew. In Zech. 11.4-14, Yahweh instructs the prophet to act as a shepherd for the people, but Israel's leaders cheaply value him and repudiate their divinely chosen leader in the presence of the Lord. Thus, Judas and the Jewish leaders are guilty of betraying and shedding 'innocent blood', and thereby they implicate themselves for their rejection of Jesus as the divinely appointed shepherd.

66. In the words of C.A. Evans, 'Jesus and Zechariah', p. 386, 'the eschatological perspective of Zechariah, especially its anticipation of the gathering of Israel's exiles, again suits Jesus' program. However, Jesus has interpreted the blood of God's covenant in the light of the words that speak of striking the shepherd. Jesus' blood will restore Israel's covenant relationship with God and will make possible the nation's renewal.'

67. On the citation of Zech. 11.12-13 in Mt. 27.9-10, see pp. 47-69.

CONCLUSION

The Gospel of Matthew uses the Old Testament extensively, citing it at least forty times and alluding to it as many as three hundred times. Yet the study of Matthew's use of the Old Testament has focused on the ten so-called formula quotations, each of which is introduced by a similar redactional formula, functions as editorial commentary from the evangelist, and exhibits a text form further from the LXX than other references to the Old Testament in Matthew. Furthermore, recent studies have recognized the neglect of other important aspects of the use of the Old Testament in Matthew, calling for the study of Matthew's citations, allusions, and thematic elements inspired by Old Testament texts.

A prophetic book with notable influence on the Gospel of Matthew is Zechariah, from which come two of the ten formula quotations, Mt. 21.5 and 27.9-10, and one explicit citation, Mt. 26.31. In fact, only Isaiah among prophetic books is quoted in Matthew more often than Zechariah. In addition to these three citations, Matthew alludes to Zechariah at least eight times. However, the use of Zechariah in the Gospel of Matthew has not been fully described. Of the works that deal with the use of Zechariah in the New Testament, only one specifically addresses Matthew's use of Zechariah. Therefore, this study also examined the use of Zechariah in the Gospel of Matthew, analyzing the explicit citations from Zechariah, considering the presence and intention of textual and conceptual allusions, and describing the theological function of Matthew's use of important themes in Zechariah.

The first chapter examined three citations from Zechariah. Using a comparative exegetical methodology, the chapter assessed the early Jewish and early Christian interpretations of the citations from Zechariah and analyzed the interpretation of these texts from Zechariah in Matthew's Gospel. The first of these citations, Mt. 21.5, cites Zech. 9.9, which announces the king's procession into Jerusalem for the purpose of bringing peace and salvation to all nations (Zech. 9.10-17). Triumphant and victorious, the humble king rides into Jerusalem on a donkey's colt, portraying the king's legitimate reign (cf. Gen. 49.10-11). In early Jewish interpretation, few texts refer to Zech. 9.9. The Dead Sea sectarians interpret Gen. 49.10 as relating to the legitimate leader in the line of David, but no clear connection of Gen. 49.10 with

Zech. 9.9 can be confirmed. Three rabbinic texts use Zech. 9.9 to emphasize the lowliness of the Messiah's coming; one, *b. Sanh.* 98a, suggests that the Messiah's riding on a donkey would indicate that people are not worthy of the Messiah's coming, and two of them, *Gen. Rab.* 98.9 (on Gen. 49.11) and *Gen. Rab.* 99.8 (on Gen. 49.11), connect Zech. 9.9 with a messianic interpretation of the donkey tethered to the vine in Gen. 49.11. In early Christian interpretation, Zech. 9.9 is used to demonstrate the fulfillment of Old Testament prophecy in the life and ministry of Jesus Christ and thereby to prove his divinity (Justin, *1 Apol.* 32.6; 35.10-11; *Dial.* 53.2-4; 88.6; Irenaeus, *Haer.* 3.19.2; 4.33.1, 12; *Epid.* 65). Justin (*Dial.* 53.3) uses Zech. 9.9 to underscore the humility and lowliness of Jesus' entry into Jerusalem, and elsewhere, *1 Apol.* 32.6, he connects Zech. 9.9 with Gen. 49.10-11 to show that Jesus is the legitimate ruler of the Jews and construes the presence of two donkeys as allegorical symbols for Jews and Gentiles.

In the New Testament, only Mt. 21.5 and Jn 12.15 cite Zech. 9.9. Both use it to explain Jesus' entry into Jerusalem on a donkey, drawing attention to the humble nature of Jesus' kingship (even though Jn 12.15 omits all three descriptors of the king in Zech. 9.9, even 'humble') and affirming that Jesus' kingship extends beyond Jerusalem to 'the ends of the earth' (Zech. 9.10). In Mt. 21.5, the citation follows Matthew's characteristic formula and translates well the MT with the possible exception of the word 'humble'. The citation begins with wording from Isa. 62.11, with which it announces to Israel that Jesus is king of Israel, who, according to Matthew, has rejected Jesus. The wording selected (and omitted) from Zech. 9.9 highlights the humble character of Jesus, who rides on a donkey's colt, and this wording, read in view of Gen. 49.11, identifies Jesus as the legitimate Davidic heir. Theologically, the citation of Zech. 9.9 in Mt. 21.5 explains the significance of Jesus' entry into Jerusalem. Matthew presents Jesus riding into Jerusalem on a donkey—a deliberate and symbolic action—to typify the humble character of his kingship and to denote the legitimacy of his reign.

The second of Matthew's citations, Mt. 27.9-10, cites Zech. 11.12-13, which is part of a symbolic prophetic action. The prophet requests a wage for his service as shepherd. The sheep merchants weigh out a wage of thirty pieces of silver, an amount that signifies a trivial and thereby insulting amount. At the instruction of Yahweh, the prophet throws the silver to the potter, signifying contempt for the wage and Yahweh's rejection of those who offered it. In early Jewish interpretation, two rabbinic writings consider conflicting interpretations of the thirty pieces of silver in Zech. 11.12-13 (*b. Hull.* 92a and *Gen. Rab.* 98.9 [on Gen. 49.11]); the thirty pieces of silver either refer to thirty commandments or to thirty righteous men, this second interpretation being similar to the written records of deeds in *Tg.* Zech. 11.12-13. In early Christian interpretation, Zech. 11.12-13 is apparently ignored except for Irenaeus (*Epid.* 81.7), who also attributes the citation to Jeremiah and refers to the monetary amount as 'thirty *staters*', an alteration appearing in several manuscripts at Mt. 26.15.

In the New Testament, only Mt. 27.9-10 cites Zech. 11.13. The citation is introduced with Matthew's characteristic formula, but the wording is similar to the formula in Mt. 2.17, the only other formula quotation from Jeremiah. Both Mt. 2.17 and 27.9 begin with the adverb 'then' to avoid ascribing the fulfilling event in question to a divine plan. While the citation is from Zech. 11.13, Matthew has attributed it to Jeremiah to denote the allusion to Jer. 19.1-13, which shares with Mt. 27.3-10 the judgment against those guilty of shedding or betraying 'innocent blood'. The citation of Zech. 11.12-13 in Mt. 27.9-10 has been substantially modified to accommodate the citation to its narrative context, to clarify the identity of the referents in the cited text, and to explain the purchase of the potter's field. The citation itself focuses on the thirty pieces of silver and their use for the purchase of the potter's field by the chief priests, who implicate themselves in Jesus' death, even though they act according to the divine purpose. Theologically, Mt. 27.9-10 cites Zech. 11.12-13, with an allusion to Jer. 19.1-13, to explain the betrayal of Judas and the rejection of Jesus by the Jewish leaders. Just as Israel's religious leaders have cheaply valued and repudiated the prophet acting as their shepherd, so do Judas and the Jewish leaders implicate themselves by betraying and shedding 'innocent blood' (Mt. 27.4). Although their actions attest to their guilt, these very actions take place within the purpose of God.

The third of Matthew's citations, Mt. 26.31, cites Zech. 13.7. The poem in Zech. 13.7-9 begins with Yahweh summoning the sword as an instrument of divine judgment against the shepherd and draws attention to the result of the shepherd's death: the sheep are scattered and refined, through suffering, into the people of Yahweh. In early Jewish interpretation, Zech. 13.7 is cited only twice. The *Damascus Document* (CD B XIX, 7-9) quotes Zech. 13.7, which the sectarians probably understood to refer to the death of their leader, the Teacher of Righteousness, and to their own persecution resulting from his death. The minor tractate *'Abot de Rabbi Nathan* cites Zech. 13.7 as a tribute to R. Simeon at his death (*'Abot R. Nat.* A §38), but this eulogistic use of Zech. 13.7 is isolated and distant from its original context. In early Christian interpretation, Zech. 13.7 is cited three times. *Barnabas* 5.12, which may display some literary dependence on Mt. 26.31, cites Zech. 13.7 in reference to the suffering of Jesus Christ in the flesh and the responsibility of the Jews for Jesus' death. Justin (*Dial.* 53.6) and Irenaeus (*Epid.* 76) understand the crucifixion of Christ and the dispersion of the disciples as fulfilling Zech. 13.7, but both writers seem to quote the verse from a source other than Matthew.

In the New Testament, both Mt. 26.31 and Mk 14.27 cite Zech. 13.7 in the context of Jesus' prediction of his death, the disciples' dispersion, and Peter's denial. In both gospels, the introductory formula ('it is written') and the citation appear on the lips of Jesus, rather than in the words of the evangelist. In Matthew, the prediction is less ambiguous, since Mt. 26.31 adds the pronoun 'you', the causal phrase 'because of me', and the temporal phrase 'this night'. Matthew 26.31 cites Zech. 13.7 with only two minor modifications from the MT. The citation begins with 'I will strike' instead of 'Strike' to emphasize that the judgment against the shepherd and the scattering of the sheep is initiated by Yahweh. The citation also adds the phrase 'of the flock', an allusion to the gathering of the scattered sheep in Ezek. 34.12-13, a text with similarities to Jesus' promise to go ahead of the disciples to Galilee after he is raised up (Mt. 26.32). Furthermore, the context of Mt. 26.31-35 clarifies certain referents within the citation itself: 'strike' refers to Jesus' death, 'shepherd' refers to Jesus, the 'sheep' are the disciples, and the disciples are 'scattered' when they become deserters at the arrest of Jesus (Mt. 26.56). Theologically, the citation of Zech. 13.7 in Mt. 26.31 explains Jesus' prediction about the desertion of the disciples. Just as the tragic death of the shepherd has a devastating effect on the sheep in Zech. 13.7, so does the arrest and death of Jesus cause the flight of his disciples. Their desertion happens within the divine plan, but so too does their restoration, since Mt. 26.31 may presuppose the context of Zech. 13.7-9, in which a remnant is purified through testing and becomes the renewed people of Yahweh.

The second chapter of this study employed seven methodological criteria for discerning the presence of Old Testament allusions in the New Testament. Of the 18 potential allusions to Zechariah in Matthew, only eight can be confirmed as intentional allusions, and these eight allusions occur between Mt. 21.5 and 27.9-10, the first and last citations from Zechariah. Two of the allusions relate to Matthew's citations from Zechariah. Matthew 26.15, with the phrase 'thirty pieces of silver', anticipates the citation of Zech. 11.12-13 in Mt. 27.9-10. Matthew 26.56 connects contextually with the citation of Zech. 13.7 in Mt. 26.31 and includes the desertion of the disciples among those events in the Passion Narrative that fulfill the Old Testament. Two of the allusions describe Jesus' death and its accomplishment. Matthew 23.35 conflates the prophet Zechariah with Zechariah son of Jehoiada (2 Chron. 24.20-22) in anticipation of Jesus' own violent death. Also, the allusion to Zech. 9.11 in Mt. 26.28 evokes the bloody death of Jesus the shepherd, by whose death the covenant is established in the context of messianic victory. Four of the allusions reflect an eschatological use of material from Zechariah and transfer roles and descriptions typically reserved for Yahweh to Jesus the Son of Man. Specifically, Mt. 24.30 alludes to Zech. 12.10-14 to describe the reaction of universal mourning at the Son of Man's coming. Matthew 24.31 alludes to Zech. 2.6 to signify the universal gathering of the elect from the four winds. Matthew 24.36 alludes to Zech. 14.7 to emphasize that the chronological arrival of the day of Yahweh is unknown by anyone, except the Father. Finally, Mt. 25.31 alludes to Zech. 14.5 to depict the coming of the Son of Man at the Parousia in the manner of Yahweh's coming with the angels.

The third chapter of this study described the thematic and theological function of Matthew's use of Zechariah in the portrayal of Jesus and his mission. In particular, the presentation of the Davidic king and the rejection of the divinely appointed shepherd in Zechariah has influenced the theology of Matthew and its presentation of Jesus as coming king and rejected shepherd. The term 'king' occurs eight times in Matthew in relation to the kingship of Jesus. The magi search for the child born king of the Jews (Mt. 2.2). Jesus enters Jerusalem as the humble king mounted on a donkey (Mt. 21.5). In the Passion Narrative, Jesus is mockingly but ironically called 'king' four times (Mt. 27.11, 29, 37, 42). The Son of Man comes with all the angels to judge all the nations as a king presiding over his court (Mt. 25.34, 40). Three additional allusions to Zechariah also relate to Matthew's portrayal of Jesus as the humble king who awaits enthronement. Matthew 24.30 alludes to Zech. 12.10-14 and depicts the reaction of universal mourning at the Son of Man's coming. Matthew 24.31 alludes to Zech. 2.11 (2.15 MT) and describes the universal gathering of the elect from the four winds. Finally, Mt. 24.36 alludes to Zech. 14.7 and identifies the coming day of Yahweh as the Parousia, a day whose arrival is known only by Yahweh. Thus, Matthew explicitly develops the nature of Jesus' kingship but in such a way to emphasize the humility of the Davidic king whose enthronement comes at a time unknown to the king himself.

The word 'shepherd' occurs four times in Matthew's application of the shepherd metaphor to Jesus. The chief priests and scribes identify Bethlehem as the birthplace of the Davidic leader who shepherds the people of Israel (Mt. 2.6). Jesus' description of the people 'like sheep without a shepherd' (Mt. 9.36) indicts the Jewish leaders for their failure to shepherd God's people and confirms Jesus as the Davidic shepherd who heals the sick and gathers 'the lost sheep of the house of Israel' (Mt. 10.6). The Son of Man comes with all the angels to judge all the nations as a shepherd separates sheep from goats (Mt. 25.32). With a citation from Zech. 13.7, Jesus compares the flight of the disciples to the scattering of sheep and identifies himself as the shepherd who is struck and dies (Mt. 26.31). In addition, Matthew extends this shepherd image with several other texts from Zechariah. Matthew 23.35 conflates the postexilic prophet Zechariah (Zech. 1.1, 7) with Zechariah son of Jehoiada in order to connect the shedding of the righteous blood of the Old Testament martyrs with the betrayal of Jesus' innocent blood and his own violent death. In the context of the citation of Zech. 13.7 in Mt. 26.31, Mt. 26.28 alludes to Zech. 9.11 and envisions the bloody death of

Jesus the shepherd as the means by which the covenant is established with the purified people of God. Matthew 26.51 alludes to Zech. 11.12-13 in anticipation of its citation in Mt. 27.9-10, where the citation is expanded with allusion to Jer. 19.1-13. Just as the Jewish leaders repudiate Israel's divinely chosen shepherd in Zech. 11.4-14, Judas and the Jewish leaders implicate themselves for their rejection of Jesus as the divinely appointed shepherd in Mt. 27.3-10. In this way, Matthew explicitly develops the metaphor of Jesus as shepherd; the description emphasizes that Jesus, in contrast to the failed Jewish leaders, fulfills the expectation of a future Davidic leader from Bethlehem. Although Jesus dies by the sword of divine judgment, he ultimately gathers the scattered people of God and judges all nations.

Three times the Gospel of Matthew cites from the prophetic book Zechariah. Between the first and last of these citations, Matthew alludes to Zechariah eight times. In addition, Matthew uses themes prominent in Zechariah in the portrayal of Jesus' ministry, death, and eschatological reign. Collectively, these citations, allusions, and thematic emphases indicate a coherence between the theology of Matthew and the theology of Zechariah; moreover, they indicate an influence of the theology of Zechariah on the theology of Matthew. Indeed, Matthew's indebtedness to Zechariah as an author 'remote in time' and 'alien in language' demonstrates Matthew's authorial adeptness in making something better.[1] The messianic vision found in the prophetic oracles of Zechariah includes the restoration of the humble Davidic king, the smiting of the divinely appointed shepherd, the creation of a renewed remnant, and the worship of Yahweh by all nations. Matthew finds this prophetic presentation particularly compelling for his own representation of Jesus as the fulfillment of Zechariah's shepherd-king and the realization of Zechariah's eschatological hopes.

1. T.S. Eliot, 'Philip Massinger', in *idem, Selected Prose of T.S. Eliot* (ed. Frank Kermode; New York: Harcourt Brace Jovanovich, 1975), p. 153.

BIBLIOGRAPHY

Texts, Translations, and Reference Works

Abegg, Martin G., Peter W. Flint and Eugene C. Ulrich (eds.), *The Dead Sea Scrolls Bible: The Oldest Known Bible* (San Francisco: Harper, 1999).

—*The Greek New Testament* (Stuttgart: Deutsche Bibelgesellschaft, 4th edn, 1994).

Aland, Barbara, Kurt Aland, Johannes Karavidopoulos, Carlo M. Martini and Bruce M. Metzger (eds.), *The Greek New Testament* (Stuttgart: Deutsche Bibelgesellschaft, 4th edn, 1994), pp. 887-90.

Aland, Kurt (ed.), *Synopsis Quattuor Evangeliorum* (Stuttgart: Deutsche Bibelgesellschaft, 9th edn, 1976).

—*Vollständige Konkordanz zum griechischen Neuen Testament* (2 vols.; Berlin: W. de Gruyter, 1977–83).

Aland, Kurt, and Barbara Aland, *The Text of the New Testament* (trans. Erroll F. Rhodes; Grand Rapids: Eerdmans, 2nd edn, 1989).

Allenbach, Jean, André Pautler and Centre d'analyse et de documentation patristiques (eds.), *Biblia patristica: index des citations et allusions bibliques dans le littérature patristique* (7 vols.; Paris: Centre national de la recherche scientifique, 2000).

Archer, Gleason L., and G.C. Chirichigno, *Old Testament Quotations in the New Testament: A Complete Survey* (Chicago: Moody, 1983).

Aune, David E., *The New Testament in Its Literary Environment* (Library of Early Christianity; Philadelphia: Westminster Press, 1987).

Bailey, James L., and Lyle D. Vander Broek, *Literary Forms in the New Testament* (Louisville, KY: Westminster/John Knox Press, 1992).

Balz, Horst, and Gerhard Schneider (eds.), *Exegetical Dictionary of the New Testament* (3 vols.; Grand Rapids: Eerdmans, 1990–93).

Barthélemy, Dominique, *Critique textuelle de l'Ancien Testament* (OBO, 50; 3 vols.; Fribourg Suisse: Éditions Universitaires, 1982–92).

Boothroyd, B., *Biblia Hebraica, or Hebrew Scriptures of the Old Testament, without Points after the Text of Kennicott, with the Chief Various Readings, Selected from His Collation of Hebrew MSS, from that of De Rossi, and from the Ancient Versions* (2 vols.; Pentefract: Boothroyd, 1810–16).

Borgen, Peder, Kåre Fuglseth and Roald Skarsten, *The Philo Index: A Complete Greek Word Index to the Writings of Philo of Alexandria* (Grand Rapids: Eerdmans, 2000).

Boring, M. Eugene, Klaus Berger and Carsten Colpe (eds.), *Hellenistic Commentary to the New Testament* (Nashville: Abingdon Press, 1995).

Bratcher, Robert G. (ed.), *Old Testament Quotations in the New Testament* (New York: United Bible Societies, 3rd edn, 1987).

Brooks, James A., and Carlton L. Winbery, *Syntax of New Testament Greek* (Lanthan, MD: University Press of America, 1979).

Carson, D.A., Douglas J. Moo and Leon Morris, *An Introduction to the New Testament* (Grand Rapids: Zondervan, 1992).

Cathcart, Kevin, and Robert P. Gordon, *The Targum of the Minor Prophets* (ArBib, 14; Wilmington, DE: Michael Glazier, 1989).

Charles, R.H., *The Greek Versions of the Testaments of the Twelve Patriarchs* (Oxford: Clarendon Press, 1908; repr., Oxford: Clarendon Press, 1960).

Charlesworth, James H. (ed.), *The Dead Sea Scrolls: Hebrew, Aramaic, and Greek Texts with English Translations*. I. *Rule of the Community and Related Documents* (PTSDSSP; Louisville, KY: Westminster/John Knox Press, 1994).

—*The Dead Sea Scrolls: Hebrew, Aramaic, and Greek Texts with English Translations*. II. *Damascus Document, War Scrolls, and Related Documents* (PTSDSSP; Louisville, KY: Westminster/John Knox Press, 1995).

—*The Dead Sea Scrolls: Hebrew, Aramaic, and Greek Texts with English Translations*. IVA. *Pseudepigraphic and Non-Masoretic Psalms and Prayers* (PTSDSSP; Louisville, KY: Westminster/John Knox Press, 1997).

—*The Dead Sea Scrolls: Hebrew, Aramaic, and Greek Texts with English Translations*. VIB. *Pesharim, Other Commentaries, and Related Documents* (PTSDSSP; Louisville, KY: Westminster/John Knox Press, 2002).

—*Jesus and the Dead Sea Scrolls* (ABRL; New York: Doubleday, 1992).

Charlesworth, James H., *et al.* (eds.), *Graphic Concordance to the Dead Sea Scrolls* (PTSDSSP; Louisville, KY: Westminster/John Knox Press, 1991).

Clines, David J.A. (ed.), *The Dictionary of Classical Hebrew* (8 vols.; Sheffield: Sheffield Academic Press, 1993–).

Comfort, Philip Wesley, *Early Manuscripts and the Modern Translations of the New Testament* (Grand Rapids: Baker Book House, 1990).

Cranford, Lorin L., *Exegeting the New Testament: A Seminar Working Model with Expanded Research Bibliography* (Worth: Scripta, 2nd edn, 1991).

Danby, Herbert, *The Mishnah* (Oxford: Oxford University Press, 1933).

Denis, Albert-Marie, *Concordance grecque des pseudépigraphes d'ancien testament* (Leuven: Leuven University Press, 1987).

Dittmar, Wilhelm, *Vetus Testamentum in Novo: Die alttestamentlichen Parallelen des Neuen Testaments im Wortlaut der Urtexte und der Septuaginta* (Göttingen: Vandenhoeck & Ruprecht, 1903).

Elliger, Karl, and Wilhelm Rudolph (eds.), *Biblia Hebraica Stuttgartensia* (Stuttgart: Deutsche Bibelges ellschaft, 1984).

Elliot, J.K. (ed.), *The Apocryphal Jesus: Legends of the Early Church* (Oxford: Oxford University Press, 1996).

Epstein, Isidore (ed.), *The Babylonian Talmud* (18 vols.; London: Soncino, 1978).

Evans, Craig A., *Jesus* (IBR Bibliographies, 5; Grand Rapids: Baker Book House, 1992).

—*Noncanonical Writings and New Testament Interpretation* (Peabody, MA: Hendrickson, 1992).

Fitzmyer, Joseph A., *The Dead Sea Scrolls: Major Publications and Tools for Study* (SBLRBS, 20; Atlanta: Scholars Press, rev. edn, 1990).

Forestell, J. Terence, *Targumic Traditions and the New Testament: An Annotated Bibliography with a New Testament Index* (SBL Aramaic Studies, 4; Chico, CA: Scholars Press, 1979).

Freedman, H., and Maurice Simon (eds.), *Midrash Rabbah* (10 vols.; New York: Soncino, 3rd edn, 1983).

Freedman, David Noel (ed.), *The Anchor Bible Dictionary* (6 vols.; New York: Double-day, 1992).

Funk, Robert W., Roy W. Hoover and the Jesus Seminar, *The Five Gospels: The Search for the Authentic Words of Jesus* (San Francisco: Harper & Row, 1993).

Funk, Robert W., and the Jesus Seminar, *The Acts of Jesus: The Search for the Authentic Deeds of Jesus* (San Francisco: HarperCollins, 1998).

García Martínez, Florentino, *The Dead Sea Scrolls Translated: The Qumran Texts in English* (trans. Wilfred G.E. Watson; Grand Rapids: Eerdmans, 2nd edn, 1996).

García Martínez, Florentino, and Eibert J.C. Tigchelaar (eds.), *The Dead Sea Scrolls Study Edition* (2 vols.; Leiden: E.J. Brill, 1997–98).

GRAMCORD Greek New Testament for Windows with Bible Companion Version 1.2m (Vancouver, WA: GRAMCORD Institute, 1996).

Harris, R. Laird, Gleason L. Archer, Jr, and Bruce K. Waltke (eds.), *Theological Wordbook of the Old Testament* (2 vols.; Chicago: Moody, 1980).

Hatch, Edwin, and Henry A. Redpath, *A Concordance to the Septuagint and the Other Greek Versions of the Old Testament* (2 vols.; Oxford: Clarendon Press, 1897; repr., Graz: Akademische Druck-u. Verlagsanstalt, 1975).

Hawkins, John C., *Horae Synopticae: Contributions to the Study of the Synoptic Problem* (Oxford: Clarendon Press, 2nd edn, 1901; repr., Grand Rapids: Baker Book House, 1968).

Hebel, Udo J., *Intertextuality, Allusion, and Quotation: An International Bibliography of Critical Studies* (Bibliographies and Indexes in World Literature, 18; New York: Greenwood, 1989).

Hennecke, Edgar, Wilhelm Schneemelcher and R. McL. Wilson (eds.), *New Testament Apocrypha* (2 vols.; Louisville, KY: Westminster/John Knox Press, 2nd edn, 1991).

Hoffmann, Paul, Thomas Hieke and Ulrich Bauer, *Synoptic Concordance: A Greek Concordance to the First Three Gospels in Synoptic Arrangement, Statistically Evaluated, Including Occurrences in Acts* (4 vols.; Berlin: W. de Gruyter, 1999–2000).

Holmes, Michael W. (ed.), *The Apostolic Fathers: Greek Texts and English Translations of their Writings* (trans. J.B. Lightfoot and J.R. Harmer; Grand Rapids: Baker Book House, 2nd edn, 1992).

Hübner, Hans, *Vetus Testamentum in Novo*. II. *Corpus Paulinum* (Göttingen: Vandenhoeck & Ruprecht, 1997).

Hühn, Eugen, *Die alttestamentlichen Citate und Reminiscenzen im Neuen Testament* (Tübingen: Mohr Siebeck, 1900).

Irenaeus, *The Demonstration of the Apostolic Preaching* (trans. J. Armitage Robinson; New York: Macmillan, 1920).

Jansma, Taeke, *Inquiry into the Hebrew Text and the Ancient Versions of Zechariah IX–XIV* (Leiden: E.J. Brill, 1949).

Jastrow, Marcus, *A Dictionary of the Targumim, the Talmud Babli and Yershalmi, and the Midrashic Literature* (2 vols.; New York: Judaica, 1950).

Jenni, Ernst, and Claus Westermann (eds.), *Theological Lexicon of the Old Testament* (trans. Mark E. Brodie; 3 vols.; Peabody, MA: Hendrickson, 1997).

Jonge, Marinus de, *The Testaments of the Twelve Patriarchs: A Critical Edition of the Greek Text* (PVTG; Leiden: E.J. Brill, 1978).

JPS Hebrew–English Tanakh (Philadelphia: The Jewish Publication Society of America, 2nd edn, 1999).

Kautzsch, E. (ed.), *Gesenius' Hebrew Grammar* (trans. A.E. Cowley; Oxford: Clarendon Press, 2nd edn, 1910).

Kelso, James L., *The Ceramic Vocabulary of the Old Testament* (BASORSup, 5-6; New Haven, CT: American Schools of Oriental Research, 1948).

Kennicott, Benjamin, *Vetus Testamentum Hebraicum, cum variis lectionibus* (2 vols.; Oxonii: E typographeo Clarendoniano, 1776–80).

Kohlenberger, John R., III, Edward W. Goodrick and James A. Swanson, *The Exhaustive Concordance to the Greek New Testament* (Grand Rapids: Zondervan, 1995).

Lamsa, George, *The Holy Bible: From the Ancient Eastern Text* (Harper & Row, 1968).

Levine, Étan, *The Aramaic Version of Lamentations* (New York: Sepher-Hermon, 1976).

Lightfoot, John, *A Commentary on the New Testament from the Talmud and Hebraica* (4 vols.; Peabody, MA: Hendrickson, 1979).

Louw, Johannes P., and Eugene A. Nida (eds.), *Greek–English Lexicon of the New Testament Based on Semantic Domains* (2 vols.; New York: United Bible Societies, 2nd edn, 1989).

Marcovich, Miroslav (ed.), *Iustini Martyris Apologiae pro christianis* (PTS, 38; Berlin: W. de Gruyter, 1994)

—*Iustini Martyris Dialogus cum Tryphone* (PTS, 47; Berlin: W. de Gruyter, 1997).

McKnight, Scot, and Matthew C. Williams, *The Synoptic Gospels: An Annotated Bibliography* (IBR Bibliographies, 6; Grand Rapids: Baker Book House, 2000).

McLean, Bradley H., *Citations and Allusions to Jewish Scripture in Early Christian and Jewish Writings through 180 C.E.* (Lewiston, NY: Edwin Mellen Press, 1992).

Melito of Sardis, *On Pascha and Fragments* (trans. Stuart George Hall; OECT; Oxford: Clarendon Press, 1979).

Metzger, Bruce M., *A Textual Commentary on the Greek New Testament* (Stuttgart: Deutsche Bibelgesellschaft, 2nd edn, 1994).

Metzger, Bruce M., and Roland F. Murphy (eds.), *The New Oxford Annotated Apocrypha: The Apocryphal/Deuterocanonical Books of the Old Testament: New Revised Standard Version* (New York: Oxford University Press, 1991).

The Midrash on Psalms (trans. William G. Braude; Yale Judaica, 13; 2 vols.; New Haven: Yale University Press, 1959).

Milik, J.T (ed.), *The Books of Enoch* (Oxford: Clarendon Press, 1976).

Montefiore, C.G., and H. Loewe, *A Rabbinic Anthology* (New York: Schocken Books, 1974).

Moulton, James H. (ed.), *A Grammar of New Testament Greek* (4 vols.; Edinburgh: T. & T. Clark, 3rd edn, 1908–1976).

Moulton, James H., and George Milligan, *The Vocabulary of the Greek New Testament* (London: Hodder & Stoughton, 1930; repr., Grand Rapids: Eerdmans, 1963).

Mulder, Martin Jan (ed.), *Mikra: Text, Translation, Reading and Interpretation of the Hebrew Bible in Ancient Judaism and Early Christianity* (CRINT, 2.1; Assen: Van Gorcum, 1988).

Muraoka, Takamitsu, *A Greek–English Lexicon of the Septuagint (Twelve Prophets)* (Leuven: Peeters, 1993).

Neirynck, F., J. Verheyden and R. Corstjens (eds.), *The Gospel of Matthew and the Sayings of Source Q: A Cumulative Bibliography 1950–1995* (BETL, 140; 2 vols.; Leuven: Leuven University Press, 1998).

Neusner, Jacob, and William Scott Green (eds.), *Dictionary of Judaism in the Biblical Period* (New York: Macmillan, 1996).

The Old Testament in Syriac according to the Peshitta Version (ed. Peshitta Institute; 5 vols.; Leiden: E.J. Brill, 1972–98).

Origen, *Origenis Hexaplorum quae supersunt: sive Veterum interpretum graecorum in totum Vetus Testamentum fragmenta* (ed. Fridericus Field; Hildesheim: Georg Olms, 1964).

Pesikta Rabbati: Discourses for Feasts, Fasts, and Special Sabbaths (trans. William G. Braude; Yale Judaica, 18; 2 vols.; New Haven: Yale University Press, 1968).

Pirke de-Rabbi Eliezer (trans. Gerald Friedlander; New York: Sepher-Hermon, 4th edn, 1981).

Porter, Stanley E. (ed.), *Handbook to Exegesis of the New Testament* (NTTS, 25; Leiden: E.J. Brill, 1997).

Rabin, Chaim, *The Zadokite Documents* (Oxford: Clarendon Press, 2nd edn, 1958).

Rahlfs, Alfred (ed.), *Septuaginta* (Stuttgart: Deutsche Bibelgesellschaft, 1979).

Reider, Joseph, and Nigel Turner, *An Index to Aquila* (VTSup, 12; Leiden: E.J. Brill, 1966).

Rengstorf, Karl Heinrich, *A Complete Concordance to Flavius Josephus* (4 vols.; Leiden: E.J. Brill, 1973–83).

Roberts, Alexander, and James Donaldson (eds.), *The Ante-Nicene Fathers* (10 vols.; Grand Rapids: Eerdmans, 1974).

Rogers, Cleon L., Jr, and Cleon L. Rogers, III, *The New Linguistic and Exegetical Key to the Greek New Testament* (Grand Rapids: Zondervan, 1998).

Rossi, Johannis B. de, *Variae lectiones Veteris Testamenti* (4 vols.; Parma: Ex Regio typographeo, 1784–88; repr., Amsterdam: Philo, 1969).

Roth, Cecil (ed.), *Encyclopaedia Judaica* (16 vols.; Jerusalem: Keter, 1972).

Ryken, Leland, *Words of Delight: A Literary Introduction to the Bible* (Grand Rapids: Baker Book House, 2nd edn, 1992).

Ryken, Leland, James C. Wilhoit and Tremper Longman, III (eds.), *Dictionary of Biblical Imagery* (Downers Grove, IL: Intervarsity Press, 1998).

Safrai, Shmuel (ed.), *The Literature of the Sages*. I. *Oral Tora, Halakha, Mishna, Tosefta, Talmud, External Tractates* (CRINT, 2.3; Assen: Van Gorcum, 1987).

Schechter, Solomon, *Fragments of a Zadokite Work* (DJS, 1; Cambridge: Cambridge University Press, 1910).

Sperber, Alexander, *The Bible in Aramaic* (4 vols.; Leiden: E.J. Brill, 1959–73).

Stemberger, Günter, *Introduction to the Talmud and Midrash* (trans. and ed. Markus Bockmuehl; Edinburgh: T. & T. Clark, 2nd edn, 1996).

Stone, Michael E. (ed.), *Jewish Writings of the Second Temple Period: Apocrypha, Pseudepigrapha, Qumran Sectarian Writings, Philo, Josephus* (CRINT, 2.2; Assen: Van Gorcum, 1984).

Thompson, J. David, *A Critical Concordance to the Septuagint: Zechariah* (The Computer Bible, 87; Lewiston, NY: Edwin Mellen Press, 2001).

Torrey, Charles Culter, *The Lives of the Prophets* (JBL Monograph Series, 1; Philadelphia: Society of Biblical Literature and Exegesis, 1946).

Tov, Emanuel, *The Greek Minor Prophets Scroll from Nahal Hever (8HevXIIgr)* (DJD, 8; Oxford: Clarendon Press, 1990).

Toy, Crawford Howell, *Quotations in the New Testament* (New York: Charles Scribner's Sons, 1884).

Turpie, David McCalman, *The Old Testament in the New: A Contribution to Biblical Criticism and Interpretation* (London: Williams & Norgate, 1868).

Ulrich, Eugene, *et al.*, *Qumran Cave 4. X. The Prophets* (DJD, 15; Oxford: Clarendon Press, 1997).

Vermes, Geza, *The Complete Dead Sea Scrolls in English* (New York: Penguin Books, 1997).

Wallace, Daniel B., *Greek Grammar Beyond the Basics: An Exegetical Syntax of the New Testament* (Grand Rapids: Zondervan, 1996).

Weitzman, M.P., *The Syriac Version of the Old Testament: An Introduction* (UCOP, 56; Cambridge: Cambridge University Press, 1999).

Wise, Michael, Martin Abegg, Jr, and Edward Cook, *The Dead Sea Scrolls: A New Translation* (New York: HarperCollins, 1996).

Zerwick, Max, and Mary Grosvenor, *A Grammatical Analysis of the Greek New Testament* (Rome: Editrice Pontificio Istituto Biblico, 3rd edn, 1988).

Zimmermann, Heinrich, *Neutestamentliche Methodenlehre: Darstellung der historisch-kritischen Methode* (rev. Klaus Kliesch; Stuttgart: Katholisches Bibelwerk, 7th edn, 1982).

Secondary Literature

Achtemeier, Elizabeth, *Nahum–Micah* (Interpretation: A Biblical Commentary for Teaching and Preaching; Atlanta: John Knox Press, 1986).

Ahlström, G.W., 'אֶדֶר', *VT* 17 (1967), pp. 1-7.

Albright, William Foxwell, 'The Names "Nazareth" and "Nazoraean"'', *JBL* 65 (1946), pp. 397-401.

Allegro, J.M. 'Further Messianic References in Qumran Literature', *JBL* 75 (1956), pp. 174-87.

Allison, Dale C., Jr, *The End of the Ages Has Come: An Early Interpretation of the Passion and Resurrection of Jesus* (Philadelphia: Fortress Press, 1985).

—*The Intertextual Jesus: Scripture in Q* (Harrisburg, PA: Trinity Press International, 2000).

—*Jesus of Nazareth: Millenarian Prophet* (Minneapolis: Fortress Press, 1998).

—*The New Moses: A Matthean Typology* (Minneapolis: Fortress Press, 1993).

—*Scriptural Allusions in the New Testament: Light from the Dead Sea Scrolls* (The Dead Sea Scrolls and Christian Origins Library, 5; North Richland Hills, TX: BIBAL, 2000).

—'The Son of God as Israel: A Note on Matthean Christology', *Irish Biblical Studies* 9 (1987), pp. 74-81.

Amaru, Betsy Halpern, 'The Killing of the Prophets: Unraveling a Midrash', *HUCA* 54 (1983), pp. 153-80.

Anderson, Janice C., *Matthew's Narrative Web: Over, and Over, and Over Again* (JSNTSup, 91; Sheffield: Sheffield Academic Press, 1994).

Andiñach, Pablo R., 'Zechariah', in Farmer (ed.), *The International Bible Commentary*, pp. 1186-98.

Bailey, Jon Nelson. 'Vowing Away the Fifth Commandment: Matthew 15.3-6//Mark 7.9-13', *RestQ* 42 (2000), pp. 193-209.

Baker, David L., *Two Testaments, One Bible: A Study of the Theological Relationship between the Old and the New Testaments* (Downers Grove, IL: Intervarsity Press, 1991).

Balch, David L. (ed.), *Social History of the Matthean Community: Cross-Disciplinary Approaches* (Minneapolis: Fortress Press, 1989).

Baldwin, Joyce G., *Haggai, Zechariah, Malachi: An Introduction and Commentary* (TOTC, 24; Downers Grove, IL: Intervarsity Press, 1982).

Bammel, Ernst, 'The *Titulus*', in Bammel and Moule (eds.), *Jesus and the Politics of His Day*, pp. 353-64.

Bammel, Ernst. and C.F.D. Moule (eds.), *Jesus and the Politics of His Day* (New York: Cambridge University Press, 1984).

Baron, David, 'Four Precious Titles of the Messiah', in *idem, Rays of Messiah's Glory: Christ in the Old Testament* (London: Hodder & Stoughton, 1988), pp. 151-78.

Bartnicki, Roman, 'Das Zitat von Zach 9.9-10 und die Tiere im Bericht von Matthäus über dem Einzug Jesu in Jerusalem', *NovT* 18 (1976), pp. 161-66.

Bauckham, Richard (ed.), *The Gospels for All Christians: Rethinking the Gospel Audiences* (Grand Rapids: Eerdmans, 1998).

Bauder, Wolfgang, 'πραΰς', in *NIDNTT*, II, pp. 256-59.

Bauer, David R., *The Structure of Matthew's Gospel: A Study in Literary Design* (JSNTSup, 31; Sheffield: Almond Press, 1988).

Baumgarten, Joseph M., and Daniel R. Schwartz, 'Damascus Document (CD)', in Charlesworth (ed.), *The Dead Sea Scrolls*, II, p. 25.

Baumstark, Anton, 'Die Zitate des Mt.-Evangeliums aus dem Zwölfprophetenbuch', *Bib* 37 (1956), pp. 296-313.

Baxter, Wayne S., 'Mosaic Imagery in the Gospel of Matthew', *TJ* 20 (1999), pp. 69-83.

Beale, G.K. (ed.), *The Right Doctrine from the Wrong Texts?* (Grand Rapids: Baker Book House, 1994).

Beare, Francis Wright, *The Gospel according to Matthew: A Commentary* (Oxford: Basil Blackwell, 1981).

Beker, J. Christiaan, 'Echoes and Intertextuality: On the Role of Scripture in Paul's Theology', in Craig A. Evans and James A. Sanders (eds.), *Paul and the Scriptures of Israel* (JSNTSup, 83; SSEJC, 1; Sheffield: Sheffield Academic Press, 1993), pp. 64-69.

Bellinger, William H., Jr, and William R. Farmer (eds.), *Jesus and the Suffering Servant: Isaiah 53 and Christian Origins* (Harrisburg, PA: Trinity Press International, 1998).

Benoit, Pierre, *L'Évangile selon Saint Matthieu* (Paris: Cerf, 1950).

—'The Death of Judas', in *idem, Jesus and the Gospel* (trans. Benet Weatherhead; 2 vols.; New York: Herder & Herder, 1973–74), I, pp. 189-207.

Ben-Porat, Ziva, 'The Poetics of Literary Allusion', *PTL: A Journal for Descriptive Poetics and Theory of Literature* 1 (1976), pp. 105-28.

Best, E., and R. McL. Wilson (eds.), *Text and Interpretation: Studies in the New Testament Present to Matthew Black* (Cambridge: Cambridge University Press, 1979).

Betz, Hans Dieter, *The Sermon on the Mount: A Commentary on the Sermon on the Mount, including the Sermon on the Plain* (ed. Adela Yarbro Collins; Hermeneia; Minneapolis: Fortress Press, 1995).

Betz, Otto, and Gerald F. Hawthorne (eds.), *Tradition and Interpretation in the New Testament: Essays in Honor of E. Earle Ellis for His Sixtieth Birthday* (Grand Rapids: Eerdmans, 1987).

Beuken, W.A.M., *Haggai–Sacharja 1–8: Studien zur Überlieferungsgeschichte der frühnachexilischen Prophetie* (SSN, 10; Assen: Van Gorcum, 1968).

Birch, Bruce C., Walter Brueggemann, Terence E. Fretheim and David L. Petersen, *A Theological Introduction to the Old Testament* (Nashville: Abingdon Press, 1999).

Black, Mark C., 'The Rejected and Slain Messiah who is Coming with His Angels: The Messianic Exegesis of Zechariah 9–14 in the Passion Narratives' (PhD dissertation, Emory University, 1990).

Black, Matthew, 'The Christological Use of the Old Testament in the New Testament', *NTS* 18 (1971), pp. 1-14.

—'The Theological Appropriation of the Old Testament by the New Testament', *SJT* 39 (1986), pp. 1-17.

Black, Stephanie L., *Sentence Conjunction in the Gospel of Matthew: καί, δέ, τότε, γάρ, οὖν and Asyndeton in Narrative Discourse* (JSNTSup, 216; SNTG, 9; Sheffield: Sheffield Academic Press, 2002).

Blank, Sheldon H., 'The Death of Zechariah in Rabbinic Literature', *HUCA* 12–13 (1937–38), pp. 327-46.

Blenkinsopp, Joseph, *A History of Prophecy in Israel* (Louisville, KY: Westminster/John Knox Press, rev. edn, 1996).

Bloch, Reneé, 'Midrash', in William S. Green (ed.), *Approaches to Ancient Judaism: Theory and Practice* (BJS, 1; Missoula, MT: Scholars Press, 1978), pp. 29-50.

Blomberg, Craig L., 'Interpreting Old Testament Prophetic Literature in Matthew: Double Fulfillment', *TJ* NS 23 (2002), pp. 17-33.

—*Jesus and the Gospels: An Introduction and Survey* (Nashville: Broadman & Holman, 1997).

—*Matthew* (NAC, 22; Nashville: Broadman, 1992).

Bock, Darrell L., *Blasphemy and Exaltation in Judaism and the Final Examination of Jesus: A Philological-Historical Study of the Key Jewish Themes Impacting Mark 14.61-64* (WUNT, 2.106; Tübingen: Mohr Siebeck, 1998).

—*Jesus according to Scripture: Restoring the Portrait from the Gospels* (Downers Grove, IL: Intervarsity Press, 2002).

—*Proclamation from Prophecy and Pattern: Lucan Old Testament Christology* (JSNTSup, 12; Sheffield: JSOT Press, 1987).

Boismard, Marie-Emile, 'Les citations targumiques dans le quatrième Évangile', *RB* 66 (1959), pp. 374-78.

Borgen, Peder, 'The Place of the Old Testament in the Formation of New Testament Theology: Response to Barnabas Lindars', *NTS* 23 (1976), pp. 67-75.

Bracewell, Ronald E., 'Shepherd Imagery in the Synoptic Gospels' (PhD dissertation, Southern Baptist Theological Seminary, 1983).

Brooks, Stephenson H., *Matthew's Community: The Evidence of His Special Sayings Material* (JSNTSup, 16; Sheffield: JSOT Press, 1987).

Broshi, Magen (ed.), *The Damascus Document Reconsidered* (Jerusalem: Israel Exploration Society, 1992).

Brown, Raymond E., *The Birth of the Messiah: A Commentary on the Infancy Narratives in Matthew and Luke* (ABRL; New York: Doubleday, 1993).

—*A Crucified Christ in Holy Week: Essays on the Four Gospel Passion Narratives* (Collegeville, MN: Liturgical Press, 1986).

—*The Death of the Messiah: A Commentary on the Passion Narratives in the Four Gospels* (ABRL; 2 vols.; New York: Doubleday, 1994).

—*The Gospel according to John* (AB, 29; 2 vols.; Garden City, NY: Doubleday, 1966).

—*An Introduction to the New Testament* (ABRL; New York: Doubleday, 1997).

Brownlee, William H., 'Messianic Motifs of Qumran and the New Testament', *NTS* 3 (1956), pp. 12-30.

Bruce, F.F., *Biblical Exegesis in the Qumran Texts* (Grand Rapids: Eerdmans, 1959).

—'The Book of Zechariah and the Passion Narratives', *BJRL* 43 (1960–61), pp. 336-53.

—*New Testament Development of Old Testament Themes* (Grand Rapids: Eerdmans, 1968).

Bruner, Frederick Dale, *Matthew* (2 vols.; Dallas: Word Books, 1987–90).

Buchanan, George Wesley, *The Gospel of Matthew* (MBCNTS, 1; 2 vols.; Lewiston, NY: Edwin Mellen Press, 1996).

—*Introduction to Intertextuality* (Mellen Biblical Press Series, 26; Lewiston, NY: Edwin Mellen Press, 1994).

—*Typology and the Gospel* (Lanham, MD: University Press of America, 1987).

—'The Use of Rabbinic Literature for New Testament Research', *Biblical Theology Bulletin* 7 (1977), pp. 110-22.

Bultmann, Rudolf, *The History of the Synoptic Tradition* (trans. John Marsh; Oxford: Basil Blackwell, 1968).

Buren, Paul Matthews van, *According to the Scriptures: The Origin of the Gospel and the Church's Old Testament* (Grand Rapids: Eerdmans, 1998).

Burridge, Richard A., *Four Gospels, One Jesus? A Symbolic Reading* (Grand Rapids: Eerdmans, 1994).

Butterworth, Mike, *Structure and the Book of Zechariah* (JSOTSup, 180; Sheffield: JSOT Press, 1992).

Cangh, Jean-Marie van, 'La Bible de Matthieu: Les citations de l'accomplissement', *Revue théologique de Louvain* 6 (1965), pp. 205-11.

Capes, David B., 'Intertextual Echoes in the Matthean Baptismal Narrative', *BBR* 9 (1999), pp. 37-49.

Cargal, T.B. '"His Blood Be upon Us and upon Our Children": A Matthean Double Entendre?', *NTS* 37 (1991), pp. 101-12.

Carroll, John T., and Joel B. Green, *The Death of Jesus in Early Christianity* (Peabody, MA: Hendrickson, 1995).

Carroll, Robert P., Review of *Jeremiah in Matthew's Gospel* by Michael Knowles, *Expository Times* 105 (1994), pp. 247.

Carson, D.A., *Matthew*, in Frank E. Gaebelein (ed.), *Expositor's Bible Commentary*. VIII. *Matthew, Mark, Luke* (Grand Rapids: Zondervan, 1984), pp. 1-599.

Carson, D.A., and H.G.M. Williamson (eds.), *It is Written: Scripture Citing Scripture: Essays in Honour of Barnabas Lindars* (Cambridge: Cambridge University Press, 1988).

Carter, Warren, *Matthew: Storyteller, Interpreter, Evangelist* (Peabody, MA: Hendrickson, 1996).

Catchpole, David R., 'The "Triumphal' Entry"', in Bammel and Moule (eds.), *Jesus and the Politics of His Day*, pp. 319-34.

Chajes, Z.H., *The Student's Guide through the Talmud* (trans. Jacob Shachter; London: East and West Library, 1952).

Chapman, John, 'Zacharias, Slain between the Temple and the Altar', *JTS* 13 (1912), pp. 398-410.

Charlesworth, James H., 'The Concept of the Messiah in the Pseudepigrapha', *ANRW* 19.2.188-218. Part 2, *Principat*, 19.1 (Berlin: W. de Gruyter, 1987).

—*The Old Testament Pseudepigrapha and the New Testament* (Cambridge: Cambridge University Press, 1985).

Charlesworth, James H., *et al.* (eds.), *The Messiah: Developments in Earliest Judaism and Christianity* (First Princeton Symposium on Judaism and Christian Origins; Minneapolis: Fortress Press, 1992).

Charlesworth, James H., and Walter P. Weaver (eds.), *The Old and New Testaments: Their Relationship and the 'Intertestamental' Literature* (Faith and Scholarship Colloquies Series; Valley Forge, PA: Trinity Press International, 1993).

Childs, Brevard S., *Biblical Theology of the Old and New Testaments* (Minneapolis: Fortress Press, 1993).

—*Introduction to the Old Testament as Scripture* (Philadelphia: Fortress Press, 1979).

—*The New Testament As Canon: An Introduction* (Philadelphia: Fortress Press, 1985).

—*Old Testament Theology in a Canonical Context* (Philadelphia: Fortress Press, 1986).

Chilton, Bruce, *The Temple of Jesus: His Sacrificial Program within a Cultural History of Sacrifice* (University Park, PA: Pennsylvania State University Press, 1992).

Chilton, Bruce, and Craig A. Evans (eds.), *Authenticating the Activities of Jesus* (NTTS, 28.2; Leiden: E.J. Brill, 1999).

—*Authenticating the Words of Jesus* (NTTS, 28.1; Leiden: E.J. Brill, 1999).

Chisholm, Robert B., 'שׁלך', in *NIDOTTE*, IV, pp. 127-28.

Claudel, Gérard, Review of *Jeremiah in Matthew's Gospel*, by Michael Knowles, *Bib* 76 (1995), pp. 427-30.

Coggins, R.J., *Haggai, Zechariah, Malachi* (OTG; Sheffield: Sheffield Academic Press, 1987).

Cohen, A., *The Twelve Prophets* (rev. A.J. Rosenberg; Soncino Books of the Bible; New York: Soncino, 2nd edn, 1994).

Cohen, Norman M., *Jewish Bible Personages in the New Testament* (Lanham, MD: University Press of America, 1989).

Coleman, Robert O., 'Matthew's Use of the Old Testament', *Southwestern Journal of Theology* 5 (1962), pp. 29-39.

Collins, John J. (ed.), *The Encyclopedia of Apocalypticism. I. The Origin of Apocalypticism in Judaism and Christianity* (ed. John J. Collins, B. McGinn and S.J. Stein; 3 vols.; New York: Continuum, 1998).

Collins, L.L, Jr, 'The Significance of the Use of Isaiah in the Gospel of Matthew' (ThD dissertation, Southwestern Baptist Theological Seminary, 1973).

Conard, Audrey, 'The Fate of Judas: Matthew 27.3-10', *Toronto Journal of Theology* 7 (1991), pp. 158-68.

Conrad, Edgar W., *Zechariah* (Readings: A New Biblical Commentary; Sheffield: Sheffield Academic Press, 1999).

Cook, Stephen L., 'The Metamorphosis of a Shepherd: The Tradition History of Zechariah 11.17 + 13.7-9', *CBQ* 55 (1993), pp. 453-66.

Cope, O. Lamar, *Matthew: A Scribe Trained for the Kingdom of Heaven* (CBQ Monograph Series, 5; Washington, DC: Catholic Biblical Association of America, 1976).

Cothenet, E., 'Les prophètes chrétiens dans l'évangile selon Saint Matthieu', in Didier (ed.), *L'Évangile selon Matthieu*, pp. 281-308.

Court, J.M., 'Right and Left: The Implications for Matthew 25.31-46', *NTS* 31 (1985), pp. 223-33.

Cowley, Roger W., 'The "Blood of Zechariah" (Mt 23.35) in Ethiopian Exegetical Tradition', in Elizabeth A. Livingstone (ed.), *Studia Patristica XVIII* (4 vols.; Kalamazoo, MI: Cistercian Publications, 1985), I, pp. 293-302.

Cozart, Richard Mark, 'The Use of Zechariah in the Gospel of Matthew by Quotation and Allusion' (ThM thesis, Dallas Theological Seminary, 1982).

Crossan, John Dominic, *The Historical Jesus: The Life of a Mediterranean Jewish Peasant* (San Francisco: HarperSanFrancisco, 1991).

Cummings, John T., 'The Tassel of His Cloak: Mark, Luke, Matthew—Zechariah', in Elizabeth A. Livingstone (ed.), *Studia Biblica 1978* (JSNTSup, 2; 3 vols.; Sheffield: JSOT Press, 1978), II, pp. 47-61.

Cunliffe-Jones, Hubert, *A Word for our Time? Zechariah 9–14, the New Testament and Today* (London: Athlone Press, 1973).

Curtis, John Briggs, 'An Investigation of the Mount of Olives in the Judaeo-Christian Tradition', *HUCA* 28 (1957), pp. 137-80.

Daube, David, *The New Testament and Rabbinic Judaism* (London: University of London Press, 1956; repr., Peabody, MA: Hendrickson, 1994).

Davies, Margaret, *Matthew* (Readings: A New Bible Commentary; Sheffield: Sheffield Academic Press, 1993).

—'Stereotyping the Other: The "Pharisees" in the Gospel according to Matthew', in J. Cheryl Exum and Stephen D. Moore (eds.), *Biblical Studies/Cultural Studies: The Third Sheffield Colloquium* (JSOTSup, 266; GCT, 7; Sheffield: Sheffield Academic Press, 1998), pp. 415-32.

Davies, Philip R., *The Damascus Covenant: An Interpretation of the 'Damascus Document'* (JSOTSup, 25; Sheffield: JSOT Press, 1982).

Davies, W.D., and Dale C. Allison, Jr, *The Gospel according to Saint Matthew* (ICC; 3 vols.; Edinburgh: T. & T. Clark, 1988–97).

Day, John, 'Prophecy', in Carson and Williamson (eds.), *It is Written*, pp. 39-55.

Delcor, Matthias, 'Les allusions à Alexandre le Grand dans Zach 9.1-8', *VT* 1 (1951), pp. 110-24.

—'Deux passages difficiles: Zacharie 12.11 et 11.13', *VT* 3 (1953), pp. 67-77.

—'Un problème de critique textuelle et d'exégèse: Zach 12.10 et aspicient ad me quem confixerunt', *RB* 58 (1951), pp. 189-99.

Delitzsch, Franz, *Neue Untersuchungen über Enstehung und Anlage der kanonischen Evangelien. I. Das Matthaeus-Evangelium* (Leipzig: Dörffling & Granke, 1853).

Delkurt, Holger, *Sacharjas Nachtgesichte: Zur Aufnahme und Abwandlung prophetischer Traditionen* (BZAW, 302; Berlin: W. de Gruyter, 2000).

Delling, Gerhard, 'μάγος', in *TDNT*, IV, pp. 356-59

Delorme, Jean, 'Intertextualities about Mark' (trans. Marie-Patricia Burns), in Draisma (ed.), *Intertextuality in Biblical Writings*, pp. 35-42.

Derrett, J.D.M., 'The Zeal of Thy House and the Cleansing of the Temple', *Downside Review* 95 (1977), pp. 79-94.

Desautels, L., 'La mort de Judas (Mt 27,3-10; Ac 1,15-26)', *Science et esprit* 38 (1986), pp. 221-39.

Dibelius, Martin, *From Tradition to Gospel* (trans. Bertram Lee Woolf; New York: Charles Scribner's Sons, 1935).

Didier, M., *L'Évangile selon Matthieu: Rédaction et Théologie* (BETL, 29; Gembloux: Duculot, 1972).

Dillard, Raymond B., and Tremper Longman, III, *An Introduction to the Old Testament* (Grand Rapids: Zondervan, 1994).

Dodd, C.H., *According to the Scriptures: The Sub-Structure of New Testament Theology* (London: Nisbet, 1952).

—*The Old Testament in the New* (Philadelphia: Fortress Press, 1963).

Doeve, J.W., *Jewish Hermeneutics in the Synoptic Gospels and Acts* (Assen: Van Gorcum, 1954).

Donaldson, Terence L., *Jesus on the Mountain: A Study in Matthean Theology* (JSNTSup, 8; Sheffield: JSOT Press, 1985).

Dorsey, David A., *The Literary Structure of the Old Testament: A Commentary on Genesis–Malachi* (Grand Rapids: Baker Book House, 1999).

Draisma, Sipke (ed.), *Intertextuality in Biblical Writings: Essays in Honour of Bas van Iersel* (Kampen: Uitgeversmaatschappij J.K. Kok, 1989).

Duff, Paul Brooks, 'The March of the Divine Warrior and the Advent of the Greco-Roman Kings: Mark's Account of the Jesus' Entry into Jerusalem', *JBL* 111 (1992), pp. 55-71.

Duguid, Ian M., *Ezekiel and the Leaders of Israel* (VTSup, 56; Leiden: E.J. Brill, 1994).

—'Messianic Themes in Zechariah 9–14', in Philip E. Satterthwaite, Richard S. Hess and Gordon J. Wenham (eds.), *The Lord's Anointed: Interpretation of Old Testament Messianic Texts* (THS; Grand Rapids: Baker Book House, 1995), pp. 265-80.

Dumbrell, William J., *The Faith of Israel: Its Expression in the Books of the Old Testament* (Grand Rapids: Baker Book House, 1988).

—'עָנוּ', in *NIDOTTE*, III, pp. 454-64.

Dungan, David Laird, *A History of the Synoptic Problem: The Canon, the Text, the Composition, and the Interpretation of the Gospels* (ABRL; New York: Doubleday, 1999).

Edgar, S.L., 'New Testament and Rabbinic Messianic Interpretation', *NTS* 5 (1958–59), pp. 47-54.

Edwards, Richard A., *Matthew's Narrative Portrait of Disciples: How the Text-Connoted Reader is Informed* (Harrisburg, PA: Trinity Press International, 1997).

—*Matthew's Story of Jesus* (Philadelphia: Fortress Press, 1985).

Ehrman, Bart D., *Jesus: Apocalyptic Prophet of the New Millennium* (Oxford: Oxford University Press, 1999).

Eissfeldt, Otto, *Kleine Schriften* (ed. Rudolf Sellheim and Fritz Maass; 6 vols.; Tübingen: Mohr Siebeck, 1962–79).

Elayi, Josette, 'The Phoenician Cities in the Persian Period', *JANESCU* 12 (1980), pp. 13-28.

Eldridge, V.J., 'Second Thoughts on Matthew's Formula Quotations', *Colloquium* 15.2 (1983), pp. 45-47.

—'Typology—the Key to Understanding Matthew's Formula Quotations?' *Colloquium* 15.1 (1982), pp. 43-51.

Eliot, T.S., 'Philip Massinger', in *idem*, *Selected Prose of T. S. Eliot* (ed. Frank Kermode; New York: Harcourt Brace Jovanovich, 1975).

Elliott, Mark A., *The Survivors of Israel: A Reconsideration of the Theology of Pre-Christian Judaism* (Grand Rapids: Eerdmans, 2000).

Ellis, E. Earle, 'Biblical Interpretation in the New Testament Church', in Mulder (ed.), *Mikra*, pp. 691-725.

—'How the New Testament Uses the Old', in I. Howard Marshall (ed.), *New Testament Interpretation: Essays on Principles and Methods* (Grand Rapids: Eerdmans, 1977), pp. 199-219.

—'Interpretation of the Bible Within the Bible Itself', in Farmer (ed.), *The International Bible Commentary*, pp. 53-63.

—'Jesus' Use of the Old Testament and the Genesis of New Testament Theology', *BBR* 3 (1993), pp. 59-75.

—*The Making of the New Testament Documents* (BIS, 39; Leiden: E.J. Brill, 1999).

—'Midrash, Targum and New Testament Quotations', in E. Earle Ellis and Max Wilcox (eds.), *Neotestamentica et Semitica: Studies in Honour of Matthew Black* (Edinburgh: T. & T. Clark, 1969), pp. 199-219.

—*The Old Testament in Early Christianity: Canon and Interpretation in the Light of Modern Research* (Grand Rapids: Baker Book House, 1991).

—*Paul's Use of the Old Testament* (Grand Rapids: Eerdmans, 1957; repr., Grand Rapids: Baker Book House, 1981).

—*Prophecy and Hermeneutic in Early Christianity* (Grand Rapids: Eerdmans, 1978).

Ellul, Danielle, 'Variations sur le thème de la guerre sainte dans le Deutéro-Zacharie', *Études théologiques et religieuses* 56 (1981), pp. 55-71.

Escande, Jacques, 'Judas et Pilate prisonniers d'une même structure (Mt 27,1-26)', *Foi et vie* 78.3 (1979), pp. 92-100.

Eslinger, Lyle, 'Inner-Biblical Exegesis and Inner-Biblical Allusion: The Question of Category', *VT* 42 (1992), pp. 47-58.

Evans, Craig A., 'Aspects of Exile and Restoration in the Proclamation of Jesus and the Gospels', in James M. Scott (ed.), *Exile: Old Testament, Jewish, and Christian Conceptions* (JSJSup, 56; Leiden: E.J. Brill, 1997), pp. 299-328.

—'Jesus and Zechariah's Messianic Hope', in Chilton and Evans (eds.), *Authenticating the Activities of Jesus*, pp. 373-88.

—'Old Testament in the Gospels', in *DJG*, pp. 579-90.

—'On the Quotation Formulas in the Fourth Gospel', *BZ* 26 (1982), pp. 79-83.

—'Qumran's Messiah: How Important is He?', in John J. Collins and Robert A. Kugler (eds.), *Religion in the Dead Sea Scrolls* (Grand Rapids: Eerdmans, 2000), pp. 135-49.

—*To See and Not Perceive: Isaiah 6.9-10 in Early Jewish and Christian Interpretation* (JSOTSup, 64; Sheffield: Sheffield Academic Press, 1989).

—' "The Two Sons of Oil": Early Evidence of Messianic Interpretation of Zechariah 4.14 in 4Q254 4 2', in Donald W. Perry and Eugene Ulrich (eds.), *The Provo International Conference on the Dead Sea Scrolls* (STDJ, 30; Leiden: E.J. Brill, 1999), pp. 566-75.

Evans, Craig A., and Peter W. Flint (eds.), *Eschatology, Messianism, and the Dead Sea Scrolls* (Grand Rapids: Eerdmans, 1997).

Evans, Craig A., and Stanley E. Porter (eds.), *The Synoptic Gospels: A Sheffield Reader* (The Biblical Seminar, 31; Sheffield: Sheffield Academic Press, 1995).

Evans, Craig A., and James A. Sanders (eds.), *Early Christian Interpretation of the Scriptures of Israel: Investigations and Proposals* (JSNTSup, 148; SSEJC, 5; Sheffield: Sheffield Academic Press, 1997).

—*The Function of Scripture in Early Jewish and Christian Tradition* (JSNTSup, 154; SSEJC, 6; Sheffield: Sheffield Academic Press, 1998).

Evans, Craig A., and W. Richard Stegner (eds.), *The Gospels and the Scriptures of Israel* (JSNTSup, 104; SSEJC, 1; Sheffield: JSOT Press, 1993).

Evans, Craig A., and William Stinespring (eds.), *Early Jewish and Christian Exegesis: Studies in Memory of William Hugh Brownlee* (Atlanta: Scholars Press, 1987).

Evans, Craig A., and Shemaryahu Talman (eds.), *The Quest for Context and Meaning: Studies in Biblical Intertextuality in Honor of James A. Sanders* (BIS, 28; Leiden: E.J. Brill, 1997).

Evans, Craig F., 'I Will Go before You into Galilee', *JTS* NS 5 (1954), pp. 3-18.

Fairbairn, Patrick, *The Typology of Scripture* (Edinburgh: T. & T. Clark, 5th edn, 1870).

Farmer, William R., *The Gospel of Jesus: The Pastoral Relevance of the Synoptic Problem* (Louisville, KY: Westminster/John Knox Press, 1994).

—'The Palm Branches in John 12.13', *JTS* 3 (1952–53), pp. 62-66.

—'Reflections on Isaiah 53 and the Christian Origins', in Bellinger and Farmer (eds.), *Jesus and the Suffering Servant*, pp. 260-80.

Farmer, William R. (ed.), *The International Bible Commentary: A Catholic and Ecumenical Commentary for the Twenty-First Century* (Collegeville, MN: Liturgical Press, 1998).

Ferguson, Everett, *Backgrounds of Early Christianity* (Grand Rapids: Eerdmans, 2nd edn 1993).

Finley, Thomas J., 'The Sheep Merchants of Zechariah 11', *GTJ* 3 (1982), pp. 51-65.

Fishbane, Michael A., *Biblical Interpretation in Ancient Israel* (Oxford: Clarendon Press, 1985).

—'Use, Authority, and Interpretation of Mikra at Qumran', in Mulder (ed.), *Mikra*, pp. 339-77.

Fitzmyer, Joseph A., '"4Q Testimonia" and the New Testament', in *idem*, *Essays on the Semitic Background*, pp. 59-89.

—*Essays on the Semitic Background of the New Testament* (London: Geoffrey Chapman, 1971).

—'The Use of Explicit Old Testament Quotations in Qumran Literature and in the New Testament', in *idem*, *Essays on the Semitic Background*, pp. 3-58

Floyd, Michael H., *Minor Prophets, Part 2* (The Forms of the Old Testament Literature, 22; Grand Rapids: Eerdmans, 2000).

Foster, Paul, 'The Use of Zechariah in Matthew's Gospel', in Tuckett (ed.), *The Book of Zechariah*, pp. 65-85.

Fox, Michael V., 'The Identification of Quotations in Biblical Literature', *ZAW* 92 (1980), pp. 416-31.

France, R.T., 'The Formula Quotations of Matthew 2 and the Problem of Communication', *NTS* 27 (1980–81), pp. 233-51.

—*The Gospel according to Matthew* (TNTC; Grand Rapids: Eerdmans, 1985).

—*Jesus and the Old Testament: His Application of Old Testament Passages to Himself and His Mission* (London: Tyndale, 1971).

—*Matthew: Evangelist and Teacher* (Grand Rapids: Zondervan, 1989).

France, R.T., and David Wenham (eds.), *Gospel Perspectives. III. Studies in Midrash and Historiography* (Sheffield: JSOT Press, 1983).

Frankemölle, Herbert, *Matthäus: Kommentar* (2 vols.; Düsseldorf: Patmos, 1994–97).

Freed, Edwin D., *Old Testament Quotations in the Gospel of John* (NovTSup, 11; Leiden: E.J. Brill, 1965).

Garland, David E., *The Intention of Matthew 23* (NovTSup, 52; Leiden: E.J. Brill, 1979).

—*One Hundred Years of Study on the Passion Narratives* (Macon, GA: Mercer University Press, 1989).

Gärtner, Bertil, 'The Habakkuk Commentary (DSH) and the Gospel of Matthew', *ST* 8 (1955), pp. 1-24.

—*The Temple and the Community in Qumran and the New Testament: A Comparative Study in the Temple Symbolism of the Qumran Texts and the New Testament* (SNTSMS, 1; Cambridge: Cambridge University Press, 1965).

Gaston, Lloyd, *No Stone upon Another: Studies in the Significance of the Fall of Jerusalem in the Synoptic Gospels* (NovTSup, 23; Leiden: E.J. Brill, 1970).

Geiger, Georg, 'Falsche Zitate bei Matthäus und Lukas', in Tuckett (ed.), *The Scriptures in the Gospels*, pp. 479-86.

Gese, Hartmut, *Essays on Biblical Theology* (trans. Keith Crum; Minneapolis: Augsburg Press, 1981).

Giese, Curtis Paul, 'A Study of the Old Testament Quote in Matthew 27.9,10' (STM thesis, Concordia Seminary, 1991).

Glasson, T. Francis, 'Davidic Links with the Betrayal of Jesus', *ExpTim* 85 (1974), pp. 118-19.

Gnilka, Joachim, *Das Matthäusevangelium* (HTKNT, 1; 2 vols.; Freiburg: Herder, 1986–88).

—*Theologie des Neuen Testaments* (HTKNTSup, 5; Freiburg: Herder, 1994).

Good, Deirdre J., *Jesus the Meek King* (Harrisburg, PA: Trinity Press International, 1999).

Goppelt, Leonhard, *Theology of the New Testament* (ed. Jürgen Roloff; trans. John E. Alsup; 2 vols.; Grand Rapids: Eerdmans, 1981–82).

—*Typos: The Typological Interpretation of the Old Testament in the New* (trans. Donald H. Madvig; Grand Rapids: Eerdmans, 1982).

Gordon, Robert P., *Studies in the Targum to the Twelve Prophets: From Nahum to Malachi* (VTSup, 51; Leiden: E.J. Brill, 1994).

—'The Targum to the Minor Prophets and the Dead Sea Texts: Textual and Exegetical Notes', *Revue de Qumran* 8 (1974), pp. 425-29.

Gough, Henry, *The New Testament Quotations Collated with the Scripture of the Old Testament* (London: Walton & Maberly, 1855).

Goulder, M.D., *Midrash and Lection in Matthew: The Speaker's Lectures in Biblical Studies, 1969–71* (London: SPCK, 1974).

—'Sections and Lections in Matthew', *JSNT* 76 (1999), pp. 79-96.

Graham, Susan L., 'A Strange Salvation: Intertextual Allusion in Mt 27,39-43', in Tuckett (ed.), *The Scriptures in the Gospels*, pp. 501-11.

Grant, Robert M., 'The Coming of the Kingdom', *JBL* 67 (1948), pp. 297-303.

Green, Joel B., *The Death of Jesus: Tradition and Interpretation in the Passion Narrative* (WUNT, 2.33; Tübingen: Mohr Siebeck, 1988).

Grimsley, Brent, 'The Matthean Fulfillment Citations: New Testament Abuse of the Old?' (MDiv thesis, Denver Conservative Baptist Seminary, 1991).

Guelich, Robert A., *The Sermon on the Mount: A Foundation for Understanding* (Waco, TX: Word Books, 1982).

Gundry, Robert H., *Mark: A Commentary on His Apology for the Cross* (Grand Rapids: Eerdmans, 1993).

—*Matthew: A Commentary on His Handbook for a Mixed Church under Persecution* (Grand Rapids: Eerdmans, 2nd edn, 1994).

—*Matthew: A Commentary on His Literary and Theological Art* (Grand Rapids: Eerdmans, 1982).

—*The Use of the Old Testament in St Matthew's Gospel with Special Reference to the Messianic Hope* (NovTSup, 18; Leiden: E.J. Brill, 1967).

Haenchen, E., 'Matthäus 23', *ZTK* 48 (1951), pp. 38-63.

Hagner, Donald A., *Matthew 1–13* (WBC, 33A; Dallas: Word Books, 1993).

—*Matthew 14–28* (WBC, 33B; Dallas: Word Books, 1995).

Hahlen, Mark A., 'The Background and Use of Equine Imagery in Zechariah', *SCJ* 3 (2000), pp. 243-60.

Ham, Clay Alan, 'The Last Supper in Matthew', *BBR* 10.1 (2000), pp. 53-69.

—'The Title "Son of Man" in the Gospel of John', *SCJ* 1 (1998), pp. 67-84.

Hanson, A.T., *Jesus Christ in the Old Testament* (London: SPCK, 1965).

—*The Living Utterances of God: The New Testament Exegesis of the Old* (London: Darton, Longman & Todd, 1983).

—*The New Testament Interpretation of Scripture* (London: SPCK, 1980).

Hanson, Paul D., 'In Defiance of Death: Zechariah's Symbolic Universe', in John H. Marks and Robert Good (eds.), *Love and Death in the Ancient Near East* (Guilford, CT: Four Quarters, 1986), pp. 173-79.

—*The Dawn of Apocalyptic* (Philadelphia: Fortress Press, 1975).

Harrington, Daniel J., *The Gospel of Matthew* (SP, 1; Collegeville, MN: Liturgical Press, 1991).

—Review of *Jeremiah in Matthew's Gospel*, by Michael Knowles, *CBQ* 56 (1994), pp. 601-602.

Harris, J. Rendel, *Testimonies* (2 vols.; Cambridge: Cambridge University Press, 1916–20).

Hartmann, Lars, 'Scriptural Exegesis in the Gospel of Matthew and the Problem of Communication', in Didier (ed.), *L'Évangile selon Matthieu*, pp. 131-52.

Harvey, A.E., *Jesus and the Constraints of History* (Philadelphia: Westminster Press, 1982).

Hays, Richard B., 'Criteria for Identifying Allusions and Echoes of the Text of Isaiah in the Letters of Paul' (paper presented at the Isaiah 53 and Christian Origins Conference, Baylor University, Waco, TX, February 1996).

—*Echoes of Scripture in the Letters of Paul* (New Haven: Yale University Press, 1989).

Heil, John Paul, *The Death and Resurrection of Jesus: A Narrative-Critical Reading of Matthew 26–28* (Minneapolis: Fortress Press, 1991).

—'Ezekiel 34 and the Narrative Strategy of the Shepherd and Sheep Metaphor in Matthew', *CBQ* 55 (1993), pp. 698-708.

Hengel, Martin, and Anna Maria Schwemer, *Der messianische Anspruch Jesu und die Anfänge der Christologie: vier Studien* (WUNT, 138; Tübingen: Mohr Siebeck, 2001).

Hengstenberg, Ernst Wilhelm; *Christology of the Old Testament and a Commentary on the Messianic Predictions* (trans. Theod. Meyer and James Martin; 4 vols.; Edinburgh: T. & T. Clark, 2nd edn, 1856–58; repr., Grand Rapids: Kregel, 1956).

Heschel, Abraham J., *The Prophets* (2 vols.; New York: Harper & Row, 1962).

Hill, David, *The Gospel of Matthew* (New Century Bible Commentary; Grand Rapids: Eerdmans, 1972).

—'Jesus and Josephus "Messianic Prophets"', in Best and McL. Wilson (eds.), *Text and Interpretation*, pp. 143-54.

Hillyer, Norman, 'Matthew's Use of the Old Testament', *EvQ* 36 (1964), pp. 12-26.

Hoffman, Yair, 'The Technique of Quotation and Citation as an Interpretive Device', in Benjamin Uffenheimer and Henning Graf Reventlow (eds.), *Creative Biblical Exegesis: Christian and Jewish Hermeneutics through the Centuries* (JSOTSup, 59; Sheffield: JSOT Press, 1988), pp. 71-79.

Holmgren, Frederick Carlson, *The Old Testament and the Significance of Jesus* (Grand Rapids: Eerdmans, 1999).

Holtzmann, H.J., *Die Synoptiker—Die Apostelgeschichte* (HCNT, 1; Freiburg: Mohr Siebeck, 1889).

Hooker, Morna D., *The Signs of a Prophet: The Prophet Actions of Jesus* (London: SCM Press, 1997).

Horgan, Maurya P., 'Isaiah Pesher 3 (4Q163 = 4QpIsac)', in Charlesworth (ed.), *The Dead Sea Scrolls*, pp. 47-82.

Horsley, Richard A., ' "Like One of the Prophets of Old": Two Types of Popular Prophets at the Time of Jesus', *CBQ* 47 (1985), pp. 435-63.

—'Popular Messianic Movements around the Time of Jesus', *CBQ* 46 (1984), pp. 471-95.

—'Popular Prophetic Movements at the Time of Jesus: Their Principal Features and Social Origins', *JSNT* 26 (1986), pp. 3-27.

House, Paul R., *Old Testament Theology* (Downers Grove, IL: Intervarsity Press, 1998).

Howard, George, *The Gospel of Matthew according to a Primitive Hebrew Text* (Macon, GA: Mercer University Press, 1987).

Howell, David B., *Matthew's Inclusive Story: A Study in the Narrative Rhetoric of the First Gospel* (JSNTSup, 42; Sheffield: JSOT Press, 1990).

Hübner, Hans, *Biblische Theologie des Neuen Testaments* (3 vols.; Göttingen: Vandenhoeck & Ruprecht, 1990–95).

—*Das Gesetz in der synoptischen Tradition: Studien zur These einer progressiven Qumranisierung und Judaisierung innerhalb der synoptischen Tradition* (Göttingen: Vandenhoeck & Ruprecht, 2nd edn, 1986).

Hutch, Hugh Ross, 'The Old Testament Quotation in Matthew 27.9,10', *Biblical World* 1 (1893), pp. 345-54.

Instone-Brewer, David, *Techniques and Assumptions in Jewish Exegesis before 70 C.E.* (TSAJ, 30; Tübingen: Mohr Siebeck, 1992).

—'The Two Asses of Zechariah 9.9 in Matthew 21', *TynBul* 54 (2003), pp. 87-98.

Jeremias, Joachim, 'ποιμήν', in *TDNT*, VI, pp. 485-502.

Johnson, David H., 'Shepherd, Sheep', in *DJG*, pp. 751-54.

Johnson, Franklin, *The Quotations of the New Testament from the Old: Considered in the Light of General Literature* (Philadelphia: American Baptist Publication Society, 1896).

Johnson, Sherman E., 'The Biblical Quotations in Matthew', *HTR* 36 (1943), pp. 135-53.

Jones, Ivor H., Review of *Jeremiah in Matthew's Gospel*, by Michael Knowles, *JTS* 47 (1996), pp. 602-604.

Jonge, Marinus de, 'Christian Influence in the Testaments of the Twelve Patriarchs', in *idem* (ed.), *Studies on the Testaments of the Twelve Patriarchs: Text and Interpretation* (SVTP, 3; Leiden: E.J. Brill, 1975), pp. 193-246.

—*Christology in Context: The Earliest Christian Response to Jesus* (Philadelphia: Westminster Press, 1988).

Joosten, Jan, 'The Old Testament Quotations in the Old Syriac and Peshitta Gospels', *Textus* 15 (1990), pp. 55-76.

Juel, David, *Messianic Exegesis: Christological Interpretation of the Old Testament in Early Christianity* (Philadelphia: Fortress Press, 1988).

Kaiser, Walter C., Jr, *The Messiah in the Old Testament* (Studies in Old Testament Biblical Theology; Grand Rapids: Zondervan, 1995).

—*The Uses of the Old Testament in the New* (Chicago: Moody, 1985).

Kampen, John, 'A Reexamination of the Relationship between Matthew 5.21-48 and the Dead Sea Scrolls', in *SBL Seminar Papers, 1990* (SBLSP, 29; Chico, CA: Scholars Press, 1990), pp. 34-59.

Kealy, Seán P., *Matthew's Gospel and the History of Biblical Interpretation* (Mellen Biblical Press Series, 55; 2 vols.; Lewiston, NY: Edwin Mellen Press, 1997).

Keener, Craig S., *A Commentary on the Gospel of Matthew* (Grand Rapids: Eerdmans, 1999).

—*The IVP Bible Background Commentary: New Testament* (Downers Grove, IL: Intervarsity Press, 1993).

Kent, Homer A., 'Matthew's Use of the Old Testament', *Bibliotheca Sacra* 121 (1964), pp. 34-43.

Kilpatrick, George D., *The Origins of the Gospel according to St Matthew* (Oxford: Clarendon Press, 1946).

Kim, Seyoon, 'Jesus, Sayings of', in *DPL*, pp. 474-92.

—'Jesus—The Son of God, the Stone, the Son of Man, and the Servant: The Role of Zechariah in the Self-Identification of Jesus', in Betz and Hawthorne (eds.), *Tradition and Interpretation*, pp. 134-48.

Kimchi, David, *Commentary upon the Prophecies of Zechariah* (trans. A. M'Caul; London: James Duncan, 1837).

Kingsbury, Jack Dean, 'The Composition and Christology of Matt 28.6-20', *JBL* 93 (1974), pp. 573-84.

—*Matthew: Structure, Christology, Kingdom* (Philadelphia: Fortress Press, 2nd edn, 1988).

Knibb, Michael A., 'The Exile in the Literature of the Intertestamental Period', *Heythrop Journal* 17 (1976), pp. 253-72.

Knowles, Michael, *Jeremiah in Matthew's Gospel: The Rejected-Prophet Motif in Matthaean Redaction* (JSNTSup, 68; Sheffield: Sheffield Academic Press, 1993).

Krause, Deborah, 'The One Who Comes Unbinding the Blessing of Judah: Mark 11.1-10 as a Midrash on Genesis 49.11, Zechariah 9.9, and Psalm 118.25-26', in Evans and Sanders (eds.), *Early Christian Interpretation*, pp. 141-53.

Kugel, James L., and Rowan A. Greer, *Early Biblical Interpretation* (LEC, 3; Philadelphia: Westminster Press, 1986).

Kunz, Andreas, *Ablehnung des Krieges: Untersuchungen zu Sacharja 9 und 10* (Herders biblische Studien, 17; Freiburg: Herder, 1998).

Laborde, Raymond P., 'The Use of Zechariah 11.12-13 in Matthew 27.9-10: A Study in Biblical Hermeneutics' (ThM thesis, Grace Theological Seminary, 1983).

Lachs, Samuel Tobias, *A Rabbinic Commentary on the New Testament: The Gospels of Matthew, Mark, and Luke* (Hoboken, NJ: Ktav, 1987).

Lamarche, Paul, *Zacharie IX–XIV: Structure litteraire et messianisme* (Études bibliques; Paris: J. Gabalda, 1961).

Lane, William L., *The Gospel According to Mark* (NICNT; Grand Rapids: Eerdmans, 1974).

Larkin, Katrina J.A., *The Eschatology of Second Zechariah: A Study of the Formation of a Mantological Wisdom Anthology* (CBET, 6; Kampen: Kok Pharos, 1994).

LaSor, William S., David A. Hubbard and Frederic W. Bush, *Old Testament Survey: The Message, Form, and Background of the Old Testament* (Grand Rapids: Eerdmans, 2nd edn, 1996).

Légasse, S., 'L'oracle contre "cette génération" (Mt 23,34-36, par. Lc 11,49-51) et la polémique judéo-chrétienne dans la Source des Logia', in Joël Delobel (ed.), *Logia: Les paroles de Jésus—The Sayings of Jesus. Mémorial Joseph Coppens* (BETL, 59; Leuven: Leuven University Press, 1982), pp. 237-56.

Léon-Dufour, Xavier, *Sharing the Eucharistic Bread: The Witness of the New Testament* (trans. Matthew J.O'Connell; New York: Paulist Press, 1987).

Leske, Adrian M., 'The Beatitudes, Salt, and Light in Matthew and Luke', in Eugene H. Lovering, Jr (ed.), *Society of Biblical Literature 1991 Seminar Papers* (SBLSP, 30; Atlanta: Scholars Press, 1991), pp. 816-39.

—'Context and Meaning of Zechariah 9.9', *CBQ* 62 (2000), pp. 663-78.

—'The Influence of Isaiah on Christian Theology in Matthew and Luke', in William R. Farmer (ed.), *Crisis in Christology: Essays in Quest of Resolution* (Livonia, MI: Dove, 1995), pp. 241-69.

—'Isaiah and Matthew: The Prophetic Influence in the First Gospel: A Report on Current Research', in William and Farmer (eds.), *Jesus and the Suffering Servant*, pp. 152-69.

—'Matthew', in Farmer (ed.), *The International Bible Commentary*, pp. 1253-330.

Leupold, H.C., *Exposition of Zechariah* (Grand Rapids: Baker Book House, 1956).

Lindars, Barnabas, *New Testament Apologetic: The Doctrinal Significance of the Old Testament Quotations* (Philadelphia: Westminster Press, 1961).

—'The Place of the Old Testament in the Formation of New Testament Theology: Prolegomena', *NTS* 23 (1976), pp. 59-66.

Lipiński, E., 'Recherches sur le livre de Zacharie', *VT* 20 (1970), pp. 25-55.

Long, Thomas G., *Matthew* (Westminster Bible Companion; Louisville, KY: Westminster John Knox Press, 1997).

Longenecker, Richard N., 'Can We Reproduce the Exegesis of the New Testament?', *TynBul* 21 (1970), pp. 3-38.

—*Biblical Exegesis in the Apostolic Period* (Grand Rapids: Eerdmans, 2nd edn, 1999).

Longman, Tremper, III, 'The Divine Warrior: The New Testament Use of an Old Testament Motif', *Westminster Theological Journal* 44 (1982), pp. 290-307.

Love, Mark Cameron, *The Evasive Text: Zechariah 1–8 and the Frustrated Reader* (JSOTSup, 296; Sheffield: JSOT Press, 1999).

Luke, K., 'Thirty Pieces of Silver (Zch. 11.12f)', *Indian Theological Studies* 19 (1982), pp. 15-32.

Luz, Ulrich, *Das Evangelium nach Matthäus* (EKKNT, 1; 3 vols.; Zürich: Benziger, 1985–2000).

—*Matthew 1–7: A Commentary* (trans. Wilhelm C. Linss; Minneapolis: Augsburg Press, 1989).

—*The Theology of the Gospel of Matthew* (trans. J. Bradford Robinson; Cambridge: Cambridge University Press, 1995).

Mackay, Cameron, 'Zechariah in Relation to Ezekiel 40–48', *EvQ* 40 (1968), pp. 197-210.

Malina, Bruce, and Jerome H. Neyrey, *Calling Jesus Names: The Social Value of Labels in Matthew* (Sonoma, CA: Polebridge, 1988).

Malina, Bruce, and Richard L. Rohrbaugh, *Social Science Commentary on the Synoptic Gospels* (Minneapolis: Fortress Press, 1992).

Mánek, Jindrich, 'Composite Quotations in the New Testament and Their Purpose', *CV* 13.3-4 (1970), pp. 181-88.

Manns, Frédéric, 'Un midrash chrétien: le récit de la mort de Judas', *RevScRel* 54 (1980), pp. 197-203.

Marcus, Joel, 'The Old Testament and the Death of Jesus: The Role of Scripture in the Gospel Passion Narratives', in Carroll and Green (eds.), *The Death of Jesus*, pp. 205-33.

Marshall, I. Howard, 'An Assessment of Recent Developments', in Carson and Williamson (eds.), pp. 1-21.

—*Last Supper and Lord's Supper* (Exeter: Paternoster Press, 1980).

Martin, Francis, 'The Image of Shepherd in the Gospel of Saint Matthew', *ScEs* 27 (1975), pp. 261-301.

Martins, Elmer, *God's Design: A Focus on Old Testament Theology* (North Richland Hills, TX: BIBAL, 3rd edn, 1998).

Mason, Rex A., *The Books of Haggai, Zechariah, and Malachi* (Cambridge Bible Commentary; Cambridge: Cambridge University Press, 1977).

—'The Relation of Zech. 9–14 to Proto-Zechariah', *ZAW* 88 (1976), pp. 227-39.

—'The Use of Earlier Biblical Material in Zechariah IX–XIV: A Study in Inner Biblical Exegesis' (PhD dissertation, University of London, 1973).

—'Some Examples of Inner Biblical Exegesis in Zech. IX–XIV', in Elizabeth A. Livingstone (ed.), *Studia Evangelica VII: Papers Presented to the Fifth International Congress on Biblical Studies Held at Oxford. 1973* (TUGAL, 126; Berlin: Akademie, 1982), pp. 343-54.

Massaux, Édouard, *The Influence of the Gospel of Saint Matthew on Christian Literature Before Saint Irenaeus* (ed. Arthur J. Bellinzoni; trans. Norman J. Belval and Suzanne Hecht; NGS, 5; 3 vols.; Macon: Mercer University Press, 1990–93).

Massebieau, Eugene, *Examen des citations de l'ancien testament dans l'évangile selon Saint Matthieu* (Paris: Libraire Fischbacher, 1885).

Matera, Frank J., *Passion Narratives and Gospel Theologies: Interpreting the Synoptics through their Passion Stories* (Theological Inquiries; New York: Paulist Press, 1986).

McCann, David C., 'Matthew's Use of the Old Testament in Matthew 27.1-10' (ThM thesis, Dallas Theological Seminary, 1984).

McCasland, Selby Vernon, 'Matthew Twists the Scriptures', *JBL* 80 (1961), pp. 143-48.

McComiskey, Thomas Edward, *Zechariah*, in *idem*, *The Minor Prophets: An Exegetical and Expository Commentary*. III. *Zephaniah, Haggai, Zechariah, and Malachi* (Grand Rapids: Baker Book House, 1998).

McConnell, Richard S., *Law and Prophecy in Matthew's Gospel: The Authority and Use of the Old Testament in the Gospel of Saint Matthew* (Basel: Friedrich Reinhardt, 1969).

McNamara, Martin, *The New Testament and the Palestinian Targum to the Pentateuch* (AnBib, 27; Rome: Pontifical Biblical Institute, 1966).

McNeil, A., 'Τότε in St Matthew', *JTS* 12 (1911), pp. 127-28.

McNicol, Allan J., David L. Dungan and David B. Peabody, with a preface by William R. Farmer, *Beyond the Q Impasse—Luke's Use of Matthew: A Demonstration by the Research Team of the International Institute for Gospel Studies* (Valley Forge, PA: Trinity Press International, 1991).

Meier, John P., *A Marginal Jew: Rethinking the Historical Jesus* (ABRL; 2 vols.; New York: Doubleday, 1991–94).

Menken, Martinus J.J., 'The Old Testament Quotation in Jn 19,36: Sources, Redaction, Background', in F. Van Segbroeck *et al.* (eds.), *The Four Gospels 1992* (3 vols.; Leuven: Leuven University Press, 1992), III, pp. 2101-18.

—'The Old Testament Quotation in Matthew 27,9-10: Textual Form and Context', *Bib* 83 (2002), pp. 305-28.

—'The Quotations from Zech 9,9 in Mt 21,5 and in Jn 12,15', in Adelbert Denaux (ed.), *John and the Synoptics* (BETL, 101; Leuven: Leuven University Press, 1992), pp. 571-78.

—'The References to Jeremiah in the Gospel according to Matthew (Mt. 2.17; 16.14; 27.9)', *ETL* 60 (1984), pp. 5-24.

—'The Sources of the Old Testament Quotation in Matthew 2.23', *JBL* 120 (2001), pp. 451-68.

—'The Textual Form and the Meaning of the Quotation from Zechariah 12.10 in John 19.37', *CBQ* 55 (1993), pp. 494-511.

—'The Use of the Septuagint in Three Quotations in John: Jn 10,34; 12,38; 19,24', in Tuckett (ed.), *The Scriptures in the Gospels*, pp. 367-93.

Merrill, Eugene H., *Haggai, Zechariah, Malachi: An Exegetical Commentary* (Chicago: Moody, 1994).

Mettinger, Tryggve N.D., *The Dethronement of Sabaoth: Studies in the Shem and Kabod Theologies* (trans. Frederick H. Cryer; ConBOT, 18; Uppsala: C.W.K. Gleerup, 1982).

Metzger, Bruce M., 'The Formulas Introducing Quotations of Scripture in the New Testament and the Mishnah', *JBL* 70 (1951), pp. 297-307.

Meyer, Lester V., 'The Messianic Metaphors in Deutero-Zechariah' (PhD dissertation, University of Chicago, 1972).

Meyer, Paul W., 'Matthew 21.1-11', *Int* 40 (1986), pp. 180-85.

Meyers, Carol L., and Eric M. Meyers, *Haggai, Zechariah 1–8* (AB, 25B; New York: Doubleday, 1987).

—*Zechariah 9–14* (AB, 25C; New York: Doubleday, 1993).

Milik, J.T., 'Problèmes de la Littérature Hénochique à la Lumière des Fragments Araméens de Qumrân', *HTR* 64 (1971), pp. 333-78.

Miller, Jean, *Les Citations d'accomplissement dans L'Évangile de Matthieu: Quand Dieu se rend présent en toute humanité* (AnBib, 140; Rome: Editrice Pontifico Istituto Biblico, 1999).

Moloney, Francis J., *A Body Broken for a Broken People: Eucharist in the New Testament* (Peabody, MA: Hendrickson, 1990).

Montefiore, C.G., *The Synoptic Gospels* (2 vols.; London: Macmillan, 2nd edn, 1927; repr., New York: Ktav, 1968).

Moo, Douglas J., *The Old Testament in the Gospel Passion Narratives* (Sheffield: Almond Press, 1983).

—'Tradition and Old Testament in Matt. 27.3-10', in France and Wenham (eds.), *Gospel Perspectives*, III, pp. 157-75.

Moore, Michael S., and Michael L. Brown, 'חֲמוֹר', in *NIDOTTE*, II, pp. 173-74.

Morris, Leon, *The Gospel According to Matthew* (Grand Rapids: Eerdmans, 1992).

—'The Gospels and the Jewish Lectionaries', in France and Wenham (eds.), *Gospel Perspectives*, III, pp. 129-56.

Moule, C.F.D., 'Fulfilment-Words in the New Testament: Use and Abuse', *NTS* 14 (1968), pp. 293-320.

Moyise, Steve, 'Intertextuality and the Study of the Old Testament in the New Testament', in Steve Moyise (ed.), *The Old Testament in the New Testament: Essays in Honour of J.L. North* (JSNTSup, 189; Sheffield: Sheffield Academic Press, 2000), pp. 14-41.

Mulder, Martin Jan (ed.), *Mikra: Text, Translation, Reading and Interpretation of the Hebrew Bible in Ancient Judaism and Early Christianity* (CRINT, 2.1; Philadelphia: Fortress Press, 1988).

Müller, Uwe, 'Die Königsverheissung Sach 9,9-10: Ihre Bedeutung für die Herrscherverheissungen des Alten Testaments und ihr Bezug zu den Evangelien nach Matthäus und Johannes' (MA thesis, Columbia International University, 1996).

Murphy, Roland E., '*Yeser* in the Qumran Literature', *Bib* 39 (1958), pp. 334-44.

Murphy-O'Connor, Jerome, 'The Original Text of CD 7.9-8.2 = 19.5-14', *HTR* 64 (1971), pp. 379-86.

Nestle, Eberhard, 'Über Zacharias in Matth 23', *ZNW* 6 (1905), pp. 198-200.

Neusner, Jacob, *Introduction to Rabbinic Literature* (ABRL; New York: Doubleday, 1994).

—'Judaism in a Time of Crisis: Four Responses to the Destruction of the Second Temple', *Judaism* 21 (1972), pp. 313-27.

—*Judaism in the Matrix of Christianity* (Philadelphia: Fortress Press, 1986).

—*Midrash in Context: Exegesis in Formative Judaism* (Philadelphia: Fortress Press, 1983).

—*What is Midrash?* (Guides to Biblical Scholarship; Philadelphia: Fortress Press, 1987).

Neusner, Jacob, William Scott Green and Ernest S. French (eds.), *Judaisms and Their Messiahs at the Turn of the Christian Era* (Cambridge: Cambridge University Press, 1987).

New, David S., *Old Testament Quotations in the Synoptic Gospels, and the Two-Document Hypothesis* (SBLSCS, 37; Atlanta: Scholars Press, 1993).

Newman, Carey C. (ed.), *Jesus and the Restoration of Israel: A Critical Assessment of N.T. Wright's 'Jesus and the Victory of God'* (Downers Grove, IL: Intervarsity Press, 1999).

Newport, Kenneth G.C., *The Sources and Sitz im Leben of Matthew 23* (JSNTSup, 117; Sheffield: Sheffield Academic Press, 1995).

Neyrey, Jerome H., *Honor and Shame in the Gospel of Matthew* (Louisville, KY: Westminster/John Knox Press, 1997).

Nickelsburg, George W.E., *Jewish Literature between the Bible and the Mishnah: A Historical and Literary Introduction* (Philadelphia: Fortress Press, 1981).

Nolan, Brian M., *The Royal Son of God: The Christology of Matthew 1-2 in the Setting of the Gospel* (OBO, 23; Fribourg Suisse: Éditions Universitaires, 1979).

Olowola, C.A., 'The Christology of the Prophet Zechariah', *ETSI Journal* 1 (1995), pp. 1-15.

O'Rourke, J.J., 'Explicit Old Testament Citations in the Gospels', *Studia Montis Regii* 7 (1964), pp. 37-60.

—'The Fulfillment Texts in Matthew', *CBQ* 24 (1962), pp. 394-403.

—'Possible Uses of the Old Testament in the Gospels: An Overview', in Evans and Stegner (eds.), *The Gospels and the Scriptures*, pp. 14-25.

Orton, David E., *The Understanding Scribe: Matthew and the Apocalyptic Ideal* (JSNTSup, 25; Sheffield: Sheffield Academic Press, 1989).

Osgood, Howard, *Quotations of the Old Testament in the New Testament* (Rochester, NY: Andrews, 1889).

Otzen, Benedikt, *Studien über Deuterosacharja* (ATDan, 6; Copenhagen: Prostant apud Munksgaard, 1965).

Overman, J. Andrew, *Matthew's Gospel and Formative Judaism: The Social World of the Matthean Community* (Minneapolis: Fortress Press, 1990).

Parsons, Mikeal, 'The Critical Use of the Rabbinic Literature in New Testament Studies', *PRSt* 12 (1985), pp. 84-102.

Pasco, Allan H., *Allusion: A Literary Graft* (Toronto: University of Toronto Press, 1994).

Patte, Daniel, *Early Jewish Hermeneutic in Palestine* (SBLDS, 22; Missoula, MT: Scholars Press, 1975).

—*The Gospel according to Matthew: A Structural Commentary on Matthew's Faith* (Philadelphia: Fortress Press, 1987).

Paulien, Jon, 'Elusive Allusions: The Problematic Use of the Old Testament in Revelation', *BR* 33 (1988), pp. 37-53.

Peels, H.G.L., 'The Blood "from Abel to Zechariah" (Matthew 23.35; Luke 11.50f) and the Canon of the Old Testament', *ZAW* 113 (2001), pp. 583-601.

Perrine, Laurence, and Thomas R. Arp., *Literature: Structure, Sound, and Sense* (San Diego: Harcourt Brace Jovanovich, 5th edn, 1988).

Person, Raymond F., *Second Zechariah and the Deuteronomic School* (JSOTSup, 167; Sheffield: JSOT Press, 1993).

Pesch, Rudolf, 'Eine alttestamentliche Ausführungsformel im Matthäus-Evangelium', *BZ* 10 (1966), pp. 220-45.

—'Eine alttestamentliche Ausführungsformel im Matthäus-Evangelium (Schluß)', *BZ* 11 (1967), pp. 79-95.

—'Der Gottessohn im matthäischen Evangelienprolog (Mt. 1–2): Beobachtungen zu den Zitationsformeln der Reflexionzitate', *Bib* 48 (1967), pp. 395-420.

—' "He Will Be Called a Nazorean": Messianic Exegesis in Matthew 1–2', in Evans and Stegner (eds.), *The Gospels and the Scriptures*, pp. 129-78.

Petersen, David L., *Haggai and Zechariah 1–9: A Commentary* (OTL; Philadelphia: Westminster Press, 1984).

—*Zechariah 9–14 and Malachi: A Commentary* (OTL; Louisville, KY: Westminster/John Knox Press, 1995).

—'Zechariah's Visions: A Theological Perspective', *VT* 34 (1984), pp. 195-206.

Pierce, Ronald W., 'A Thematic Development of the Haggai—Zechariah—Malachi Corpus', *JETS* 27 (1984), pp. 401-11.

Porter, Paul A., *Metaphors and Monsters: A Literary-Critical Study of Daniel 7 and 8* (ConBOT, 20; Lund: C.W.K. Gleerup, 1983; repr., Toronto: Paul A. Porter, 1985).

Porter, Stanley E., 'The Use of the Old Testament in the New Testament: A Brief Comment on Method and Terminology', in Evans and Sanders (eds.), *Early Christian Interpretation*, pp. 79-96.

Portnoy, Stephen L., and David L. Petersen, 'Biblical Texts and Statistical Analysis: Zechariah and Beyond', *JBL* 103 (1984), pp. 11-21.

Powell, Mark Allan, 'The Magi as Kings: An Adventure in Reader-Response Criticism', *CBQ* 62 (2000), pp. 459-80.

Quesnel, Michael, 'Les citations de Jérémie dans l'évangile selon saint Matthieu', *EstBib* 47 (1989), pp. 513-27.

Radday, Yehuda T., and Dieter Wickermann, 'The Unity of Zechariah Examined in the Light of Statistical Linguistics', *ZAW* 87 (1975), pp. 30-55.

Redditt, Paul Lewis, *Haggai, Zechariah and Malachi* (NCB; Grand Rapids: Eerdmans, 1995).

Reiner, Erica, 'Thirty Pieces of Silver', *JAOS* 88 (1968), pp. 186-90.

Reynolds, Kent A., 'The Relationship of Isaiah 62.11 to Zechariah 9.9: Generative Source or Formulaic Parallel?' (MA thesis, Columbia Biblical Seminary, 1997).

Ridderbos, Herman N., *The Gospel according to John: A Theological Commentary* (trans. John Vriend; Grand Rapids: Eerdmans, 1997).

—*Matthew* (trans. Ray Togtman; Grand Rapids: Zondervan, 1987).

Ringgren, Helmer, with a foreward by James H. Charlesworth, *The Faith of Qumran: Theology of the Dead Sea Scrolls* (trans. Emilie T. Sander; New York: Crossroad, expanded edn, 1995).

—*The Messiah in the Old Testament* (SBT; London: SCM Press, 1956).

Roth, Cecil, 'The Cleansing of the Temple and Zechariah 14.21', *NovT* 4 (1960), pp. 174-81.

Rothfuchs, Wilhelm, *Die Erfüllungszitate des Matthäus-Evangeliums: Eine biblisch-theologische Untersuchung* (BWANT, 8; Stuttgart: Kohlhammer, 1969).

Ruffin, Michael L., 'Symbolism in Zechariah: A Study in Functional Unity' (PhD dissertation, Southern Baptist Theological Seminary, 1986).

Sabourin, Leopold, *The Gospel according to St Matthew* (Bandra, Bombey: St Paul, 1982).

Sæbø, Magne, *Sacharja 9–14: Untersuchungen von Text und Form* (WMANT, 34; Neukirchen–Vluyn: Neukirchener Verlag, 1969).

Sand, Alexander, *Das Evangelium nach Matthäus* (Regensburger Neues Testament; Regensburg: Friedrich Pustet, 1986).

—*Das Gesetz und die Propheten: Untersuchungen zur Theologie des Evangeliums nach Matthäus* (Regensburg: F. Pustet, 1974).

Sanders, E.P., *Jesus and Judaism* (Philadelphia: Fortress Press, 1985).

—*Judaism: Practice and Belief 63 B.C.E.–66 C.E.* (Philadelphia: Trinity Press International, 1992).

Sanders, James A., 'Ναζωραῖος in Matthew 2.23', in Evans and Stegner (eds.), *The Gospels and the Scriptures*, pp. 116-28.

Savran, George W., *Telling and Retelling: Quotation in Biblical Narrative* (Indiana Studies in Biblical Literature; Bloomington: Indiana University Press, 1988).

Schaefer, Konrad R., 'Zechariah 14: A Study in Allusion', *CBQ* 57 (1995), pp. 66-91.

Schenk, Wolfgang, 'ἀρνέομαι', in *EDNT*, I, pp. 154-55.

Schlatter, Adolf von, *Der Evangelist Matthäus: seine Sprache, sein Ziel, seine Selb-ststständigkeit: ein Kommentar zum ersten Evangelium* (Stuttgart: Calwer, 6th edn, 1963).

Schmidt, Werner H., *Old Testament Introduction* (trans. Matthew J. O'Connell and David J. Reimer; New York: W. de Gruyter, 2nd edn, 1999).

—'יצר', in *TLOT*, II, p. 566.

Schnackenburg, Rudolf, *Matthäusevangelium* (Die neue Echter Bibel; 2 vols.; Würzburg: Echter, 1985).

Schroeder, Roy P., 'The "Worthless" Shepherd: A Study of Mark 14.27', *Currents in Theology and Mission* 2 (1975), pp. 342-44.

Schultz, Richard L., *The Search for Quotation: Verbal Parallels in the Prophets* (JSOTSup, 180; Sheffield: Sheffield Academic Press, 1999).

Selman, Martin, 'Zechariah: Theology of', in *NIDOTTE*, IV, pp. 1303-307.

Senior, Donald, 'A Case Study in Matthean Creativity: Matthew 27.3-10', *BR* 19 (1974), pp. 23-36.

—'The Death of Jesus and the Resurrection of the Holy Ones (MT 27.51-53)', *CBQ* 38 (1976), pp. 312-29.

—'The Fate of the Betrayer: A Redactional Study of Matt. XXVII, 3-10', *ETL* 48 (1972), pp. 372-426.

—'The Lure of the Formula Quotations: Re-assessing Matthew's Use of the Old Testament with the Passion Narrative as Test Case', in Tuckett (ed.), *The Scriptures in the Gospels*, pp. 89-115.

—*Matthew* (ANTC; Nashville: Abingdon Press, 1998).

—*The Passion Narrative according to Matthew: A Redactional Study* (BETL, 39; Leuven: Leuven University Press, 1975).

—'The Passion Narrative in the Gospel of Matthew', in Didier (ed.), *L'Évangile selon Matthieu*, pp. 343-58.

—*The Passion of Jesus in the Gospel of Matthew* (Wilmington, DE: Michael Glazier, 1985).

—*What are they Saying about Matthew?* (New York: Paulist Press, rev edn, 1996).

Siebeneck, Robert T., 'The Messianism of Aggeus and Proto-Zacharias', *CBQ* 19 (1957), pp. 312-28.

Silva, Moisés, 'The New Testament Use of the Old Testament', in D.A. Carson and John D. Woodbridge (eds.), *Scripture and Truth* (Grand Rapids: Baker Book House, 1992), pp. 147-62.

—'Old Testament in Paul', in *DPL*, pp. 630-42.

Sim, David C., *Apocalyptic Eschatology in the Gospel of Matthew* (SNTSMS, 88; Cambridge: Cambridge University Press, 1996).

—*The Gospel of Matthew and Christian Judaism: The History and Social Setting of the Matthean Community* (Studies of the New Testament and its World; Edinburgh: T. & T. Clark, 1998).

Simonetti, Manlio (ed.), *Matthew 1–13* (ACCS; New Testament, 1a; Downers Grove, IL: Intervarsity Press, 2001).

—*Matthew 14–28* (ACCS; New Testament, 1b; Downers Grove, IL: Intervarsity Press, 2002).

Skarsaune, Oskar, *In the Shadow of the Temple: Jewish Influences on Early Christianity* (Downers Grove, IL: Intervarsity Press, 2002).

—*The Proof from Prophecy: A Study in Justin Martyr's Proof-Text Tradition: Text-Type, Provenance, Theological Profile* (NovTSup, 56; Leiden: E.J. Brill, 1987).

Smith, Dwight Moody, Jr, 'The Use of the Old Testament in the New', in James M. Efird (ed.), *The Use of the Old Testament in the New and Other Essays: Studies in Honor of William Franklin Stinespring* (Durham, NC: Duke University Press, 1972), pp. 3-65.

Smith, Ralph L., *Micah–Malachi* (WBC, 32; Waco, TX: Word Books, 1984).

Snodgrass, Klyne, 'The Use of the Old Testament in the New', in David Alan Black and David S. Dockery (eds.), *New Testament Criticism and Interpretation* (Grand Rapids: Zondervan, 1991), pp. 409-34.

Soares Prabhu, George M., *The Formula Quotations in the Infancy Narratives of Matthew: An Enquiry into the Tradition History of Mt. 1–2* (AnBib, 63; Rome: Pontifical Biblical Institute, 1976).

Sperber, Alexander, 'New Testament and Septuagint', *JBL* 59 (1940), pp. 193-293.

Stanley, Christopher D., *Paul and the Language of Scripture: Citation Technique in the Pauline Epistles and Contemporary Literature* (SNTSMS, 74; Cambridge: Cambridge University Press, 1993).

Stanton, Graham, *A Gospel for a New People: Studies in Matthew* (Edinburgh: T. & T. Clark, 1992).

—*The Interpretation of Matthew* (Studies in New Testament Interpretation; Edinburgh: T. & T. Clark, 2nd edn, 1995).

—'Matthew', in Carson and Williamson (eds.), *It is Written*, pp. 205-19.

—'The Origin and Purpose of Matthew's Gospel: Matthean Scholarship from 1945-80', *ANRW* 25.3.1889-951. Part 2, *Principat*, 25.3 (Berlin: W. de Gruyter, 1985).

Steinmann, Andrew Erwin, 'The Shape of Things to Come: The Genre of the Historical Apocalypse in Ancient Jewish and Christian Literature' (PhD dissertation, University of Michigan, 1990).

Stendahl, Krister, *The School of St Matthew, and its Use of the Old Testament* (ASNU, 20; Lund: C.W.K. Gleerup, 1954; repr., Philadelphia: Fortress Press, 1968).

Strecker, Georg, 'The Concept of History in Matthew', *JAAR* 35 (1967), pp. 219-30.

—'Das Geschichtsverständnis des Matthäus', *EvT* 26 (1966), pp. 57-74.

—*Der Weg der Gerechtigkeit: Untersuchungen zur Theologie des Matthäus* (FRLANT, 82; Göttingen: Vandenhoeck & Ruprecht, 3rd edn, 1971).

Stuhlmacher, Peter, *Biblische Theologie des neuen Testaments. I. Grundlegung von Jesus zu Paulus* (Göttingen: Vandenhoeck & Ruprecht, 1992).

—*Jesus of Nazareth—Christ of Faith* (trans. Siegfried S. Schatzmann; Peabody, MA: Hendrickson, 1993).

Stuhlmueller, Carroll, *Rebuilding with Hope: A Commentary on the Books of Haggai and Zechariah* (ITC; Grand Rapids: Eerdmans, 1988).

Sundberg, Albert C., Jr, 'On Testimonies', *NovT* 3 (1959), pp. 268-81.

Sutcliffe, Edmund F., 'Matthew 27.9', *JTS* 3 (1952), pp. 227-28.

Swartley, Willard M., 'Intertextuality in Early Christian Literature', in *DLNT*, pp. 536-42.

—*Israel's Scripture Traditions and the Synoptic Gospels: Story Shaping Story* (Peabody, MA: Hendrickson, 1994).

Sweeney, Marvin A., *The Twelve Prophets* (BerOl; 2 vols.; Collegeville, MN: Liturgical Press, 2000).

Telford, William R., *The Barren Temple and the Withered Tree: A Redaction-Critical Analysis of the Cursing of the Fig Tree Pericope in Mark's Gospel and its Relation to the Cleansing of the Temple Tradition* (JSNTSup, 1; Sheffield: JSOT Press, 1980).

Tevis, Dennis Gordon, 'An Analysis of Words and Phrases Characteristic of the Gospel of Matthew' (PhD dissertation, Southern Methodist University, 1983).

Thomson, J.G., 'The Shepherd-Ruler Concept in the Old Testament and its Application in the New Testament', *SJT* 8 (1955), pp. 406-18.

Tilborg, Sjef van, *The Jewish Leaders in Matthew* (Leiden: E.J. Brill, 1972).

—'Matthew 27.3-10: An Intertextual Reading', in Draisma (ed.), *Intertextuality in Biblical Writings*, pp. 159-74.

Tollington, Janet E., *Tradition and Innovation in Haggai and Zechariah 1–8* (JSOTSup, 150; Sheffield: Sheffield Academic Press, 1993).

Tooley, Wilfred, 'The Shepherd and Sheep Image in the Teaching of Jesus', *NovT* 7 (1964), pp. 15-25.

Torrey, Charles Culter, 'The Foundry of the Second Temple at Jerusalem', *JBL* 55 (1936), pp. 247-60.

Trilling, Wolfgang, 'Der Einzug in Jerusalem Mt 21,1-17', in J. Blinzer, O. Kuss and F. Mussner (eds.), *Neutestamentliche Aufsätze: Festschrift für Josef Schmid zum 70. Geburtstag* (Regensburg: Friedrich Pustet, 1963), pp. 303-309.

Tuckett, Christopher M., 'Zechariah 12.10 and the New Testament', in *idem* (ed.), *The Book of Zechariah and its Influence* (Burlington, VT: Ashgate, 2003), pp. 111-21.

Tuckett, Christopher M. (ed.), *The Scriptures in the Gospels* (BETL, 131; Leuven: Leuven University Press, 1997).

Unnik, W.C. van, 'The Death of Judas in St Matthew's Gospel', in M.H. Shepherd and E.C. Hobbs (eds.), *Gospel Studies in Honor of Sherman Elbridge Johnson* (AthRSup, 3; Evanston, IL: Anglican Theological Review, 1974), pp. 44-57.

Upton, John A., 'The Potter's Field and the Death of Judas', *Concordia Journal* 8 (1982), pp. 213-19.

Van Segbroeck, Frans, 'Les citations d'accomplissement dans l'évangile selon Matthieu d'après trois ouvrages récents', in Didier (ed.), *L'Évangile selon Matthieu*, pp. 107-30.

Vanhoozer, Kevin, *Is There a Meaning in This Text? The Bible, the Reader, and the Morality of Literary Knowledge* (Grand Rapids: Zondervan, 1998).

Vardaman, Jerry, 'A New Inscription which Mentions Pilate as "Prefect"', *JBL* 81 (1962), pp. 70-71.

Vermes, Geza, 'Bible and Midrash: Early Old Testament Exegesis', in P.R. Ackroyd and C.F. Evans (eds.), *The Cambridge History of the Bible*. I. *From the Beginnings to Jerome* (Cambridge: Cambridge University Press, 1970), pp. 199-231.

—*An Introduction to the Complete Dead Sea Scrolls* (Minneapolis: Fortress Press, 1999).

—*Jesus and the World of Judaism* (Philadelphia: Fortress Press, 1983).

—'Jewish Literature and New Testament Exegesis: Reflections on Methodology', *JJS* 33 (1982), pp. 361-76.

—*Scripture and Tradition in Judaism: Haggadic Studies* (StPB, 4; Leiden: E.J. Brill, 2nd edn, 1983).

Verseput, Donald, *The Rejection of the Humble Messianic King: A Study of the Composition of Matthew 11–12* (EurUS, 23; Theology, 291; Frankfurt: Peter Lang, 1986).

Vischer Wilhelm, *The Witness of the Old Testament to Christ* (London: Lutterworth, 1949).

Voelz, James W., 'Multiple Signs and Double Texts: Elements of Intertextuality', in Draisma (ed.), *Intertextuality in Biblical Writings*, pp. 27-34.

Vorster, Willed S., 'Intertextuality and Redaktionsgeschichte', in Draisma (ed.), *Intertextuality in Biblical Writings*, pp. 15-26.

Waard, Jan de, *A Comparative Study of the Old Testament Text in the Dead Sea Scrolls and in the New Testament* (STDJ, 4; Leiden: E.J. Brill, 1965).

Wainwright, Elaine M., *Toward a Feminist Critical Reading of the Gospel according to Matthew* (BZNW, 60; Berlin: W. de Gruyter, 1991).

Walter, Nikolaus, 'Paul and the Early Christian Jesus-Tradition', in A.J.M. Wedderburn (ed.), *Paul and Jesus: Collected Essays* (JSNTSup, 37; Sheffield: JSOT Press, 1989), pp. 51-80.

Wellhausen, Julius, *Das Evangelium Matthaei*, 2nd edn, in *Evangelienkommentare* (Berlin: Georg Reimer, 1904–14; repr., Berlin: W. de Gruyter, 1987).

Wengst, Klaus, 'Aspects of the Last Judgment in the Gospel according to Matthew', in Henning Graf Reventlow (ed.), *Eschatology in the Bible and in Jewish and Christian Tradition* (JSOTSup, 243; Sheffield: Sheffield Academic Press, 1997), pp. 233-45.

Wenham, David, 'Paul's Use of the Jesus Tradition: Three Samples', in David Wenham (ed.), *Gospel Perspectives. V. The Jesus Tradition Outside the Gospels* (Sheffield: JSOT Press, 1984), pp. 7-37.

Wenham, J.W., 'When Were the Saints Raised?', *JTS* 32 (1981), pp. 150-52.

Weren, Wim, 'Jesus' Entry into Jerusalem: Matthew 21,1-17 in the Light of the Hebrew Bible and the Septuagint', in Tuckett (ed.), *The Scriptures in the Gospels*, pp. 117-41.

Westcott, B.F., *An Introduction to the Study of the Gospels* (London: Macmillan, 7th edn, 1888).

Wiefel, Wolfgang, *Das Evangelium nach Matthäus* (THKNT, 1; Leipzig: Evangelische Verlagsanstalt, 1998).

Wilcox, Max, 'On Investigating the Use of the Old Testament in the New Testament', in Best and McL. Wilson (eds.), *Text and Interpretation*, pp. 231-43.

—'Text Form', in Carson and Williamson (eds.), *It is Written*, pp. 193-203.

Witherington, Ben, III, *The Christology of Jesus* (Minneapolis: Fortress Press, 1990).

—*Jesus the Seer: The Progress of Prophecy* (Peabody, MA: Hendrickson, 1999).

Witt, Douglas A., 'Zechariah 12–14: Its Origins, Growth, and Theological Significance' (PhD dissertation, Vanderbuilt University, 1991).

Wolde, Ellen van, 'Trendy Intertextuality?', in Draisma (ed.), *Intertextuality in Biblical Writings*, pp. 43-49.

Wong, Chan-Kok, 'The Interpretation of Zechariah 3, 4 and 6 in the New Testament and Early Christianity' (PhD dissertation, Westminster Theological Seminary, 1992).

Woodward, Stephen, 'The Provenance of the Term "Saints": A *Religionsgeschichtliche* Study', *JETS* 24 (1981), pp. 107-16.

Wright, Christopher J.H., *Knowing Jesus through the Old Testament* (Downers Grove, IL: Intervarsity Press, 1992).

Wright, N.T., *Christian Origins and the Question of God. II. Jesus and the Victory of God* (Minneapolis: Fortress Press, 1996).

Yarchin, William, 'קר', in *NIDOTTE*, II, pp. 522-25.

Zahn, Theodor, *Das Evangelium des Matthäus* (KNT, 1; Leipzig: Deichert, 4th edn, 1922).

—*Introduction to the New Testament* (trans. Melancthon Williams Jacobus *et al.*; 3 vols.; Edinburgh: T. & T. Clark, 1909; repr., Minneapolis: Klock & Klock, 1977).

Zimmerli, Walther, *Ezekiel 2: A Commentary on the Book of the Prophet Ezekiel Chapters 25–48* (trans. James D. Martin; ed. Paul D. Hanson and Leonard Jay Greenspoon; Hermeneia; Philadelphia: Fortress Press, 1983).

—'Prophetic Proclamation and Reinterpretation', in D.A. Knight (ed.), *Tradition and Theology in the Old Testament* (Philadelphia: Fortress Press, 1977), pp. 69-100.

Zucker, David J., 'Jesus and Jeremiah in the Matthean Tradition', *JES* 27 (1990), pp. 288-305.

INDEXES

INDEX OF REFERENCES

INDEX OF AUTHORS